Organizational Reputation in the Public Sector

A favorable reputation is an asset of importance that no public sector entity can afford to neglect because it gives power, autonomy, and access to critical resources. However, reputations must be built, maintained, and protected. As a result, public sector organizations in most OECD countries have increased their capacity for managing reputation. This edited volume seeks to describe, explain, and critically analyze the significance of organizational reputation and reputation-management activities in the public sector.

This book provides a comprehensive first look at how reputation management efforts in public organizations play out, focusing on public agencies as formal organizations with their own hierarchies, identities, and cultures—existing in a network of other public organizations with similar or different functions, power, and reputations. From this unique perspective, the chapters in this volume examine issues such as organizational identity, power, actors, politics, and stakeholders within the public sector. Paying specific attention to strategies and processes, and illustrating with examples from the countries of Belgium, Denmark, Norway, Ireland, Israel, and Sweden, the book deepens our understanding of reputation management efforts at various levels of government.

Arild Wæraas is Professor of Organization Theory and Leadership at the Norwegian University of Life Sciences, Norway. His research interests are reputation, organizational identity, and organizational fields. His latest publications include "Being All Things to All Customers: Building Reputation in an Institutionalized Field" (co-authored, *British Journal of Management*) and "Trapped in Conformity? Translating Reputation Management into Practice" (co-authored, *Scandinavian Journal of Management*).

Moshe Maor is Professor of Political Science at the Hebrew University of Jerusalem, Israel, and the holder of the Wolfson Family Chair of Public Administration. His areas of expertise are bureaucratic politics, public policy, and comparative politics. His latest publications include "Organizational Reputation, Regulatory Talk and Strategic Silence" (co-authored; J-PART) and "Organizational Reputation, the Content of Public Allegations and Regulatory Communication" (co-authored, J-PART). Maor is also a member of the Council for Higher Education in Israel.

Routledge Critical Studies in Public Management

Edited by Stephen Osborne

The study and practice of public management has undergone profound changes across the world. Over the last quarter century, we have seen

- increasing criticism of public administration as the overarching framework for the provision of public services,
- the rise (and critical appraisal) of the 'New Public Management' as an emergent paradigm for the provision of public services,
- the transformation of the 'public sector' into the cross-sectoral provision of public services, and
- the growth of the governance of inter-organizational relationships as an essential element in the provision of public services

In reality, these trends have not so much replaced each other as elided or coexisted together—the public policy process has not gone away as a legitimate topic of study, intra-organizational management continues to be essential to the efficient provision of public services, and the governance of inter-organizational and inter-sectoral relationships is now essential to the effective provision of these services.

Further, while the study of public management has been enriched by the contribution of a range of insights from the 'mainstream' management literature, it has also contributed to this literature in such areas as networks and inter-organizational collaboration, innovation, and stakeholder theory.

This series is dedicated to presenting and critiquing this important body of theory and empirical study. It will publish books that both explore and evaluate the emergent and developing nature of public administration, management, and governance (in theory and practice) and examine the relationship with and contribution to the overarching disciplines of management and organizational sociology.

Books in the series will be of interest to academics and researchers in this field, students undertaking advanced studies of it as part of their undergraduate or postgraduate degree, and reflective policy makers and practitioners.

1 **Unbundled Government**
A critical analysis of the global trend to agencies, quangos and contractualisation
Edited by Christopher Pollitt and Colin Talbot

2 **The Study of Public Management in Europe and the US**
A competitive analysis of national distinctiveness
Edited by Walter Kickert

3 **Managing Complex Governance Systems**
Dynamics, self-organization and coevolution in public investments
Edited by Geert Teisman, Arwin van Buuren and Lasse Gerrits

4 **Making Public Services Management Critical**
Edited by Graeme Currie, Jackie Ford, Nancy Harding and Mark Learmonth

5 **Social Accounting and Public Management**
Accountability for the common good
Edited by Stephen P. Osborne and Amanda Ball

6 **Public Management and Complexity Theory**
Richer decision-making in public services
Mary Lee Rhodes, Joanne Murphy, Jenny Muir, John A. Murray

7 **New Public Governance, the Third Sector, and Co-Production**
Edited by Victor Pestoff, Taco Brandsen, and Bram Verschuere

8 **Branding in Governance and Public Management**
Jasper Eshuis and Erik-Hans Klijn

9 **Public Policy beyond the Financial Crisis**
An international comparative study
Philip Haynes

10 **Rethinking Public-Private Partnerships**
Strategies for turbulent times
Edited by Carsten Greve and Graeme Hodge

11 **Public-Private Partnerships in the USA**
Lessons to be learned for the United Kingdom
Anthony Wall

12 **Trust and Confidence in Government and Public Services**
Edited by Sue Llewellyn, Stephen Brookes, and Ann Mahon

13 **Critical Leadership**
Dynamics of leader–follower relations in a public organization
Paul Evans, John Hassard and Paula Hyde

14 **Policy Transfer and Learning in Public Policy and Management**
International contexts, content and development
Edited by Peter Carroll and Richard Common

15 **Crossing Boundaries in Public Management and Policy**
The international experience
Edited by Janine O'Flynn, Deborah Blackman and John Halligan

16 **Public-Private Partnerships in the European Union**
Christopher Bovis

17 **Network Theory in the Public Sector**
Building new theoretical frameworks
Edited by Robyn Keast, Myrna Mandell and Robert Agranoff

18 **Public Administration Reformation**
Market demand from public organizations
Edited by Yogesh K. Dwivedi, Mahmud A. Shareef, Sanjay K. Pandey, and Vinod Kumar

19 **Public Innovation Through Collaboration and Design**
Edited by Christopher Ansell and Jacob Torfing

20 **Strategic Management in Public Organizations**
European practices and perspectives
Edited by Paul Joyce and Anne Drumaux

21 **Organizational Reputation in the Public Sector**
Edited by Arild Wæraas and Moshe Maor

Organizational Reputation in the Public Sector

Edited by Arild Wæraas and Moshe Maor

NEW YORK AND LONDON

First published 2015
by Routledge
711 Third Avenue, New York, NY 10017

and by Routledge
2 Park Square, Milton Park, Abingdon, Oxon OX14 4RN

*Routledge is an imprint of the Taylor & Francis Group,
an informa business*

© 2015 Taylor & Francis

The right of the editors to be identified as the author of the editorial
material, and of the authors for their individual chapters, has been asserted
in accordance with sections 77 and 78 of the Copyright, Designs and
Patents Act 1988.

All rights reserved. No part of this book may be reprinted or reproduced or
utilised in any form or by any electronic, mechanical, or other means, now
known or hereafter invented, including photocopying and recording, or in
any information storage or retrieval system, without permission in writing
from the publishers.

Trademark Notice: Product or corporate names may be trademarks or
registered trademarks, and are used only for identification and explanation
without intent to infringe.

Library of Congress Cataloging-in-Publication Data
A catalog record for this book has been requested

ISBN: 978-0-415-72977-2 (hbk)
ISBN: 978-1-315-85082-5 (ebk)

Typeset in Sabon
by Apex CoVantage, LLC

Contents

	Foreword	ix
	DANIEL CARPENTER	
	Preface	xiii
1	**Understanding Organizational Reputation in a Public Sector Context**	1
	ARILD WÆRAAS AND MOSHE MAOR	

Part I
Theoretical Perspectives   15

2	**Theorizing Bureaucratic Reputation**	17
	MOSHE MAOR	
3	**Actors and Strategies of the Bureaucratic Reputation Game**	37
	LUCIO PICCI	
4	**Driving Forces, Critiques, and Paradoxes of Reputation Management in Public Organizations**	54
	HALDOR BYRKJEFLOT	

Part II
Reputation Management in Central Government Agencies   75

5	**The Relationship between an Irish Government Department and Its Newly Established Agency: A Reputational Perspective**	77
	CIARA O'DWYER	
6	**Reputation Management in Times of Crisis: How the Police Handled the Norwegian Terrorist Attack in 2011**	95
	TOM CHRISTENSEN AND PER LÆGREID	

viii *Contents*

7 How Organizational Reputation and Trust May Affect
the Autonomy of Independent Regulators: The Case of
the Flemish Energy Regulator 118

KOEN VERHOEST, JAN ROMMEL, AND JAN BOON

8 Organizational Reputation, Public Protest, and
the Strategic Use of Regulatory Communication 139

YAEL SCHANIN

Part III
Reputation Management in Local Government 161

9 Struggles behind the Scenes: Reputation Management in
Swedish Hospitals 163

MARIA BLOMGREN, TINA HEDMO, AND CAROLINE WAKS

10 Dealing with Stakeholders in Local Government: Three
Norwegian Cases of Municipal Reputation Management 185

HILDE BJØRNÅ

11 Investigating the Politics of Reputation Management in
Local Government: The Case of Denmark 203

HEIDI HOULBERG SALOMONSEN AND JEPPE AGGER NIELSEN

12 Municipal Reputation Building in Norway: A Reputation
Commons Tragedy? 227

ARILD WÆRAAS

Contributors 245
Index 247

Foreword

From the vantage of 2014, the appearance of *Organizational Reputation in the Public Sector* is both a surprising and gratifying development.

Surprising: When in 1998 and 1999 I refashioned a dissertation on corporate identity in executive departments into a book on reputation and bureaucratic autonomy, reputation was a concept only occasionally mentioned in the literature on public agencies. The reigning theoretical configurations of the time were legislative dominance in the political science literature (accompanied by the insistence of others that executive actors also played a significant role) and neutral competence and public-service motivation in the public administration literature. The state of theorization and of empirical research remained disappointing, with political scientists in particular running from agency to agency trying to demonstrate 'political control' or the lack thereof. I saw the need for an alternative theory, but I was far from certain that reputation was the right alternative, or that it would succeed.

Gratifying: Reputation-based theories have not entirely supplanted these earlier models—nor would I wish them to, in a world where no single theory can explain all organizational behavior, public or private. Yet accounts premised upon organizational image have now become a standard reference for explaining the decisions of agencies, the varying success of government and administrative strategies, the discretion and deference that agencies are accorded by politicians and political institutions, the alliances and liaisons that agencies make (or do not), the coming and going of personnel, and even the life and death of agencies themselves. As Arild Wæraas and Moshe Maor explain in their thoughtful introduction to this volume, I was not the first to happen upon this insight. Scholars ranging from Herbert Simon to James Q. Wilson to Martha Derthick, among others, had written of the importance of reputations to agency function and dysfunction. What those scattered remarks lacked was a theoretical framework that integrated various observations, proposed causal mechanisms, advanced hypotheses for testing, and directed our attention to certain variables and measures. Those accounts also lacked an in-depth empirical analysis of reputations themselves, which requires attention to the multiple audiences in which reputations live. A decade and a half of scholarship has gone a long way toward filling these gaps.

x *Foreword*

What this collection of studies shows more than anything is that the baton has truly been passed. The true advances in the study of organizational reputation are occurring not just outside my office, but often outside of North America. This is not to gainsay the crucial work on organizational reputation being done by American scholars such as George Krause, Susan Moffitt, Colin Moore, and others. It is to say that the work of scholars in Denmark, France, Israel, the Netherlands, Norway, Sweden, and other locales is increasingly 'where the action is.' This globalization of discourse can only be a good thing, and it is my fervent hope that policy makers and scholars in the United States will better open their eyes and ears to consider the valuable research and rich policy lessons being produced elsewhere in the world.

From my own view, I think the literature on organizational reputation does need some improvements, and I am pleased to see progress in this direction being made in the present volume.

BETTER DIFFERENTIATION IN EMPIRICAL ACCOUNTS

A critical challenge that arises in assessing any social science theory is the problem of observational equivalence. In the older debates over whether agencies were politically dominated by a legislature or politically autonomous, critics were rightly concerned that what looked like evidence for one claim was in fact consistent with a range of models. Hence the observation that Congress paid little attention to agencies (few hearings, for instance), while being used as evidence for agencies' autonomy, was in fact consistent with strong control (in which case there would be little need for hearings). For reputation-based accounts, too, scholars need to examine alternative explanations of the facts that are usually offered as evidence for the account. Do public managers and agencies care not so much about reputation but really about "getting it right," regardless of whether anyone notices? If so, they might show responsiveness to criticism of their performance in either case. Do agencies pursue ceremonial restructuring not only to mollify audiences and critics but also because it is the cheapest manner of reform from a cost standpoint? As is so often the case when alternative explanations arise, the focus must be placed ever more squarely upon measurement, both quantitative and quantitative. What does a reputation look like, such that we can tell it apart from the 'facts of performance'? Where would a reputation-based account conflict with other accounts?

FOCUS ON MULTIPLE AUDIENCES, MULTIPLE IDENTITIES

If the focus on reputations is to be extended to richer and more nuanced models and empirical studies, the idea that agencies can have more than one reputation will need to be advanced. By definition, the public organizations we study have multiple officials and representatives, and they have plural publics. As political scientists, public management scholars, sociologists, anthropologists, economists, and other analysts train their eyes ever more on financial regulatory agencies and central banks, for instance, we must be wary of reducing the agencies themselves to their leaders and top appointees, and we must be equally wary of reducing their audiences into some sloppy amalgam of 'Wall Street' and global capital acting as if it were a unitary force.

NORMATIVE THEORY

A major weakness of reputation-based theory, to my reading (and I include my own writings in the criticism), lies in the lack of prescriptions for organizational change and structure. As the theory is better developed, it will become ever more critical to explain to politicians, reform commissions, and our students what the 'upshot' is of reputation-based theory, and what difference it makes for how practitioners and authorities should approach their work. As Professors Wæraas and Byrkjeflot have written recently, the translation from positivist understanding of how agencies behave in our studies to how we should try to restructure them, their cultures, or their incentives is fraught with mapping and translation issues. Yet given the evident force of organizational reputations in administrative life, that attempt must be carried forward.

I close here, in deep appreciation of Professor Wæraas and Professor Maor, who have taken up international leadership of this strain of research. As the baton has been passed, it is time for me to get out of the way and cheer on the athletes as they complete the next lap of many to come.

Daniel Carpenter

Preface

This book began with a simple observation: Whereas there are a number of books about reputation management in a business setting, very few provide an exclusive focus on organizational reputation in a public sector setting. With the exception of Daniel Carpenter's pioneering works, we were aware of none. Yet reputation management in practice is certainly not something that is exclusive to the private sector. Public sector organizations of all kinds, ranging from central government agencies and ministries to public educational institutions and even municipalities, engage in activities to build, maintain, and protect their reputations. And although there is an emerging body of research on these activities, it does not have the characteristics of a coherent field of research. So, we felt it was necessary to increase our knowledge of the reputational strategies and efforts of public bureaucracies in the form of an edited collection of contributions from colleagues who share our interest in reputation in the public sector.

An edited volume is the joint efforts among the editors, the contributors, and the publisher. This volume is no exception: It has been more than a three-year-long process of numerous revisions, email exchanges, meetings, telephone and Skype calls, seminars, and even a conference. We started out in 2011 with some ideas that we shared with colleagues and subsequently developed into a book proposal. Because Arild was involved in a research project on municipal reputation and brand management financed by the Norwegian Research Council, the idea was to publish an edited volume on this topic exclusively. However, the attention quickly shifted toward reputation-management strategies and processes in a broader sense (although, as the observant reader will notice, the book includes a separate section on reputation management in local government). In July 2012, we signed the contract with Routledge. In April 2013, we chaired a panel on reputation management in the public sector at the XVII IRSPM conference in Prague, which turned out to be a successful event that significantly moved our project forward. And finally, in June of this year, we were ready to submit all chapters.

We want to thank all the contributors to this volume for their efforts and patience. Bringing together researchers from different academic disciplines and countries is always a challenge, especially when the field of research is xiv *Preface*

emerging and somewhat fragmented. However, in our case we are pleased to say that the hard work has paid off. We do want to acknowledge the efforts of the contributors to adhere to our guidelines and produce chapters of high quality that we believe will contribute to this emerging field of research. In addition, we want to thank the editorial team at Routledge for their help and encouragements along the way: Manjula Raman, Lauren Verity, and especially Laura Stearns, who was positive to the idea of a book on organizational reputation in the public sector from the very beginning. We also appreciate the financial support of the Norwegian Research Council in the development of this book. Last, but not least, we want to thank our families for their support and understanding during this long process.

1 Understanding Organizational Reputation in a Public Sector Context

Arild Wæraas and Moshe Maor

INTRODUCTION

When the term *reputation* is used about public sector organizations, the connotation that most likely comes to mind is 'bad.' Because government organizations have been associated with negatively charged words such as *inefficiency, bureaucracy, waste, incompetence,* and *rigidity* for so long, it is hard to imagine that public entities would have an interest in improving and protecting their reputation at all. However, as this book will emphasize, public entities are in fact concerned with their reputations and have begun to implement measures to nurture, maintain, and protect them. Research from multiple countries and institutional contexts presents mounting evidence that public sector organizations have become more cognizant of the value of a favorable reputation and, as a result, are gradually treating the management of reputation as a concern of strategic importance. The definition of unique competencies, development of communication strategies, careful timing of decisions, use of reputation-management consultants, and systematic use of media training and reputation measurement indices are only some of the visible activities that attest to the assumed importance of cultivating a favorable reputation.

The notion that public sector organizations benefit from a favorable reputation is not original. As noted by Carpenter and Krause (2012), reputation is discussed in several classic texts, including Simon, Smithburg, and Thompson ([1950] 1991); Kaufman (1981); and Wilson (1989). A more systematic, theoretical, and empirical focus did not emerge until after the millennium shift through the works of Carpenter (2001, 2002). Along with subsequent contributions (Carpenter 2010; Carpenter and Krause 2012; Gilad and Yogev 2012; Maor 2007, 2010, 2011; Gilad, Maor, and Ben-Nun Bloom 2013; Maor, Gilad, and Ben-Nun Bloom 2013; Maor and Sulitzeanu-Kenan 2013, 2014; Moffitt 2010; Picci 2011; Wæraas and Byrkjeflot 2012), these works form an emerging field of research that is not concerned with the general standing of political bodies or the public sector as a whole. Instead, the field draws attention to the reputation of individual administrative entities that behave more or less as autonomous actors within the

2 Arild Wæraas and Moshe Maor

political-administrative system. Although these entities are not all competing with each other, all of them can be assumed to benefit from cultivating and protecting a favorable reputation. These entities include bureaucratic organizations such as executive departments and ministries, central and local government agencies and units, regulatory agencies at various levels, public health care institutions, and educational institutions.

The benefits of enjoying a favorable reputation in the public sector context and the growing interest of public sector organizations in managing their reputation provide important background for this book. Our knowledge of these topics and their implications is limited. Compared to the field of corporate reputation, which has its own conference (The International Conference on Corporate Reputation, Brand Identity, and Competitiveness) and its own academic journal (*Corporate Reputation Review*), the field of reputation that pertains specifically to public bureaucracies is currently an emerging and immature, yet promising, field of research. Given that we currently find ourselves in a "reputation society" (Masum and Tovey 2011)—where decision making is characterized by increasing emphasis on track records—scholarly attention to the reputation of public sector organizations is warranted. How reputations are formed, how they are built and protected, and how they matter are only some of the key questions that need to be addressed in more detail. By searching for answers to these questions, it is our hope that this book will provide the basis for a more coherent field of research.

In the remaining sections of this chapter, we discuss the concept of reputation as it has been defined in business studies. We then give a more detailed introduction to the existing research on organizational reputation in the public sector, followed by a presentation of the various contributions in this volume.

WHAT IS ORGANIZATIONAL REPUTATION?

Despite the considerable amount of scholarly work published on organizational reputation, researchers are still debating its meaning. Definitions and uses are at times quite divergent, and reputation can easily be conflated with related concepts such as image, prestige, legitimacy, and status (Deephouse and Suchman 2008; Dutton and Dukerich 1991; Rindova, Pollock, and Hayward 2006). This terminology confusion creates a challenge for researchers who seek to describe and analyze the significance of reputation and reputation management in the private as well as the public sector. The picture becomes even more complex when considering that the concept of reputation is approached from a variety of academic disciplines. Fields such as corporate communication, strategy, management, marketing, economics, and organization studies investigate different aspects of reputation, each with their own traditions of doing research and analyzing the phenomenon

(Lange, Lee, and Dai 2010; Rhee and Valdez 2009; Rindova et al. 2005; Walker 2010).

In a review of 54 articles published on reputation, Walker (2010) finds that Fombrun's definition of reputation from 1996 is more frequently referenced than other definitions. Fombrun (1996, 72) defined reputation as a "collective representation of a firm's past actions and results that describe the firm's ability to deliver valuable outcomes to multiple stakeholders." According to Walker, Fombrun's definition emphasizes that reputation is (1) based on perceptions, (2) the aggregate perception of all stakeholders, and (3) comparative. Walker (2010) adds two additional dimensions: Reputation is (4) either positive or negative and (5) stable and enduring. Similarly, Deephouse and Suchman (2008) note that reputation is fundamentally (1) a continuous measure, by placing each actor on a continuum from worst to best; (2) rival, in the sense that an organization's reputation can increase only at another organization's expense; (3) differentiating, in the sense that reputation encourages organizations to distinguish themselves from their peers; and (4) economic, in the sense of being a strategic resource that contributes to competitive advantage. Fombrun (2012, 100) refines his own 1996 definition in the following way: "A corporate reputation is a collective assessment of a company's attractiveness to a specific group of stakeholders relative to a reference group of companies with which the company competes for resources." With this definition, Fombrun accentuates the comparative and competitive nature of reputation (c.f. Deephouse and Suchman 2008).

Different theoretical perspectives highlight the multifaceted aspects of reputation. Definitions tend to fall into one of three overarching perspectives: the economics, social constructivist, and institutional perspectives (Rindova and Martins 2012): From the *economics* perspective, reputation is formed among stakeholder groups as a result of actions chosen by the organization. Organizations signal their 'true' attributes through these actions, forming reputations with "specific stakeholders regarding specific characteristics" (Noe 2012, 116). Their reputation is a valuable asset or resource that enables them to achieve positive outcomes. As they decide which actions to take vis-à-vis their stakeholders to reach these outcomes, they are assumed to be able to control their own reputational signals. Organizations are players in a market and rely on these signals to judge and predict each other's competitive abilities and economic behavior (Weigelt and Camerer 1988).

From the *social constructivist* perspective, reputation refers to more than lower-level, attribute-specific perceptions. Organizational reputation is analyzed at the collective stakeholder level and is understood as a socially constructed aggregate product (Power 2007; Rao 1994; Rindova and Martins 2012; Rindova, Pollack, and Hayward 2006), referring to collective knowledge or recognition rather than an assessment of a relevant attribute. From this perspective, reputations are derived not only from the actions of organizations but also from social interactions between stakeholder groups. As stakeholders and organizations interact, a range of information,

4 Arild Wæraas and Moshe Maor

meanings, and interpretations is created, shared, and confirmed. Consequently, in contrast to the economics perspective, the social constructivist perspective assumes that organizations have a lower degree of control over their own reputation.

The *institutional* perspective shares the social-constructivist view that reputation is associated with collective knowledge and recognition, but emphasizes the larger macro-cultural context in which organizations compete and from which reputations develop (Fombrun 2012). Powerful institutional intermediaries within organizational fields such as monitoring organizations, the media, and financial analysts are important sources of reputation formation by disseminating 'objective' information about organizational attributes (Elsbach and Kramer 1996; Rindova and Martins 2012). Reputations refer to organizations' relative positions in rankings created by these intermediaries. The institutional perspective calls attention to these relative positions by, for example, highlighting the various responses undertaken by organizations when they perceive their position to be incorrect or unjustified (Elsbach and Kramer 1996; Martins 2005).

RESEARCH ON ORGANIZATIONAL REPUTATION IN THE PUBLIC SECTOR

All three perspectives on reputation can be identified in the literature on bureaucratic and administrative reputation. Two main research traditions have emerged: the political science and the organizational. Whereas the first shares notable viewpoints with the economics perspective on reputation, the other is inspired by the social constructivist and institutional perspectives.

The *political science* approach focuses empirically on executive agencies and their standing within a political-administrative system (Carpenter 2001, 2010; Gilad and Yogev 2012; Maor 2007, 2010, 2011, 2014; Maor, Gilad, and Ben-Nun Bloom 2012; Maor and Sulitzeanu-Kenan 2013, 2014; Moffitt 2010). In this approach, there are no disagreements among scholars over Carpenter's (2010, 45) definition of organizational reputation as "a set of symbolic beliefs about the unique or separable capacities, roles, and obligations of an organization, where these beliefs are embedded in audience networks." "Reputation uniqueness" according to Carpenter (2001, 5) refers to the demonstration by agencies that they can create solutions (e.g., expertise, efficiency) and provide services (e.g., moral protection) found nowhere else in the polity. Reputations provide governmental agencies with decisive benefits on top of their formal authority and powers. Reputations "are valuable political assets—they can be used to generate public support, to achieve delegated autonomy and discretion from politicians, to protect the agency from political attack, and to recruit and retain valued employees" (Carpenter 2002, 491).

The theoretical premise of studies within this tradition is that governmental agencies are generally rational and politically conscious organizations. The derived research examines how agencies' strategic balancing of their overall reputations is undertaken through their response to reputational threats based on their understanding of their distinct reputations. Suffice to mention that studies demonstrate that executive agencies endogenously construct their jurisdictions (Maor 2010), the public visibility of their errors (Maor 2011), and their decision duration insofar as regulatory enforcement is concerned (Maor and Sulitzeanu-Kenan 2013). Recently, studies have been directed at how agencies' strategic balancing of their overall reputations is undertaken through their *selective response* (i.e., choice between levels of a particular type of response) or *differential response* (i.e., choice between types of responses) to certain external signals. This stream of research tries to show how reputational concerns translate into actions by governmental agencies, by focusing on the internal shaping of administrative organizations' uneven responsiveness to—and management of—their multiple audiences. Findings show how agencies tend to keep silent regarding issues on which they generally enjoy a strong reputation and on issues that lie outside their distinct jurisdiction, while responding to opinions about core functional areas in which their reputation is weaker and areas wherein their reputation is still evolving (Maor, Gilad, and Ben-Nun Bloom 2013). This is a classic example of a selective response. Regarding differential response, Gilad, Maor, and Ben-Nun Bloom (2013) highlight how agencies have a greater propensity to acknowledge problems, yet mostly shift blame to others when faced with claims that regulation is overly lenient (namely, underregulation), and to deny allegations that regulation is excessive. And Maor and Sulitzeanu-Kenan (2014) demonstrate that the effect of negative media coverage on agency outputs is moderated by the level of previous-year agency outputs, i.e., negative coverage is followed by an increase in agency outputs when previous year outputs are below average and a decrease in agency outputs when previous year outputs are above average. These two types of agency response to reputational threats appear to be the result of the agency's increased interest in change following reputational threats, which is channeled to activities that are internally identified as lagging (e.g., public relations during natural disasters, consumer engagement, or stakeholder consultation).

Works drawing on the *organizational* approach to reputation also focus on public agencies but tend to treat any public sector entity as an 'organization' in search of a stronger reputation, and reputation management as an 'organizational' and taken-for-granted prescription with allegedly universal validity ready to be installed in any context (Wæraas and Byrkjeflot 2012). Hence, the focus includes all kinds of administrative units in the public sector ranging from ministries and central government agencies (Luoma-aho 2007, 2008; Wæraas 2013) to public health care units (Arnold et al. 2003; Byrkjeflot and Angell 2007; Luoma-aho 2013; Wæraas and Sataøen 2014)

6   Arild Wæraas and Moshe Maor

to local government units (Nielsen and Salomonsen 2012; Kuoppakangas, Suomi, and Horton 2013; Ryan 2007) to higher education (Aula and Tienari 2011; Wæraas and Solbakk 2009). Furthermore, instead of focusing on specific attributes of reputation, the research within this tradition emphasizes the general standing of public organizations and the overall socially constructed and aggregate nature of reputation. Consequently, the rationality and degrees of freedom of the individual organization in controlling its own reputation are downplayed. In many cases, the starting point for analysis is the problematic reputation of a public sector entity, or the growing awareness of public sector entities in general concerning the significance of managing reputation. The research focus is directed at how public entities cope with the challenges of reputation and how they develop strategies for influencing various aspects of reputation formation. In so doing, studies draw inspiration from corporate communication and branding literatures, looking more at the symbolic management of reputation and branding than the significance or impact of reputation on other variables (Avery and Lariscy 2010; Byrkjeflot and Angell 2007; Nielsen and Salomonsen 2012; Wæraas, Bjørnå, and Moldenæs 2014; Whelan et al. 2010). Increased competition in the public sector between different entities (e.g., between schools, hospitals, child care units, municipalities) following New Public Management reforms is generally seen as a major background for engaging in reputation-management strategies. However, works also acknowledge the social imitation processes underpinning the diffusion of reputation management and the various carriers that help spread this idea, such as popular management books, management gurus, and consultants (Wæraas and Byrkjeflot 2012).

PURPOSE AND PLAN OF BOOK

In sum, the existing body of literature on organizational reputation in the public sector is still in its infancy, suffering from theoretical fragmentation and with works being written from diverging research traditions with few cross-references. The lack of an overall research agenda represents a challenge for bringing researchers together. Indeed, the authors of this book come from such diverse disciplines as political science, public administration, organization studies, business studies, corporate communication, and economics, all relying on different traditions of theorizing and doing research, and working out of different countries and cultural contexts. The result is an eclectic volume that represents a polyphony of voices. We share the view that collaboration and fertilization across disciplinary boundaries is necessary to kick-start this emerging field toward a more unified path. A large puzzle needs to be laid, and our book and its contributions are all pieces of this larger puzzle whose picture, we hope, will become clearer.

The purpose of this book is not only to bring together contributions from various disciplines but also to take a first comprehensive step toward a more unified research domain on organizational reputation in the public sector. To do so, this book seeks answers to a number of questions. Some of the most important ones are the following:

- How can organizational reputation in the public sector be conceptualized and theorized?
- How do public sector organizations build and manage their reputations?
- What are the main strategies of reputation management that are available to public sector organizations?
- How do newly established public sector organizations build their reputation?
- How do public sector organizations respond to reputational threats?
- Do public sector organizations benefit from a good reputation, and how?
- What characterizes reputation management in times of severe crises?
- What goes on 'behind the scenes' when public sector organizations manage their reputation?
- How do stakeholder expectations shape reputation management?
- What is the role of politicians in reputation management?
- How do shared reputations affect reputation management?

The chapters of this book are organized into three parts. The first part, "Theoretical Perspectives," establishes the notion of bureaucratic reputation and delves into its theoretical dimensions. In chapter two, Moshe Maor seeks to evaluate where we are in understanding the reputation of public sector organizations. After highlighting different kinds of pressures that agencies regularly face in order to gauge the (in)security of reputation, he elaborates on the key insights of the literature, focusing on reputation management through changes in the timing and observability of agency decisions, as well as through changes in agency outputs. He also identifies five problems in applying bureaucratic reputation theories to public sector organizations. The chapter concludes with a section that highlights a number of substantive areas that are ripe for further scholarly exploration.

Chapter three, written by Lucio Picci, opens up the black box of reputation in a public sector setting. After describing the bureaucratic reputation game and defining the incentives, preferences, and strategies of the actors involved in these games, he discusses the organizational outputs of the strategies that are pursued. Public organizations might benefit more from having a 'satisficing' reputation: one that is good enough to escape criticism from audiences but not so good as to generate opposition from those actors whose interests are at odds with the organization's mission. Picci subsequently discusses how various reputational incentives may be strengthened, paying specific attention to a key issue he refers to as the overall legibility problem.

8 *Arild Wæraas and Moshe Maor*

In chapter four, Haldor Byrkjeflot invites a critical examination of popular reputation-management prescriptions, or 'recipes,' that have spread from the private to the public sector through consulting firms and management gurus. He discusses why reputation-management recipes have increased in popularity in recent years and highlights several problems and paradoxes arising from their proliferation. Because reputation management will most likely continue to have an important impact on public organizations in the foreseeable future, developing alternative ideals that are more attuned to public institutions' characteristics and values is a challenge. The chapter ends with a review of eight paradoxes associated with the adoption of reputation-management recipes in the public sector.

The second part of this book examines reputation-management processes in central government entities. It begins with Ciara O'Dwyer's chapter, which is a study of the efforts of a newly established agency in Ireland to develop its reputation. The agency sought to develop a strong reputation by developing positive working relations with key stakeholders, working collaboratively and transparently, highlighting technical competence, and prioritizing the public interest. However, it failed to fully understand the importance of its relationship with its parent government department, thus threatening its ability to manage its reputation effectively. These findings indicate that agencies can develop a strong reputation but must be mindful of the extent to which central government can exert control over its operations.

Chapter six is written by Tom Christensen and Per Lægreid. They address the reputation-management efforts of the Norwegian police following the terrorist attack on July 22, 2011. The police were criticized for being too self-congratulatory and lacking in empathy concerning both the way they handled the crisis and how they presented their own handling of it. Analyzing the response strategies from an instrumental and a cultural perspective, the chapter concludes that the reputation management of the police was primarily shaped by symbolic and cultural factors. Moreover, although the reputation-management efforts essentially failed, the impact on overall trust was minimal.

In chapter seven, Koen Verhoest, Jan Rommel, and Jan Boon investigate the relationship between reputation, trust, and agency autonomy. Building on a case study of the Flemish electricity and gas regulator, the authors seek to explain the policy autonomy of this agency. Its autonomy and collaboration with the political principal, the Flemish Minister of Energy, are much stronger than what could be expected, thus representing an empirical puzzle. Examining the role of reputation and trust in this regard, and discussing key differences and similarities between the two concepts, the authors find that the agency relied on reputation as a trust-building mechanism. This resulted in more de facto policy autonomy and deeper forms of collaboration.

Chapter eight is written by Yael Schanin. She examines how mass protest affects a bureaucratic organization's strategies and, more specifically,

Understanding Organizational Reputation 9

how organizational reputation affects the way a bureaucratic organization reacts to public protest. These questions are examined in a study of how a social protest affected the communication policy and the regulatory policy of the Banking Supervision Department in the Bank of Israel. Employing both quantitative and qualitative methods, the chapter analyzes the change in the Israeli banking regulator's responses to expressions of public opinion and the change in the regulator's regulatory operation after the social protest. One important finding is that media policy takes care of short-term reputational threats, whereas regulatory policy takes care of long-term reputational threats.

The third part of the book aims to shed light on reputation management in local government. Chapter nine, written by Maria Blomgren, Tina Hedmo, and Caroline Waks, takes us 'behind the scene' of reputation-management processes in Swedish regional hospitals. It investigates how the internal complexities, interactions, and dynamics are managed; which factors condition the management of these types of processes; and which implications these factors might have for organizational self-presentations. The authors reach the conclusion that reputation management in hospitals is a complex, bottom-up process involving, and being conditioned by, negotiations, the institutional embeddedness of health care, medical professions, and communication professionals.

In chapter ten, Hilde Bjørnå explores the reputation-management strategies of three Norwegian municipalities. Relying on a combination of data sources, she studies how reputation-management strategies are shaped based on the municipalities' perceptions of stakeholder group expectations and how they vary across municipal contexts. She finds that the three cases all target different stakeholders and develop their strategies accordingly. She also finds that the strategies are likely to affect the competitive standing of the municipalities and that the main challenges associated with their strategies derive from their status as political and democratic organizations.

Chapter eleven, written by Heidi Houlberg Salomonsen and Jeppe Agger Nielsen, examines the politics of reputation management in Danish local government. The authors address the interests, roles of, and relationships between the politicians and the administration in this regard. The starting point is that although very little is known about the role of politicians in reputation-management processes, there are good reasons to expect a certain level of conflict between politicians and between politicians and their administrations. However, in the Danish local government context, politicians and administrators seem to share the same interests. A key finding is that both groups are involved and that reputation management is neither a depoliticized activity nor a topic of much disagreement.

Finally, in chapter twelve, Arild Wæraas explores the significance of shared reputations in Norwegian local government. In the Norwegian municipal sector, municipalities that are members of the same region share a common reputation with members of that region. The author explores the

10 *Arild Wæraas and Moshe Maor*

significance of this reputation commons and investigates how the municipalities handle the challenge of sharing it. A key finding is that they rely more on communal strategies than differentiation strategies. The chapter concludes that municipal reputation building in Norway is not characterized by a reputation commons tragedy, despite the fact that the municipalities also focus on their own individual reputation.

In sum, these chapters offer a rich palette of the most recent research and thinking on reputation in public bureaucracies. As the reader will discover, there is much to learn about reputation issues from a number of contexts and administrative levels. However, this book is clearly only a first step toward a better understanding of the significance of reputation. Important questions and empirical as well as theoretical gaps remain. We hope that this first step will motivate both new and experienced scholars to join us in developing this emerging field.

REFERENCES

Arnold, John, Crispin Coombs, Adrian Wilkinson, John Loan-Clarke, Jennifer Park, and Diane Preston. 2003. "Corporate Images of the United Kingdom National Health Service: Implications for the Recruitment and Retention of Nursing and Allied Health Professional Staff." *Corporate Reputation Review* 6:223–238.

Aula, Hanna-Mari, and Janne Tienari. 2011. "Becoming "World-Class"? Reputation-Building in a University Merger." *Critical Perspectives on International Business* 7:7–29.

Avery, Elizabeth Johnson, and Ruthann W. Lariscy. 2010. "FEMA and the Rhetoric of Redemption: New Directions in Crisis Communication Models for Government Agencies." In *The Handbook of Crisis Communication,* edited by W. Timothy Coombs and Sherry J. Holladay, 319–333. Maiden, MA: Wiley-Blackwell.

Byrkjeflot, Haldor, and Svein Ivar Angell. 2007. "Dressing Up Hospitals as Enterprises? The Expansion and Managerialization of Communication in Norwegian Hospitals." In *Mediating Business: The Expansion of Business Journalism,* edited by Peter Kjær and Tore Slaatta, 235–264. København: Copenhagen Business Press.

Carpenter, Daniel. 2001. *The Forging of Bureaucratic Autonomy: Reputations, Networks, and Policy Formation in Executive Agencies, 1862–1928.* Princeton, NJ: Princeton University Press.

Carpenter, Daniel. 2002. "Groups, the Media, Agency Waiting Costs, and FDA Drug Approval." *American Journal of Political Science* 46:490–505.

Carpenter, Daniel. 2010. *Reputation and Power: Organizational Image and Pharmaceutical Regulation at the FDA.* Princeton, NJ: Princeton University Press.

Carpenter, Daniel, and George A. Krause. 2012. "Reputation and Public Administration." *Public Administration Review* 72:26–32.

Deephouse, David L., and Mark C. Suchman. 2008. "Legitimacy in Organizational Institutionalism." In *The SAGE Handbook of Organizational Institutionalism,* edited by Royston Greenwood, Christine Oliver, Kerstin Sahlin, and Roy Suddaby, 49–77. Thousand Oaks, CA: Sage.

Dutton, Jane E., and Janet M. Dukerich. 1991. "Keeping an Eye on the Mirror—Image and Identity in Organizational Adaptation." *Academy of Management Journal* 34:517–554.

Understanding Organizational Reputation   11

Elsbach, Kimberly D., and Roderick M. Kramer. 1996. "Members' Responses to Organizational Identity Threats: Encountering and Countering the Business Week Rankings." *Administrative Science Quarterly* 41:442.

Fombrun, Charles J. 1996. *Reputation: Realizing Value from the Corporate Image.* Boston: Harvard Business School Press.

Fombrun, Charles J. 2012. "The Building Blocks of Corporate Reputation." In *The Oxford Handbook of Corporate Reputation,* edited by Michael Barnett and Timothy C. Pollock, 94–113. Oxford: Oxford University Press.

Gilad, Sharon, and Tamar Yogev. 2012. "How Reputation Regulates Regulators: Illustrations from the Regulation of Retail Finance." In *The Oxford Handbook of Corporate Reputation,* edited by Michael Barnett and Timothy C. Pollock, 320–340. Oxford: Oxford University Press.

Gilad, Sharon, Moshe Maor, and Pazit Ben-Nun Bloom. 2013. "Organizational Reputation, the Content of Public Allegations, and Regulatory Communication." *Journal of Public Administration Research and Theory.* doi: 10.1093/jopart/mut041.

Kaufman, Herbert A. 1981. *The Administrative Behavior of Federal Bureau Chiefs.* Washington, DC: Brookings Institution.

Kuoppakangas, Päivikki, Kati Suomi, and Khim Horton. 2013. "Reputation and Legitimacy: A Comparative View of Three Municipal Enterprises in Finland." *International Journal of Public and Private Healthcare Management and Economics* 3:1–17.

Lange, Donald P., Peggy M. Lee, and Ye Dai. 2010. "Organizational Reputation: A Review." *Journal of Management* 37:153–184.

Luoma-aho, Vilma. 2007. "Neutral Reputation and Public Sector Organizations." *Corporate Reputation Review* 10:124–143.

Luoma-aho, Vilma. 2008. "Sector Reputation and Public Organisations." *International Journal of Public Sector Management* 21:446–467.

Luoma-aho, Vilma. 2013. "Expectation Management for Public Sector Organizations." *Public Relations Review* 39:248–250.

Maor, Moshe. 2007. "A Scientific Standard and an Agency's Legal Independence: Which of These Reputation Protection Mechanisms Is Less Susceptible to Political Moves?" *Public Administration* 85:961–978.

Maor, Moshe. 2010. "Organizational Reputation and Jurisdictional Claims: The Case of the U.S. Food and Drug Administration." *Governance: An International Journal of Policy, Administration, and Institutions* 23:133–159.

Maor, Moshe. 2011. "Organizational Reputations and the Observability of Public Warnings in 10 Pharmaceutical Markets." *Governance: An International Journal of Policy, Administration, and Institutions* 24:557–582.

Maor, Moshe. 2014. "The Missing Areas in the Bureaucratic Reputation Framework." Working Paper, Jerusalem: Hebrew University of Jerusalem. http://papers.ssrn.com/sol3/papers.cfm?abstract_id=2466425.

Maor, Moshe, Sharon Gilad, and Pazit Ben-Nun Bloom. 2013. "Organizational Reputation, Regulatory Talk, and Strategic Silence." *Journal of Public Administration Research and Theory* 23:581–608.

Maor, Moshe, and Raanan Sulitzeanu-Kenan. 2013. "The Effect of Salient Reputational Threats on the Pace of FDA Enforcement." *Governance: An International Journal of Policy, Administration, and Institutions* 26:31–61.

Maor, Moshe, and Raanan Sulitzeanu-Kenan. 2014. "Differential Performance Response: The Effect of Reputational Threats on Public Agency Outputs." http://papers.ssrn.com/sol3/papers.cfm?abstract_id=2441699.

Masum, Hassan, and Mark Tovey, eds. 2011. *The Reputation Society. How Online Opinions Are Reshaping the Offline World.* Cambridge, MA: MIT Press.

12   Arild Wæraas and Moshe Maor

Martins, Luis. 2005. "A Model of the Effects of Reputational Rankings on Organizational Change." *Organization Science* 16:701–720.

Moffitt, Susan L. 2010. "Promoting Agency Reputation through Public Advice: Advisory Committee Use in the FDA." *The Journal of Politics* 72:880–893.

Nielsen, Jeppe Agger, and Heidi Houlberg Salomonsen. 2012. "Why All This Communication? Explaining Strategic Communication in Danish Local Governments from an Institutional Perspective." *Scandinavian Journal of Public Administration* 16:69–89.

Noe, Thomas. 2012. "A Survey of the Economic Theory of Reputation: Its Logics and Limits." In *The Oxford Handbook of Corporate Reputation,* edited by Michael L. Barnett and Timothy G. Pollock, 114–139. Oxford: Oxford University Press.

Picci, Lucio. 2011. *Reputation-Based Governance.* Stanford, CA: Stanford University Press.

Power, Michael. 2007. *Organized Uncertainty. Designing a World of Risk Management.* London: Oxford University Press.

Rao, Hayagreeva. 1994. "The Social Construction of Reputation: Certification Contests, Legitimation and the Survival of Organizations in the American Automobile Industry 1895–1912." *Strategic Management Journal* 15:20–44.

Rhee, Mooweon, and Michael Valdez. 2009. "Contextual Factors Surrounding Reputation Damage with Potential Implications for Reputation Repair." *Academy of Management Review* 34:146–168.

Rindova, Violina P., and Luis Martins. 2012. "Show Me the Money: A Multidimensional Perspective on Reputation as an Intangible Asset." In *The Oxford Handbook of Corporate Reputation,* edited by Michael L. Barnett and Timothy C. Pollock, 16–33. Oxford: Oxford University Press.

Rindova, Violina P., Timothy C. Pollock, and M. Hayward. 2006. "Celebrity Firms: The Social Construction of Market Popularity." *Academy of Management Review* 31: 50–71.

Rindova, Violina P., Ian O. Williamson, Antoaneta P. Petkova, and Joy M. Sever. 2005. "Being Good or Being Known: An Empirical Examination of the Dimensions, Antecedents, and Consequences of Organizational Reputation." *Academy of Management Journal* 48:1033–1049.

Ryan, Barbara. 2007. "How Can the Corporate Sector Concepts of 'Reputation' and 'Trust' Be Used by Local Government? A Study to Establish a Model of Reputation Management for Local Government." *Asia Pacific Public Relations Journal* 8:37–75.

Simon, Herbert A., Donald W. Smithburg, and Victor A. Thompson. 1991 [1950]. *Public Administration.* Piscataway, NJ: Transaction.

Wæraas, Arild. 2013. "Beauty from Within? What Bureaucracies Stand For." *American Review of Public Administration.* doi: 10.1177/0275074013480843.

Wæraas, Arild, and Haldor Byrkjeflot. 2012. "Public Sector Organizations and Reputation Management: Five Problems." *International Public Management Journal* 15:186–206.

Wæraas, Arild, and Hogne L. Sataøen. 2014. "Trapped in Conformity? Translating Reputation Management into Practice." *Scandinavian Journal of Management* 30(2):242–253.

Wæraas, Arild, and Marianne N. Solbakk. 2009. "Defining the Essence of a University: Lessons from Higher Education Branding." *Higher Education* 57:449–462.

Wæraas, Arild, Hilde Bjørnå, and Turid Moldenæs. 2014. "Place, Organization, Democracy: Three Strategies for Municipal Branding." *Public Management Review.* doi: 10.1080/14719037.2014.906965.

Walker, Kent. 2010. "A Systematic Review of the Corporate Reputation Review Literature: Definition, Measurement, and Theory." *Corporate Reputation Review* 12:357–387.

Weigelt, Keith, and Colin Camerer. 1988. "Reputation and Corporate Strategy: A Review of Recent Theory and Applications." *Strategic Management Journal* 9:443–454.

Whelan, Susan, Gary Davies, Margaret Walsh, and Rita Bourke. 2010. "Public Sector Corporate Branding and Customer Orientation." *Journal of Business Research* 63:1164–1171.

Wilson, James Q. 1989. *Bureaucracy: What Government Agencies Do and Why They Do It*. New York: Basic Books.

Part I
Theoretical Perspectives

2 Theorizing Bureaucratic Reputation*

Moshe Maor

Theoretical and empirical research on bureaucratic reputation and its impact on the behavior of governmental agencies and public sector organizations (I henceforth use these two terms interchangeably) has begun to find its place in modern-day political science and bureaucracy research. A growing body of research has acknowledged the importance of reputational considerations in decision making by public entities, but has only just begun to scratch the surface of the scientific opportunities awaiting investigation of this subject. This body of research revolves around the ways reputation-sensitive public bodies function as organizations within a governmental system (Meier and Krause 2003) and directs our attention inside the black box of executive government. Carpenter (2001, 2010a) has offered some generalized answers to issues regarding reputation and regulatory power, and has summed up the contribution of this scholarly literature: "The lesson of this scholarship is that, when trying to account for a regulator's behavior, *look at the audience, and look at the threats*" (Carpenter 2010b, 832, *italics in original*).

This chapter addresses two lines of criticism regarding Carpenter's approach to bureaucratic reputation. First, he puts too much emphasis on the exogenous threats while underestimating their endogenous processing, given agencies' understanding of their distinct reputations.[1] Second, he too greatly emphasizes the institutional persistence of legislative and presidential decisions, which lend stability to autonomy, thereby lending stability to good reputation (Carpenter 2001, 18). In doing so, Carpenter can respond to claims regarding the fragile foundations of good reputation (Roberts 2006, 57; Miller 2010, 474) by directing attention to institutional persistence. However, this line of reasoning underestimates the ability of public bodies to act adaptively, strategically, and opportunistically in developing good reputations as well as in maintaining and enhancing the stability of such reputations. This chapter seeks to evaluate where we are in understanding the aforementioned lines of criticism. It therefore focuses on what I consider to be critical themes related to this criticism, which have permeated the literature on organizational reputation since the early 2000s.

18 *Moshe Maor*

Prior to that time, bureaucratic reputation in the public sector was rarely mentioned in institutional political science, which instead largely focused on political control of bureaucratic agencies by elected officials (or 'principals') and the mechanisms by which these officials could influence agency behavior (Wood 2010).[2] During that time, in small numbers, some political scientists made contributions to the study of bureaucratic reputation, including the works of Quirk (1980), Rourke (1984), Wilson (1989), Heimann (1997), and Whitford (2002). However, that has changed during the last decade, since Carpenter (2001) first noticed that agencies attempt to cultivate reputations that will enable them to gain autonomy, and theorized about it. This new wave of theoretical and empirical work is different because, whereas in models of political control the source of bureaucratic power has been the bureaucratic information advantage an agency possesses, in theories of bureaucratic reputation the source of bureaucratic power has been the unique reputation and diverse ties to interest groups and the media an agency cultivates.

In order to portray the key findings from research concerning the aforementioned lines of criticism, I focus on six tasks. First, I elaborate the main concept under study. Second, I highlight two kinds of pressures that agencies regularly face—pressures of political control derived from the institutional structure under which agencies operate, as well as pressures from the people whose confidence they try to retain—in order to gauge the (in)security of organization reputation. Third, I elaborate on the key insights of the literature that focus on reputation management through changes in the timing and observability of agency decisions, as well as through changes in agency outputs. Fourth, I discuss the main findings of the literature that revolve around reputation management by the strategic use of communication. Fifth, I briefly identify five main problems in applying bureaucratic reputation theories to public sector organizations. Last, I suggest substantive areas ripe for further scholarly exploration.

ANALYTICAL PRELUDE

Over the last 10 years or so, an important new approach has emerged within political science that puts bureaucratic reputation center stage. It is perhaps best characterized by four elements: the specific view of reputation that enables an agency that possesses it to make a claim for unique contributions to the public good; the multifaceted nature of reputation; the existence of multiple expectations by multiple audiences;[3] and the context of today's knowledge society and blame culture, which foster conditions that intensify agency concerns with reputational risk. These elements are the cornerstones of reputation-grounded and driven conceptual frameworks in political science. There are numerous questions fundamental to our understanding of these elements of bureaucratic reputation. Although I will address them, it is perhaps most critical to begin by defining the concept under study. The idea is not to provide a comprehensive, cross-disciplinary review of the literature that addresses the concept of reputation, nor to compare it with related constructs. The intent is rather to highlight the main features of this concept.

Much of the bureaucratic reputation theory is the product of Harvard University political scientist Dan Carpenter, whose methods combine historical analysis, quantitative empirical studies, and formal modeling. In this nascent subfield, there are no disagreements among scholars over Carpenter's (2010a, 45) definition of organizational reputation as a set of symbolic beliefs about the unique or separable capacities, intentions, roles, obligations, history, and mission of an organization that are embedded in a network of multiple audiences (Carpenter 2010a, 33, 45). This definition centers on the evaluation of the organization's unique character and activities by multiple audiences. Evaluation is based on past observations and experience with the organization's ability to provide unique services capably. Reputation uniqueness, according to Carpenter (2001, 5), refers to the demonstration by agencies that they can create solutions (e.g., expertise, efficiency) and provide services (e.g., moral protection) that no other agency in the polity offers. This implies that organizational reputation relies on the external audiences' perceptions of the quality of policy outcomes that these audiences really care about and the effectiveness of its actions that distinguish the organization from others in the polity. According to Carpenter and Krause (2012, 27), "what audiences see is not the perfectly tuned or visible reality of the agency." Rather, it is an image that embeds considerable uncertainty and ambiguity (Gioia, Schultz, and Corley 2000) regarding the agency's performance, the expertise of its staff, its values, and the legality of its actions (Carpenter, 2010a). "Complex public organizations are seen 'through a glass but dimly' by their manifold audiences" (Carpenter and Krause 2012, 27).

This frame of reference differs from the one that underpins the concept of legitimacy, which refers to the appropriateness or correctness of the organization's character with respect to the norms and routines required (Foreman, Whetten, and Mackey 2012). Whereas the legitimacy criteria focus on the organization's fit or similarity with established norms and expectations, the construct of reputation revolves around the way the organization stands out compared to its peers (Deephouse and Carter, 2005). Carpenter's (2010a) statement of organizational distinction is even stronger because it directs attention away from a broad, general impression and toward the key element of comparison, be it the performative, moral, procedural, or technical traits of the organization. An agency does not have a strong reputation per se, but rather a strong reputation for the protection of public safety, public health, public morality, and so on.[4] Carpenter's four faces of an agency's reputation highlight the dimensions over which the relative standing of the organization is assessed vis-à-vis other agencies.

20   *Moshe Maor*

Carpenter's statement also implies the existence of multiple reputations and, therefore, multiple expectations by external audiences regarding each of these dimensions. Each external audience selects the dimension(s) of reputation that will receive priority in its assessment of the organization. In the same vein, each organization chooses which dimension(s) will receive priority and which will not (Carpenter and Krause 2012, 27). Another aspect of multidimensionality is that agencies' reputations may vary across functional areas, such as regulatees' stability, corporate governance, and consumer protection (Maor, Gilad, and Ben-Nun Bloom 2013). Consequently, agency leaders pursue an alignment between agency policies and a carefully cultivated reputation for one or more of the aforementioned dimensions, in one or more of the agency's functional areas, which is distinct from other organizations (cf. Gilad, 2008; Gilad and Yogev 2012). They do so by delivering unique services and by avoiding visible failures (Carpenter 2001, 2002, 2004; Heimann 1997; Kaufman 1981, 76; Krause and Douglas 2005; Roberts 2006).

Government agencies can build reputations by creating a good and preferably superior track record; shadowing practices and policies pursued by agencies that possess strong reputations; affiliating with agencies and national, international, or supranational organizations that possess strong reputations; and by appointing agency heads who enjoy strong reputations (Petkova 2012; Maor 2011). If reputations are successfully formed, cultivated and managed, they become "valuable political assets—they can be used to generate public support, to achieve delegated autonomy and discretion from politicians, to protect the agency from political attack, and to recruit and retain valued employees" (Carpenter 2002, 491). Because strong reputations are powerful assets for agencies and are, in fact, equivalent to agency coalition building (Carpenter 2001, 22), many incentives exist in order to protect them. "There are other things that bureaucracies protect and 'maximize', but for many agencies . . . reputation protection serves as the simplest and most powerful dynamic governing their behavior" (Carpenter 2004, 54). Regulatory pressures in today's knowledge society and blame culture foster conditions that intensify agency concerns with reputational risk, which is defined as the possible loss of an agency's reputational capital (Fombrun 1996, 27). Such risks differ "in . . . social construction from other risk categories by being a purely 'man-made' product of social interaction and communication" (Power, Scheytt, Soin, and Sahlin 2009, 302). Such man-made products may potentially have disastrous impacts on agency survival, as they may lead to damaged reputation and, consequently, to severe budgetary cuts or auditing punishments (e.g., Banks and Weingast 1992). This is especially the case when agency failure is undertaken under conditions of high political risk and task salience—for example, during crisis response.

But even during an agency's normal operation, "satisfying some audience subset often means upsetting others or projecting ambiguity" (Carpenter and Krause 2012, 29). Therefore, each agency routinely processes criticisms

Theorizing Bureaucratic Reputation   21

from external audiences that may carry reputational risks. The prioritization of reputational risks may involve a consideration of the relative risk to society, the relative risk to the most relevant external audience, the (political) cost of damaged reputations, and the extent to which the agency is willing to expose itself, by way of policy intervention, to reputational loss. The result is an agency decision to focus its energies on handling current or future threats, over one or more functional areas, in relation to one or more external audiences (i.e., prioritizing one audience over another), by following formal or informal guidelines.

The durable bureaucratic reputation of an organization may be harmed by criticism and doubts as to its expertise, capacity, efficacy, and the quality of its goods and services, as evaluated by its salient functioning and interactions with external audiences with regard to its key activities. Agencies' incentives to avoid reputational damage are incorporated in studies of organizational reputation as an assumption—namely, that regulatory agencies are rational agents as well as politically conscious organizations interested in protecting their unique reputations (e.g., Quirk 1980; Heimann 1997; Carpenter 2010a; Maor 2010, 2011; Maor, Gilad, and Ben-Nun Bloom 2013; Maor and Sulitzeanu-Kenan 2013). Once this assumption is made, scholars turn to gauge how administrative agencies identify reputational threats and endogenously construct their reputation-protection behavior. A more nuanced picture is provided by Moffitt (2010, 882), who claims that scholars may analyze the pursuit of agency reputation in isolation from other agencies (Carpenter 2002, 2004), in competition or comparison with other agencies (Krause and Corder 2007; Krause and Douglas 2005), or as "conditions when bureaucrats' reputations depend on others . . . who reside outside of the agency as well as those within" (Moffitt 2010, 882).

Theories of bureaucratic reputation are therefore analytic expressions of the relationship between administrative agencies and their external audiences, in which the agencies protect their reputations by responding to their multiple audiences. The logic of such theories, therefore, raises critical issues related to agency decisions, such as how agencies make decisions, how they resolve goal conflicts, how external performance criteria affect agencies, how well agencies socialize their members (Meier and Krause 2003, 15), and others. The studies elaborated here—which are guided by bureaucratic reputation theories and informed by these questions—testify to the generality and promise of this approach.

THE (IN)SECURITY OF GOOD REPUTATION

In this section, I highlight two kinds of threats that agencies regularly face in order to gauge the implications an analysis of bureaucratic reputation has on research regarding political control of the bureaucracy. Administrative agencies confront varying pressures of political control that are derived from the institutional structure under which they operate, as well as pressures from the people whose confidence they try to retain. Although each type of pressure may lead to the other, it is conceptually important to distinguish between the two. For the former, because public bureaucracies are designed politically (e.g., Moe 1989, 1990; Krause 2010), elected officials are likely to apply control measures and design incentive systems in order to ensure that agencies do not drift from the goals set by elected authorities. So when the priorities of a president or of congressional majorities change, agencies may be exposed to the forces of political control. A president or a congressional committee determined to rein in the power of an administrative agency and influence its behavior have several mechanisms at their disposal, including oversight by congressional committees (e.g., Weingast and Moran 1983), appointments (e.g., Wood 1988'fire-alarm' oversight (e.g., McCubbins and Schwarz 1984), control by the president and multi-institutional policy makers (e.g., Hammond and Knot 1996), direct citizen contact (e.g., Brehm and Gates 1997), a statute (e.g., Huber and Shipan 2002), administrative procedures (e.g., McCubbins, Noll, and Weingast 1987), and personnel management institutions embedded in a political system (Gailmard and Patty 2007).

The aforementioned literature raises two questions in relation to the (in)security of bureaucratic reputation. First, can agencies' concerns with reputational considerations outweigh the political control pressures that they confront? And, specifically, how do reputation-sensitive agencies arrive at decisions given the institutional structure under which they operate and the uncertainty that is experienced by bureaucratic experts in the subject area of agency operation? Second, assuming an agency has a multifaceted reputation, which of these bases of reputation is more/less susceptible to political moves? Turning to the first question, Krause and Douglas (2005) found that reputational maintenance is more important to an agency than succumbing to political pressures and, therefore, there is no observable relationship between political insulation and bureaucratic performance. Instead, agencies employ imitative practices in order to avoid being labeled inferior. These findings were corroborated in a related study that suggests that differences in agency design at the federal level do not explain differences in the quality of administrative performance (Krause and Douglas 2006). However, Krause and Corder (2007, 130) found evidence to suggest that "Executive branch agencies . . . possess tangible incentives to bias their forecasts towards serving a president's interests at the expense of objective quality," although this bias appears unrelated to long-term changes in the level of politicization within each agency. And Wood and Waterman (1991) found that agencies situated in executive departments were most responsive to executive influence, whereas the output of independent regulatory commissions remained stable over the period examined. They concluded that "structure is important—but not overriding when multiple democratic principals jointly demand a policy outcome" (Wood and Waterman 1991, 823). So, whether Krause and Douglas' (2006) findings could be generalized to other public bodies is questionable.

Turning to the second question, Maor (2007) shows that the scientific 'gold standard' for agency decisions (i.e., a scientific fact-finding method that is the most accurate test possible)

> is less susceptible to political moves because of its important role as a legitimating device for both government ministers and regulators. Government ministers are able to address multiple audiences and even to respond to aggressive [anti-government] strategies by powerful interest groups by undermining one reputation-protection mechanism (that is, an agency's independence) without weakening the other (that is, the scientific barrier for granting full-subsidy status to treatments that lack comparative therapeutic advantage).
>
> (Maor 2007, 961)

Maor concludes that agency (formal) "independence may be regarded as a symbolic device, which government ministers can modify to appease interest groups that aggressively oppose the agency's policy" (Maor 2007, 963).

But if that is so, how can bureaucratic reputation theories explain assaults on the credibility and reputation of a regulator by elected officials? At the outset, Carpenter relies too heavily on the institutional persistence of legislative and presidential decisions that lend stability to autonomy, thereby lending stability to good reputation. According to Carpenter (2001, 18), "[w]hen politicians defer to agencies, they often do so through funding and legal mechanisms that are not easily changed or reversed on short notice." In doing so, Carpenter can respond to claims that good reputations are fragile and insecure (Roberts 2006, 57; Miller 2010, 474) because they "sit on the slippery ground of their constituents' fickle interpretations" (Fombrun 1996, 388), by directing attention to institutional persistence. However, Carpenter (2010a, 730) eloquently demonstrates how "the rise of libertarian models and conservative politics in the United States, the accretion of power to the global pharmaceutical industry, and the globalization of economic regulation have all weakened the authority and force of the [Food and Drug] Administration's capacities and actions." Newt Gingrich's shaming of the U.S. Food and Drug Administration (FDA) as America's "number one job-killer" in 1994 (p. 731) and President Bush's appointments, which undermined the scientific foundation of the FDA's decision-making process, have further weakened FDA authority. Does this experience expose the fragile foundations of good reputation? And if so, should we devote academic attention to study a phenomenon that is fragile, friable, and fleeting?

24 Moshe Maor

According to bureaucratic reputation theories, as long as the agency can provide consistent quality of activities and effectiveness of outputs over time, and be perceived by multiple audiences as doing so, agency reputation will be solidified. It will also be of value to elected officials who may infer an agency's future decisions from its past action, thereby reducing their uncertainty about the future. The problem is that it is very difficult to assess agency reputation at any given point in time. Changes in an agency's managerial and professional leadership, industry health, globalization pressures, and other unstable factors may constrain agency options and create situations where agency activities have a negative impact on some politically sensitive aspects. An agency may also run into scandals or accidents, miscalculate regulatory opportunities, and throw itself into highly emotional debates with wide-ranging moral and scientific implications. These unfortunate events may create uncertainty about agency action in the present, and this, in turn, is bound to make agency reputation of little value in reducing elected officials' uncertainty about agency actions in the future.

But reputation-sensitive agencies are adaptive, strategic, and sometimes even opportunistic actors (e.g., Oliver 1991). Their creative response is generated through interactive dynamics and mutual exchanges. They have a repository of ideas, values, and strategies that they may combine in various ways, deploy them politically, and redeploy them between different audiences, thereby redefining relations with these audiences. In the pursuit of reputation protection, they may simultaneously play multiple games (Sheingate 2007, 15), and their "actions can be moves in many games at once" (Padgett and Ansell 1993, 1263). Specifically, reputation-sensitive agencies are able to adapt in order to cope with criticisms by external audiences—that is, to accommodate themselves to the preferences of their external audiences. They are able to manipulate external audiences' opinions and shape, rather than simply accommodate external audiences' opinions, turning them into a component of agency behavior. In other words, they can act to shape the criteria by which they are assessed rather than acting only to influence their reputational ranking. And they are able to exploit opportunities with little regard for principles or consequences; for example, by trying to claim credit during another agency's crisis precisely when the crisis comes under control, or by claiming jurisdiction when judging that such a claim is perceptively timed (Maor 2010). This, in turn, enables them to initiate a change in their relations with external audiences as well as altering its direction to their own advantage.

Understanding agency behavior means understanding the execution of these strategies. Carpenter and Moore (2007), for example, have offered an illustrative example of creative response that combines all three types of agency behavior and relies on two related concepts: bureaucratic cohort and the strategic use of ambiguity. They demonstrated how a new cohort of FDA officials recruited after World War II made new demands on drug companies while framing these demands as embedded in the restrictive limits of the legal authority under which they were acting. Based on strong professional and scientific signals and ambiguous claims, they tried to change the critical coordinates of FDA operations from safety standards that were legally authorized to new drug efficacy standards. And when events led Congress to seek new standards, they were able to step into the fray with a solution already at hand.

It is therefore reasonable to expect that once reputation-sensitive agencies notice that the political pendulum is about to swing, or has plainly swung, way too far in a direction that undermines agency reputation, they will be likely to endogenously process these reputational threats and react—in an adaptive, strategic, and/or opportunistic way, or not at all—on the basis of their understanding of their distinct reputation. If successful, agency reputation will be maintained or restored. If they decide to act, agency response may include, for example, substantive refocusing of activities across functional areas, reorganization and collaborative engagements across functional areas, distinct communication strategies (Maor, Gilad, and Ben-Nun Bloom 2013; Gilad, Maor, and Ben-Nun Bloom 2013), changes in public agency outputs (Maor and Sulitzeanu-Kenan 2014), and, above all, investment in quality output across functional areas.

One has to recognize, however, that even drastic measures will not do the trick because reputation becomes a strategic asset only as a result of consistent and sustained policies, aimed at building a unique reputation, that are subjectively perceived as such by multiple audiences over an extended period of time. Given the lack of reputation rankings in the public sector (and the controversy over proxies that exist) and the lack of a consensus over performance indicators, the process of estimating the capacity of an administrative agency to address the risks and uncertainty associated with the environments within which it operates may take some time. Where risks and uncertainty of the policy domain are low and not salient, the agency's recognition and attention will take much longer to achieve. The criteria to determine agency reputation may also change, and therefore the cumulative result of agency efforts insofar as quality of activities and effectiveness of outcome are concerned may take time to be noticeable, during which agency reputation will still suffer from past performance. Needless to say, agencies may also miscalculate their reputation repair activities, thus worsening audiences' perception of the organization.

Taken together, these studies suggest that the protection of agency reputation may be an interest shared by both agency and elected officials in normal practice. When the latter are faced with the successful building of agency reputation among pivot groups, and recognize the derived electoral benefit for themselves, they may do their utmost to maintain the agency's good reputation. And this constant care and rebalancing of agency reputation may occur over decades (Carpenter 2001). Taking stock of the discussion so far, it can be argued that claims regarding the fragile foundations of good reputation should not inhibit further research in this subfield.

26   *Moshe Maor*

MANAGING REPUTATION THROUGH CHANGES IN THE TIMING OF AGENCY DECISIONS, THE PUBLIC OBSERVABILITY OF AGENCY DECISIONS, AND AGENCY OUTPUTS

The key empirical insights in reputation management may be divided into two streams: (1) reputation management through changes in decision timing, decision observability, and agency outputs, and (2) reputation management through the strategic use of communication.[5] The following set of studies examined here is drawn from the former stream.

Scholars who draw upon the predominant principal-agent approach tend to focus on the content of regulatory decisions in terms of either left-right policy differences, or as a matter of 'more' or 'less' enforcement (Bawn 1995; Moe 1985). However, public bodies have another fundamental power—the power to wait (Carpenter 2003). As Carpenter, Chattopadhyay, Moffitt, and Nall (2012, 99, *italics in original*) argue: "Agency time discretion is the abundant leeway that agencies have over *when* to make a decision, regardless of what that decision will be." Students of bureaucratic politics have investigated a wide variety of puzzles generated by this insight. Carpenter's (2002) study, for example, tries to gauge why the FDA approves some drugs more quickly than others. The assumptions underlying his model are that regulators guard their reputation for protecting the safety of consumers, and "that the approval of a truly dangerous drug will carry reputational costs for the agency that cannot be regained" (Carpenter 2002). Specifically,

> Although real-world agencies have the option to recall a bad product . . . the agency has no such option in the model here. Once the drug has done sufficient harm that it must be recalled, the agency cannot recover its reputational losses by recalling the drug. Everyone will know that the agency has made a 'bad' decision. In this respect the decision to approve a drug is reputationally irreversible.
>
> (Carpenter 2002, 492)

Carpenter finds that the FDA skillfully determines its review time so that it decreases with the "wealth of the richest organization representing the disease treated by the drug, [the] media coverage given to [the] disease, and [it is] a nonlinear function of the number of groups representing [the] disease" (Carpenter 2002, 490).

A similar set of assumptions were used in Carpenter's (2004) study, which tried to gauge whether one should infer regulatory capture when policy arrangements appear to favor well-organized and wealthy interests. In this study, Carpenter shows that regulatory agencies regularly update the information base upon which they rely when making their decisions, and proposes that even 'neutral' regulators may be rationally motivated to

Theorizing Bureaucratic Reputation 27

pursue policies that help large and established firms. This is especially the case when regulators are familiar with the reputations of these firms and are able to accurately assess the quality of the information provided by these firms to the regulators.

Carpenter's assumption that regulators cannot recover reputation losses resulting from the approval of a truly dangerous drug has also been taken for granted in a few models of drug approval regulation (e.g., Carpenter 2004, 55; Carpenter, Moffitt, Moore, Rynbrandt, Ting, Yohai, and Zucker 2010, 518). This assumption has been recently undermined by Maor's (2011) study of organizational reputation and public warnings in 10 pharmaceutical markets. Maor introduces another component of agency decision—namely, the public observability of agency decisions and errors, which directs the scholarly spotlight to the "potential calculus underlying the decision of whether or not to encourage large-scale media coverage of a regulator's decision and errors" (Maor 2011, 558). Trying to ascertain how a regulator's reputation does affect the public observability of its regulatory errors, Maor (2011, 558) finds that withdrawing a dangerous drug from the market elicits a blame-avoidance reaction for expertise-based agencies (e.g., drug regulators in the United States, Germany, and the U.K.) as well as for drug regulators that 'shadow' decisions and procedures made by regulators that have reputations for expertise (e.g., drug regulators in Israel, Canada, Switzerland, and South Africa), and a credit-claiming reaction for agencies that act as guardians of public safety *in the media* (e.g., drug regulators in Australia, New Zealand, and Ireland). He concludes that "media coverage of safety-based drug withdrawals is a function of the regulator's predominant basis of reputation. Media coverage will be lowest when the regulator has a reputation for scientific expertise in pre-approval drug evaluation (or when it 'shadows' decisions made by regulators that have reputations for expertise) and highest when it has a reputation as guarantor of public safety in the media" (Maor 2011, 558). These findings undermine Carpenter's assumption regarding the irreversibility of reputational losses by indicating that the observability of errors is, in part, an agency construction, and for some agencies, errors are not really a problem at all. At a more substantial level, Maor's (2011) research also solidifies Carpenter's idea of "critical facets of agency reputation" by demonstrating that "[T]he type of reputation an organization has plays a key role in determining its behavior" (Maor 2011, 559).

A related scholarship has also recorded agency appetite for publicity. Focusing on agency choice between public participation through the invitation of public review of agency decisions and the maintenance of secrecy, Moffitt (2010) finds that the FDA seeks public advice for tasks that risk implementation failure. According to Moffitt, "public consultations support agency efforts to distribute information outside the agency and reapportion responsibility for risky policy decisions" (2010, 891). To sum, bureaucrats pursue publicity depending on their type of reputation (Maor

28 Moshe Maor

2011) and on predictable characteristics of the policy tasks they implement (Moffitt 2010).

However insightful these studies are, they do not touch upon the conditions under which reputation is more or less likely to matter, the mechanisms that shape its effects, the meaning of the concept of 'threat' to agency reputation, and the information that negative coverage conveys to the agency: whether punishment for past actions or threat guiding future conduct (Maor and Sulitzeanu-Kenan 2013). In a recent study, Maor and Sulitzeanu-Kenan (2013) analyzed 'time-to-decision' in warning letter processes by two enforcement divisions within the FDA's Center for Drug Evaluation and Research. Trying to identify the specific aspect of the agency's reputation that is challenged—criticism over consumer protection versus criticism regarding overregulation—they found that nearly all criticism of these divisions revolves around the FDA's primary consumer protection responsibilities (i.e., under-enforcement), thus questioning the validity of the FDA's unique reputation. Based on a quantitative analysis of this type of criticism, they found that as media coverage of the FDA's consumer protection responsibilities becomes more positive, the agency takes enforcement decisions (warning letters) more slowly; in contrast, more critical media coverage leads to quicker action by the FDA. This effect is moderated by media salience; namely, it is found only for periods in which press coverage is relatively intense. Once Maor and Sulitzeanu-Kenan (2013) identified the condition in which the agency is less sensitive to external evaluations of its performance, they were able to draw attention to the context in which the relationship between organizational reputation and agency decisions operate and, more specifically, the baseline attitude of organizations to their reputation in the absence of exogenous challenges. Perhaps the most important insight of their research is that agencies may be reputationally relaxed, only to become concerned about their reputation in the advent of external criticism, or reputationally concerned, only to relax following visible public praise (Maor and Sulitzeanu-Kenan 2013).

Relatedly, Maor and Sulitzeanu-Kenan (2014) used the valence of press coverage of an agency as a dynamic measure of its reputation in order to assess the impact of reputational threats on an agency's outputs. Focusing on the main service delivery agency for the Australian government in the field of social policy over the period 2000–2010, they demonstrated that the effect of negative media coverage on agency performance is moderated by the level of its previous year outputs. Negative coverage is followed by an increase in agency outputs when previous-year outputs are below average, and a decrease in agency outputs when previous-year performance is above average. The two types of agency response to reputational threats appear to be the result of the agency's increased interest in change following reputational threats, which is channeled to activities that are internally identified as lagging (e.g., outputs,

Theorizing Bureaucratic Reputation   29

public relations, community engagements, and stakeholder consultation). These findings suggest that an agency's response to reputational threats is endogenously *differential,* among others, through changes in its organizational outputs or other activities. These findings are in line with Maor, Gilad, and Ben-Nun Bloom's (2013) as well as Gilad, Maor, and Ben-Nun Bloom's (2013) findings that reputational concerns may variably impact an agency's strategic use of communication, depending on the agency's internal considerations. Attention now turns to a brief discussion of this stream of research.

MANAGING REPUTATION THROUGH THE STRATEGIC USE OF COMMUNICATION

Given the rapidly changing way of life and the dynamic nature of the public agenda, it will be difficult for each audience to recollect and make sense of the use of an agency's communications gear and, hence, the agency's response to criticism may appear nonrecursive, complex, and fluid at times and, most importantly, random and not preprogrammed. Two recent papers suggest, however, a more nuanced picture than the aforementioned fluid response or a dualistic image of an agency as both 'good cop' and 'bad cop' (Carpenter 2010a, chapter 10).

There is little doubt that a reputation-sensitive agency hears, sees, and feels the public. There is also little doubt that over some functional areas the agency feels comfortable because it possesses a strong reputation, whereas over others it does not. Very briefly, Maor, Gilad, and Ben-Nun Bloom (2013) have demonstrated that a regulatory agency tends to keep silent regarding issues on which it generally enjoys a strong reputation and on issues that lie outside its distinct jurisdiction, while responding to opinions about core functional areas in which its reputation is weaker and areas wherein its reputation is still evolving. This implies that an agency's assessment of the relative threat to its reputation results in *selective* communication strategies (i.e., a choice between levels of a particular type of response) across functional areas. In a related study, Gilad, Maor, and Ben-Nun Bloom (2013) tried to gauge how the content of public allegations has an impact upon regulatory communication strategies, which type of allegations pose a higher threat to agency reputation, and how agencies manage these threats via communication. They found that a regulatory agency has greater propensity to acknowledge problems, yet mostly shifts blame to others when faced with claims that regulation is overly lenient (namely, underregulation), and to deny allegations that regulation is excessive. These findings highlight an agency's *differential* response (i.e., a choice between types of responses) to particular reputational threats. The findings imply that external audiences may be able to shape agency attention and trigger different agency responses by "carefully choosing how to frame their allegations—for example, as a

30 Moshe Maor

problem of overregulation versus underregulation" (Gilad, Maor, and Ben-Nun Bloom 2013, 3).

In acknowledging the intensity of reputation management through the strategic use of communication and, in particular, the complex dilemma faced by the agency whether to acknowledge problems, these two studies have addressed the issue of taking agency communication with the public beyond saccharine public statements, and into spaces where reputational dilemmas can be classified, analyzed, and faced (see also Salomonsen and Nielsen, and Blomgren et al. in this volume). Both studies show not only the interactive nature of the relations between the agency and the public but also the fact that the agency is not acting in an ad hoc way. Rather, the agency carefully designs its interaction with the public and shapes the 'common ground' that it shares with its critics. Although it remains attuned to the public's feelings and intuitions, it selectively or differentially responds in a way that retains its credibility.

ARE ALL AGENCIES REPUTATIONALLY SENSITIVE?

The discussion so far clearly demonstrates the power of Carpenter's theory. His claim that agency decisions are made endogenously because of reputational considerations has significantly widened the ambit of institutional political science. Although this subfield is still in its infancy, the foundation for a powerful theory is being put in place. It is therefore surprising that political scientists have not made much effort to criticize theories of bureaucratic reputation.

There are at least five main problems with applying bureaucratic reputation theories to public sector organizations. First, bureaucrats may be constrained in cultivating reputation by a severe lack of funding and/or by administrative (or agency-specific) culture and political executives. In other words, they may not be allowed, however willing they are, to manage their organizations with the goal of reputation advancement and protection. Second, bureaucrats may be also constrained by their own attitudes and views, especially their perception of the media as a double-edged sword. Third, some agencies may be less susceptible to reputational pressures due to their relationships with external audiences and elected officials. Passive external audiences or close ties with politicians that remove any probability of budget cuts or agency termination following poor performance may shield an agency from the consequences of reputational threats. Fourth, administrative agencies often collaborate, rendering the identification of an agency's reputation and the link between an agency and its external audiences very difficult. Fifth, reputation-protection may be undermined by agency officials' career concerns. The most obvious of these arises because the agency's head may prefer to advance a short-term reputation, whereas senior agency officials may prefer to protect the agency against long-term reputational threats. These sorts of constraints, which imply

Theorizing Bureaucratic Reputation   31

that not all agencies are willing and/or able to advance and protect their reputations, are not handled by current theories of bureaucratic reputation.

DIRECTIONS FOR FUTURE RESEARCH

Whereas the bureaucratic reputation literature that is motivated by core theoretical concerns has done much to validate Carpenter's insights, there are still questions that are ripe for further investigation. Perhaps the most obvious implications of the discussion so far is that scholars should continue to look at how bureaucratic reputation shapes agency strategies while taking into account the variance among agencies over their sensitivities to reputational threats. In this endeavor, scholars can focus on the amount of media coverage that an agency gets, as opposed to the amount of coverage that one of its problems (e.g., a disease) gets (Carpenter 2002); the valence of the coverage (positive or negative); and the specific facet of reputation that is challenged (e.g., criticism about consumer protection versus criticism about overregulation). A central question is how a weak reputation factors into agency decision making. In addition, scholars should analyze the relationship between an agency's reputation and agency behavior by using longer time periods because some variation in media coverage may be historically contingent—that is, coming from a short period of time of a decade or so. If one were to look at a few decades of criticism directed at an agency, more criticism of different sorts could be observed. Relatedly, Carpenter's (2005) call for more historical studies of administrative agencies—ranging from military agencies to large or small government agencies and revealing the importance of "reputation, prestige, professional esteem, and historical legacy as motivating factors driving bureaucratic behavior" (Carpenter 2005, 65)—should be seriously taken on board by students of bureaucratic reputations.

In addition, considerable scholarship deals solely with one agency, mainly the FDA. Scholars should analyze how the reputational considerations of one agency are similar or different from other agencies in telecommunications, environmental protection, financial security, and others, rather than just the pharmaceutical field, and from agencies that operate in policy domains where enforcement is not part of the agency's core mission (e.g., the National Aeronautics and Space Administration [NASA] and the Federal Emergency Management Agency [FEMA]). Scholars should also analyze how the reputational considerations of one agency are similar to or different from agencies entrusted with similar regulatory missions in other countries. Additionally, future research should address whether a firm's size, strength, and other traditional measures bear on the regulatory agency's reputational calculation. If, for instance, the media is more likely to cover problems of large firms, what appears to be media influence may reflect firm influence, which may invite different interpretations than a reputational one. Addressing this issue could rule out whether firm characteristics help explain agency

32 Moshe Maor

decisions. Students of bureaucracy may also see endogeneity as a potential avenue through which agencies, operating in a context of large, well-established firms, might use media coverage as part of their arsenal to punish regulated entities or to justify extending agency regulatory activities.

Much work needs to be done to unravel how an agency's basis of reputation impacts its behavior. Important questions include how an agency prioritizes its dimensions of reputation. Would an agency not cultivate a specific type of reputation because it also seeks to expand another type of reputation? A classic example is Carpenter, Chattopadhyay, Moffitt, and Nall's (2012, 101) examination of whether administrative deadlines shape an agency's decision timing by focusing on "the tradeoff between an agency's interest in using its expertise to produce accurate, valid decisions—and in protecting its long-run reputation for reliable expertise, against its interest in sufficient staff and funding and its short-run reputation for prompt action." Understanding the process by which administrative agencies strike a balance between conflicting bases of reputation (e.g., legal enforcement vs. prevention) and between different aspects of their performance (e.g., swift vs. accurate decision making) should be at the core of bureaucratic reputation research. Future research should also look at how each of the agency's multiple audiences learns about the agency's quality of decisions and effectiveness of outcomes, and how agencies enhance or limit this process. How do the information provided by administrative agencies and the communication channels they use affect this process? What are the criteria by which bureaucratic reputations are assessed by multiple audiences, and what factors explain continuity and change in these criteria? These questions are entirely uncharted realms. In addition, future research may rely on Moynihan's (2012, 572) study of interagency collaborations, which proposes that "(i)f extra-network reputation and political responsibility is more important than intra-network reputation and norms of reciprocity, blame avoidance strategies are more likely." One salient question is how reputational considerations affect the motivation of government agencies to engage in interagency collaborations and to select particular modes of collaboration?

As we are just beginning to understand the magnitude of the role of bureaucratic reputation, we are also just beginning to grasp the breadth of research opportunities available concerning this topic. I anticipate that the next 10 years will bring about pivotal research regarding this topic, and this research will redefine the manner with which administrative agencies and public bodies are viewed and studied.

NOTES

*   An earlier version of this paper was presented at the XVII IRSPM Conference, Prague, Czech Republic, April 2013. I would like to thank Sharon Gilad and participants in the panel "Reputation Management in the Public Sector" for very insightful comments. Any remaining errors are my own.

1 I thank Sharon Gilad for raising this point.
2 A notable exception is Moe's (1984) review essay entitled "The New Economics of Organization," which lays out in simple terms the role of reputation of bureaucrats as an important mechanism that facilitates the monitoring job of politicians over the bureaucracy. According to Moe (1984, 767), "[o]ne [mechanism] is the reputation of bureaucrats. Over time, politicians are able to observe bureaucratic behavior and, for many of the more important actors, arrive at tacit agreement as to their honesty, competence, ideology, innovativeness, and other qualities of relevance." This insight, however, did not trigger much research on bureaucratic reputation in the scholarly community that employs principal-agent models.
3 At present, this is an important factor that distinguishes bureaucratic reputation theories from blame-avoidance theories (Hood 2011; Carpenter and Krause 2012, 29).
4 For an alternative view of reputation as socially constructed, see Rao (1994).
5 On the problems most public organizations will face when adopting the reputation management logic, see Wæraas and Byrkjeflot (2012).

REFERENCES

Banks, Jeffrey S., and Barry R. Weingast. 1992. "The Political Control of Bureaucracies under Asymmetric Information." *American Journal of Political Science* 36:509–24.

Bawn, Kathleen. 1995. "Political Control versus Expertise: Congressional Choices about Administrative Procedures." *American Political Science Review* 89:62–73.

Brehm, John, and Scott Gates. 1997. *Working, Shirking and Sabotage: Bureaucratic Response to a Democratic Public.* Ann Arbor: University of Michigan Press.

Carpenter, Daniel P. 2001. *The Forging of Bureaucratic Autonomy: Reputations, Networks and Policy Innovation in Executive Agencies, 1862–1928.* Princeton, NJ: Princeton University Press.

Carpenter, Daniel P. 2002. "Groups, the Media, Agency Waiting Costs, and FDA Drug Approval." *American Journal of Political Science* 46:490–505.

Carpenter, Daniel P. 2003. "Why Do Bureaucrats Delay? Lessons from a Stochastic Optimal Stopping Model of Agency Timing, with Applications to the FDA." In *Politics, Policy, and Organizations Frontiers in the Scientific Study of Bureaucracy,* edited by George A. Krause and Kenneth J. Meier, 23–40. Ann Arbor, MI: University of Michigan Press.

Carpenter, Daniel P. 2004. "Protection without Capture: Dynamic Product Approval by a Politically Responsive, Learning Regulator." *American Political Science Review* 98:613–631.

Carpenter, Daniel P. 2005. "The Evolution of National Bureaucracy in the United States." In *The Institutions of American Democracy: The Executive Branch,* edited by Joel D. Aberbach and Mark A. Peterson, 41–71. New York: Oxford University Press.

Carpenter, Daniel P. 2010a. *Reputation and Power: Organizational Image and Pharmaceutical Regulation at the FDA.* Princeton: Princeton University Press.

Carpenter, Daniel P. 2010b. "Institutional Strangulation: Bureaucratic Politics and Financial Reform in the Obama Administration." *Perspectives on Politics* 8: 825–846.

Carpenter, Daniel P., and George A. Krause. 2012. "Reputation and Public Administration." *Public Administration Review* 72:26–32.

34 Moshe Maor

Carpenter, Daniel P., Jacqueline Chattopadhyay, Susan Moffitt, and Clayton Nall. 2012. "The Complications of Controlling Agency Time Discretion: FDA Review Deadlines and Postmarket Drug Safety." *American Journal of Political Science* 56: 98–114.

Carpenter, Daniel P., Susan L. Moffitt, Colin D. Moore, Ryan T. Rynbrandt, Michael M. Ting, Ian Yohai, and Evan James Zucker. 2010. "Early Entrant Protection in Approval Regulation: Theory and Evidence from FDA Drug Review." *Journal of Law Economics & Organization* 26: 515–545.

Carpenter, Daniel P., and Colin D. Moore. 2007. "Robust Action and the Strategic Use of Ambiguity in a Bureaucratic Cohort: FDA Officers and the Evolution of New Drug Regulations, 1950–1970." In *Formative Acts: American Politics in the Making,* edited by Stephen Skowronek and Matthew Glassman, 293–315. Philadelphia: University of Pennsylvania Press.

Deephouse, David L., and Suzanne M. Carter. 2005. "An Examination of Differences between Organizational Legitimacy and Organizational Reputation." *Journal of Management Studies* 42:329–360.

Fombrun, Charles J. 1996. *Reputation: Realizing Value from Corporate Image.* Cambridge, MA: Harvard Business School Press.

Foreman, Peter, David Whetten, and Alison Mackey. 2012. "An Identity-Based View of Reputation, Image, and Legitimacy: Clarifications and Distinctions among Related Constructs." In *The Oxford Handbook of Corporate Reputation,* edited by Michael L. Barnett and Timothy G. Pollock, 179–200. Oxford: Oxford University Press.

Gailmard, Sean, and John W. Patty. 2007. "Slackers and Zealots: Civil Service, Policy Discretion, and Bureaucratic Expertise." *American Journal of Political Science* 51(4): 873–889.

Gilad, Sharon. 2008. "Exchange without Capture: The UK Financial Ombudsman Service's Struggle for Accepted Domain." *Public Administration* 86:907–924.

Gilad, Sharon, Moshe Maor, and Pazit Ben-Nun Bloom. 2013. "Organizational Reputation, the Content of Public Allegations and Regulatory Communication." *Journal of Public Administration Research and Theory.* doi: 10.1093/jopart/mut041.

Gilad, Sharon, and Tamar Yogev. 2012. "How Reputation Regulates Regulators: Illustrations from the Regulation of Retail Finance." In *The Oxford Handbook of Corporate Reputation,* edited by Michael Barnett and Tim Pollock, 320–340. Oxford: Oxford University Press.

Gioia, Dennis A., Majken Schultz, and Kevin G. Corley. 2000. "Organizational Identity, Image, and Adaptive Instability." *Academy of Management Review* 25:63–81.

Hammond, Thomas H., and Jack H. Knott. 1996. "Who Controls the Bureaucracy? Presidential Power, Congressional Dominance, Legal Constraints, and Bureaucratic Autonomy in a Model of Multi-institutional Policymaking." *Journal of Law, Economics and Organization* 12:119–166.

Heimann, C.F. Larry. 1997. *Acceptable Risks: Politics, Policy and Risky Technologies.* Ann Arbor: University of Michigan Press.

Hood, Christopher. 2011. *The Blame Game: Spin, Bureaucracy, and Self-Preservation in Government.* Princeton: Princeton University Press.

Huber, John, D., and Charles R. Shipan. 2002. *Deliberate Discretion? The Institutional Foundations of Bureaucratic Autonomy.* Cambridge: Cambridge University Press.

Kaufman, Herbert. 1981. *The Administrative Behavior of Federal Bureau Chiefs.* Baltimore: Johns Hopkins University Press.

Krause, George A. 2010. "Legislative Delegation of Authority to Bureaucratic Agencies." In *The Oxford Handbook of American Bureaucracy,* edited by Robert F. Durant, 521–544. Oxford: Oxford University Press.

Krause, George A., and J. Kevin Corder. 2007. "Explaining Bureaucratic Optimism: Theory and Evidence from U.S. Federal Executive Agency Macroeconomic Forecasts." *American Political Science Review* 101:129–42.

Krause, George A., and James W. Douglas. 2005. "Institutional Design versus Reputational Effects on Bureaucratic Performance: Evidence from U.S. Government Macroeconomic and Fiscal Projections." *Journal of Public Administration Research and Theory* 15:281–306.

Krause, George A., and James W. Douglas. 2006. "Does Agency Competition Improve the Quality of Policy Analysis? Evidence from OMB and CBO Current Year Fiscal Projections." *Journal of Policy Analysis and Management* 25:53–74.

Maor, Moshe. 2007. "A Scientific Standard and an Agency's Legal Independence: Which of these Reputation-Protection Mechanisms is Less Susceptible to Political Moves?" *Public Administration* 85:961–978.

Maor, Moshe. 2010. "Organizational Reputation and Jurisdictional Claims: The Case of the U.S. Food and Drug Administration." *Governance* 23:133–159.

Maor, Moshe. 2011. "Organizational Reputations and the Observability of Public Warnings in 10 Pharmaceutical Markets." *Governance* 24:557–582.

Maor, Moshe, Sharon Gilad, and Pazit Ben-Nun Bloom. 2013. "Organizational Reputation, Regulatory Talk and Strategic Silence." *Journal of Public Administration Research and Theory* 23:581–608.

Maor, Moshe, and Raanan Sulitzeanu-Kenan. 2013. "The Effect of Salient Reputational Threats on the Pace of FDA Enforcement." *Governance* 26:31–61.

Maor, Moshe, and Raanan Sulitzeanu-Kenan. 2014. "Differential Performance Response: The Effect of Reputational Threats on Public Agency Outputs." http://papers.ssrn.com/sol3/papers.cfm?abstract_id = 2441699.

McCubbins, Mathew D., and Thomas Schwartz. 1984. "Congressional Oversight Overlooked: Policy Patrols versus Fire Alarms." *American Journal of Political Science* 28:165–179.

McCubbins, Mathew D., Roger G. Noll, and Barry R. Weingast. 1987. "Administrative Procedures as Instruments of Political Control." *Journal of Law, Economics, and Organization* 3:243–277.

Meier, Kenneth J., and George A. Krause. 2003. "The Scientific Study of Bureaucracy: An Overview." In *Politics, Policy, and Organizations: Frontier in the Scientific Study of Bureaucracy,* edited by George A. Krause and Kenneth J. Meier, 1–22. Ann Arbor: University of Michigan Press.

Miller, Gary J. 2010. Review of *Reputation and Power: Organizational Image and Pharmaceutical Regulation at the FDA* by Daniel Carpenter. *International Public Management Journal* 13:471–475.

Moe, Terry M. 1984. "The New Economics of Organization." *American Journal of Political Science* 28:739–77.

Moe, Terry M. 1985. "Control and Feedback in Economic Regulation: The Case of the NLRB." *American Political Science Review* 79:1094–117.

Moe, Terry M. 1989. "The Politics of Structural Choice: Toward a Theory of Public Bureaucracy." In *Organization Theory: From Chester Bernard to the Present and Beyond,* edited by Oliver E. Williamson, 116–45. New York, NY and Oxford: Oxford University Press.

Moe, Terry M. 1990. "The Politics of Bureaucratic Structure." In *Can the Government Govern?,* edited by John E. Chubb and Paul E. Peterson, 267–329. Washington, DC: Brookings Institution.

Moffitt, Susan L. 2010. "Promoting Agency Reputation through Public Advice: Advisory Committee Use in the FDA." *Journal of Politics* 72:880–893.

Moynihan, Donald P. 2012. "Extra-Network Organizational Reputation and Blame-Avoidance in Networks: The Hurricane Katrina Example." *Governance* 25:567–588.

36 Moshe Maor

Oliver, Christine. 1991. "Strategic Responses to Institutional Processes." *Academy of Management Review* 16:145–179.

Padgett, John F., and Christopher K. Ansell. 1993. "Robust Action and the Rise of the Medici, 1400–1434." *American Journal of Sociology* 98:1259–1319.

Petkova, Antoaneta. 2012. "From the Ground Up: Building Young Firms' Reputations." In *The Oxford Handbook of Corporate Reputation,* edited by Michael Barnett and Tim Pollock, 383–401. Oxford: Oxford University Press.

Power, Michael, Tobias Scheytt, Kim Soin, and Kerstin Sahlin. 2009. "Reputational Risk as a Logic of Organizing in Late Modernity." *Organization Studies* 30:301–324.

Quirk, Paul. 1980. "The Food and Drug Administration." In *The Politics of Regulation,* edited by James Q. Wilson, 191–234. New York: Basic Books.

Rao, Hayagreeva. 1994. "The Social Construction of Reputation: Certification Contests, Legitimation, and the Survival of Organizations in the American Automobile Industry: 1895–1912." *Strategic Management Journal* 15:29–44.

Roberts, Patrick S. 2006. "FEMA and the Prospects for Reputation-Based Autonomy." *Studies in American Political Development* 20:57–87.

Rourke, Francis E. 1984. *Bureaucracy, Politics, and Public Policy.* Boston: Little Brown & Company.

Sheingate, Adam. 2007. "The Terrain of the Political Entrepreneur." In *Formative Acts: American Politics in the Making,* edited by Stephen Skowronek and Matthew Glassman, 13–31. Philadelphia: University of Pennsylvania Press.

Wæraas, Arild, and Haldor Byrkjeflot. 2012. "Public Sector Organizations and Reputation Management: Five Problems." *International Public Management Journal* 15:186–206.

Weingast, Barry R., and Mark J. Moran. 1983. "Bureaucratic Discretion of Congressional Control? Regulatory Policymaking by the Federal Trade Commission." *Journal of Political Economy* 91:756–800.

Whitford, Andrew B. 2002. "Bureaucratic Discretion, Agency Structure, and Democratic Responsiveness: The Case of the United States Attorneys." *Journal of Public Administration Research and Theory* 12:3–27.

Wilson, James Q. 1989. *Bureaucracy: What Government Agencies Do and Why They Do It.* New York: Basic Books.

Wood, B. Dan. 1988. "The Principals, Bureaucrats, and Responsiveness in Clean Air Enforcement." *American Political Science Review* 82:213–34.

Wood, B. Dan. 2010. "Agency Theory and the Bureaucracy." In *The Oxford Handbook of American Bureaucracy,* edited by Robert F. Durant, 181–206. Oxford: Oxford University Press.

Wood B. Dan, and Richard W. Waterman. 1991. "The Dynamics of Political Control of the Bureaucracy." *American Political Science Review* 85:801–828.

3 Actors and Strategies of the Bureaucratic Reputation Game[1]

Lucio Picci

INTRODUCTION

In this chapter I provide a description of what I call the 'bureaucratic reputation game,' by defining the incentives of the relevant actors, their likely preferences, their available strategies, and how the playing out of such strategies produces organizational outputs. Such a characterization of the problem allows me to take sides in the debate on the management of the reputation of public organizations with what I hope the reader will consider some useful insights.

The main conclusions of this chapter are twofold. First, we should not take for granted that public organizations benefit from having a good reputation. On the contrary, there are reasons to expect that they, and even more so their political principals, are often 'reputation satisficers,' as opposed to maximizers. Second, when desiring to improve the reputation of a public organization, the most straightforward route is to improve the organization itself. This may sound commonsensical, but the advice should be placed in the context of those reputation-management theories that, seeing reputation as a social construct, have posited that it may be effectively shaped by communication strategies (see also Wæraas and Maor in this volume). Communication strategies do have a role in the bureaucratic reputation game, but it is a subtle one and, overall, they should be employed with great care.

In the next section, I characterize incentives and strategies along the lines of Picci (2011, chapter 2), I argue that it is useful to distinguish between the concept of reputation and that of trust, where the former can be seen as the result of a learning game in a situation where there is uncertainty about some relevant characteristics of one's counterpart. Trust, on the other hand, is usefully seen as arising from alignment of incentives within a strategic relation—such as a repeated prisoner's dilemma game. Such a characterization of concepts provides an analytical framework to study the motivations and incentives of the relevant actors and to define their set of available strategies, a task I undertake in section 3.

38   Lucio Picci

This objective, however, can't be accomplished if we adopt a simplistic 'black box' characterization of public organizations. Their working, and their resulting reputation, is the consequence of the concomitant actions of a great number of subunits and of individuals, who may (or may not) have reputational concerns of their own. To complicate the analysis further, unlike firms that, at least according to their textbook characterization, have the maximization of profit as a single and easily quantifiable goal, public organizations have objectives that are numerous, often fuzzy, and sometimes contradictory. Moreover, public organizations are strictly dependent on politics and on their public administration. As a consequence, we need both a view inside the 'black box'—in the form of a public choice model of sorts, explaining how individual incentives and actions aggregate to produce organizational outcomes—and an understanding of how a given public organization relates to the general structure of the public administration to which it belongs. This is not an easy task, and the purpose of section 3 is merely to propose sketches of solutions.

Having defined concepts, and specified actors, section 4 discusses strategies. I mostly focus on the role of reputational incentives and on how they may be strengthened. To some extent, this goal may be attained at the level of the individual public organization. Elsewhere (Picci 2011), I argue in favor of broader reforms carried out at a higher political level, with information and communication technologies serving a key enabling role. One such reform would aim at a policy space that is more 'legible' (Picci 2012), a concept that I also discuss. For reputation-enhancing, system-wide reforms, however, tensions are bound to arise. In particular, because public organizations with a better reputation tend to enjoy more autonomy (Carpenter 2001; Carpenter and Krause 2011; for a critical reading, see Maor in this volume), the political principal has to face the dilemma of whether to encourage reforms that, ultimately, would lead to less precious control. The last section summarizes and discusses the main conclusions of the chapter.

CHARACTERIZING ORGANIZATIONAL REPUTATION

I define organizational reputation as beliefs, embedded in a network of multiple audiences, about an organization's set of relevant characteristics. Such a definition is similar, but not identical, to the one adopted by Carpenter (2001, 33) and by Carpenter and Krause (2011). In the taxonomy proposed by Lange, Lee, and Dai (2011), it fits into the "being known for something" conceptualization of reputation. In that of Noe (2012), it would fall inside the precinct of the "economic theory of reputation." Also, in Wæraas and Maor (this volume, 3) it would correspond to the economics perspective, where "reputation is formed among stakeholder groups as a result of actions chosen by the organization."[2] My definition explicitly recognizes that organizations have different audiences, a theme whose relevance has been recognized in much of the literature. Considering audiences should not lead us to forget that, ultimately, reputational beliefs are formed at the individual level, although there may be ways in which they crystallize into a shared consensus within a given audience. In this respect, social constructivists have underlined the social nature of those perceptions (Wæraas and Maor in this volume), an issue that I do not consider.

The set of characteristics on which reputational beliefs are formed may be rather ample. First and foremost, we should consider the organization's capability, which we may loosely define as the quality and overall effectiveness of the organizational output. Another relevant characteristic that may give rise to reputational beliefs is the organization's adherence to its charter, that is, the degree of congruence between its stated objectives and reality. For example, a firm may be an instrument of organized crime and be employed as a money-laundering device, and the cognizant public may believe that such an objective is pursued at the expense of profit maximization. Compared to firms, public organizations give rise to many more doubts regarding their adherence to their charters. On the one hand, they have multiple and often fuzzy objectives, a characteristic that complicates monitoring. Also, they are often instruments of patronage and possibly corrupt relations with their political patrons, which may well lead to actions that are at odds with their stated charter.[3]

These organizational characteristics are certainly relevant, but they are not the only ones. For example, reputation may be not about what an organization produces but about its methods of production, and even about the overall organizational setup, which may be more or less 'appropriate' in the sense of Meyer and Rowan (1977). Moreover, the definition of the various organizational characteristics may be more or less granular. For example, my characterization of 'capability,' above, roughly comprises 'performance' and 'technical' reputation, as defined in Carpenter and Krause (2011), and the quality of the organizational output is correlated to its cost, but only imperfectly, so that quality and cost could be considered separately. The overall message is that reputation has a multidimensional character.

Also in the academic literature, reputation is typically described using value judgments such as 'good' or 'bad.' Certainly, it is a practice coherent with the everyday usage of the language, but I am convinced that it is also misleading. Reputational beliefs have different aspects that we should strive to spell out carefully, and qualifying reputation using a value judgment inadvertently conflates two questions that ought to be kept separate: on the one hand, the perceptions about a given organizational characteristic, and on the other, the preferences that the organization's audiences have about that characteristic.

As a way to avoid this pitfall, I consider four separate attributes of reputation, all of them independent of preferences. These are (1) high vs. low, (2) strong vs. weak, (3) consistent vs. nonconsistent, and (4) dispersed vs. concentrated. Reputation may be 'high' or 'low' with respect to a given

40 *Lucio Picci*

characteristic of the organization. For example, a firm may have the reputation of producing high-quality products, or of being highly adherent to its stated charter. A reputation, moreover, may be 'strong' or 'weak.' It is strong when a given perception is well established, typically because the organization produced many informative signals in the past, and it is weak otherwise. 'Consistency' is another characteristic that reputation may or may not have. Consider, for example, a public organization having only loosely defined procedures. The quality of a given output may then be contingent on the identity of the public officials involved in its production—some of them are likely to be better at improvising than others. As a consequence, such an organization may develop a reputation for having an average but highly varying quality. Last, individual reputational assessments may be more or less dispersed. At the individual level, different people may have contrasting reputational beliefs about a given organization, depending on the signals they received. In this respect, reputational assessments are bound to be more dispersed for those organizations whose characteristics vary in time. The public organization of the example above may end up having a reputation that is both inconsistent, because recurring customers will correctly perceive its time-varying quality, and dispersed, because one-time customers will take home an opinion that will depend on the occasion.

These different dimensions of reputation may be combined in various ways. For example, an organization may have a reputation for producing a given output of high quality, a reputation that may, however, be weakly established, but at the same time may be shared by most observers and audiences—that is, it may be concentrated. The same organization, however, may have an altogether different reputation with respect to a different output it produces, and with respect to different organizational characteristics, such as adherence to charter or production methods.

We expect different audiences to have different reputational perceptions. For example, regulated firms in a market may develop strong reputational beliefs about the relevant characteristics of their regulating agency, because their frequent interactions generate valuable information. Other audiences, for which that particular agency is of less importance, will probably have weaker reputational beliefs, mostly based on hearsay or media reports—following what Fombrun and Rindova (2000) call a "signal refraction process."

Not only are reputational beliefs conditional on the information set available to each audience, but, more importantly, different audiences typically have different *preferences*. For example, the preferences of a regulated utility with respect to its regulator are at odds with those of the general public, and honest citizens value the capability of a law enforcement agency quite differently from criminals. When considering the impact of the presence of multiple audiences on organizational outputs, it is necessary to distinguish carefully in what respect those audiences differ—whether in their beliefs, or in their preferences.[4]

The fact that preferences vary across audiences is the main reason why it is confusing to define a reputation 'good' or 'bad,' unless these adjectives are carefully qualified. In what follows, occasionally I use the 'good' vs. 'bad' reputation classification as a useful shorthand. I define the reputation of an organization to be good with respect to a given characteristic, if the audiences that are relevant for the organization's survival share the belief that the organizational output satisfies their preferences. If an organization has a good reputation in most relevant characteristics, we may conclude that it has a good reputation *tout court*. This shorthand should be used with prudence, because often a public organization faces powerful audiences whose preferences about the organizational output are seriously at odds with each other.

If reputation is about beliefs, we may perhaps conclude that an organization having a reputation, say, for producing high-quality output is one that the public 'trusts' to make high-quality products. In everyday usage of the language, the concepts of reputation and of trust are both semantically charged, and contiguous. Reputation has to do with beliefs about the characteristics, or 'type,' of a given player. Strategic interactions allow players to learn about other players' types. As the strategic interaction proceeds, beliefs are updated using Bayes' theorem, in the end possibly producing perfect knowledge about the other players' types (a *separating equilibrium*), or not (a *pooling equilibrium*) (Picci 2011, chapter two, and references therein). Trust, on the other hand, is better seen as arising in strategic interactions where the players have aligned incentives but do not harbor any doubts regarding other players' characteristics—in game theory parlance, when the game is of complete information. The folk theorem is a paradigmatic example of such an alignment of incentives, in showing how, under a set of conditions, players may overcome the moral hazard problem that we observe when the interaction occurs only once. However, incentives may be aligned also following the presence of strategic interactions that are not of the prisoner's dilemma type.

In fact, strategic interactions typically involve both learning, giving rise to reputational concerns, and varying degrees of alignment of incentives in the absence of learning, where trust may emerge. I will argue that such intertwining of concepts is particularly pronounced when interactions involve organizations. However, there are two reasons why it is useful to keep in mind the distinction between reputation and trust (see also Verhoest, Rommel, and Boon in this volume). First, in a learning game, strategies are costly signals having an impact on reputational beliefs, and these signals are a lever at the disposal of an organization wishing to modify its reputation. As a consequence, it is important to separate situations where such signaling may occur, from those that are better seen as resulting from various degrees of alignment of incentives. Secondly, the presence of aligned incentives, which may give rise to trust (and, more generally, to the predictability of the behavior of organizations), may in itself be an objective to be aimed at by those

42   *Lucio Picci*

entities that, within a given domain, have the capability to not only play their strategies within a given set of rules of the game but also modify those rules.

Let's note a further point of contact, and one of divergence, between the concepts of reputation and trust. Both of them lead to the predictability of behavior, but for different reasons. In the case of trust, predictability derives from the alignment of incentives: I trust you because I believe that it is in your interest to behave in a given way.[5] This also applies to the concept of reputation, but for a distinctive reason: I trust an organization enjoying the reputation of producing high-quality output not to change course, because the long-run benefit of nurturing that reputation outweighs any short-run advantage that it may have in producing shoddy output today. In the case of reputation, too, predictability of behavior derives from a reading of one's counterpart's incentives—which is natural, given the broadly defined rational choice approach that I adopt—but these incentives are specific in that they derive from the value that the producer attributes to its 'reputational capital.'

INSIDE THE ORGANIZATIONAL BLACK BOX

Carpenter and Krause (2011, 26) aptly state that an organization is not a "vessel," but a "flotilla, never easily moving in unison." What is true of organizations in general is even truer in the public sector. We ought to better understand how the behaviors of these 'vessels' may produce organizational outputs, and to do so we focus on the incentives at play, with a focus on reputational incentives. We consider the relationships between reputational beliefs on organizational characteristics and the reputation of the subunits and of the individual members of the organization. Also, we argue that the reputation of an organization may spill over to other organizations, possibly across the divide between the public and the private sectors. An understanding of these issues is important in devising reputation-management strategies, a task we take upon ourselves in the next section.

We begin by briefly considering the incentives at play at the individual level. First, obviously, public employees are subject to a hierarchy and may be punished if they do not carry out orders. By themselves, such incentives only go that far. Apart from the monitoring problem intrinsic in any principal-agent relationship, the specificity of most public sector employment contracts makes punishment threats a rather blunt weapon. Also, for this reason, other types of incentives tend to have higher salience within public organizations. Quite often, people like to work well, and honor their organization's mandate, because of their intrinsic motivations. These may be of particular relevance within public organizations, also because of a self-selection mechanism leading individuals to choose a public sector job if they feel that it can satisfy their ambitions even in the absence of strong pecuniary incentives. Last, but not least, public officials often are concerned about their career prospects, possibly following the presence of an implicit contract establishing that a good individual performance today improves prospects for a future promotion (for a formal characterization of these themes, see Dewatripont, Jewitt, and Tirole 1999a, 1999b).

Individual reputation is an essential element of career-concern motivations and may also play a role in defining intrinsic motivations. For this reason, a situation where reputational incentives are important at the individual level may also contribute to a good organizational reputation. Subunits also may desire to have a good reputation within the organization that they belong to, possibly because of their bosses' career concerns. Also, subunits may hope that by building a good reputation, they will increase their political clout within the organization and be allotted more resources. Strengthening reputational incentives at the subunit and individual level, in turn, may better align the movement of the organization's 'flotilla' and make it more consistent with the pursuit of the organizational goals.[6]

Obviously, organizational reputation is also determined by incentives that are not of a reputational nature. In particular, general alignment of incentives within the organization will produce trust and predictability of organizational outcomes, which in turn will typically be accompanied by a higher quality of output and by a better reputation. We thus see a further reason why, when we look inside the organizational black box, it is difficult to disentangle the concept of reputation from that of trust: High trust among the members and the subunits of an organization will often be conducive to a good reputation of the organization as a whole.

We now turn our attention to the relation between a single organization and the public administration—part of what Wæraas and Byrkjeflot (2012) call the "politics problem." The reputation of a public organization is not formed in isolation but depends on its overall relationship with its environment and on the reputation of other organizations in the public sector. Observing a mediocre public organization constitutes at least partial evidence that the whole public administration it belongs to is below par. Consider the following example. Barton Gellman notes in *The Washington Post* on August 15, 2013, that the U.S. National Security Agency has "broken privacy rules or overstepped its legal authority thousands of times each year since Congress granted the agency broad new powers in 2008." Arguably, this piece of news has tarnished that agency's reputation with respect to its methods, and possibly also its adherence to charter. Moreover, observing such a failure protracted in time, observers may be led to revise downward their assessment of the overall capability of the U.S. public administration to avoid serious mistakes, and to correct them when they arise. That is, changes in the reputation of a single public organization may well have externalities on the reputations of other entities belonging to the same public administration.

Such reputational externalities may encourage free-riding, an issue also recognized in Wæraas (this volume, 227), where he notes that for public

44 *Lucio Picci*

sector organizations, "because everyone benefits from an improved shared reputation without participating, while outcomes are highly uncertain, free-riding issues may block initiatives." An important aspect of these reputational externalities is that they are not confined to the public administration, and in fact they cross the divide with the private sector. One example clarifies the point. As Edward Wong notes in *The New York Times* on July 25, 2013, Chinese consumers do not trust infant milk powder produced in China, to the point that their quest abroad has created shortages in the supermarkets of several countries, and that Chinese authorities, besides "enforcing strict limits on formula imports," announced "stricter inspection procedures throughout the industry." The crisis in confidence over Chinese baby powder was sparked by a serious incident in 2008, "when six babies died and more than 300,000 children fell ill from drinking milk products that had been tainted with melamine, a toxic chemical." It is widely recognized that the problem needs fixing, and "editorials by state-run news organizations said they hoped Chinese powder makers would improve their standards so as to 'defeat' the foreign companies." The lack of trust of the Chinese public with respect to not just infant milk, but also food in general, is well summarized by a 2012 Pew Research survey, indicating that 41 percent of Chinese thought that food safety was a serious problem, compared with just 12 percent in 2008.

This journalistic account would lead us to believe that those agencies that in China are responsible for the quality of baby powder, and of food more generally, have a very bad reputation. As a consequence, all producers of baby powder in China arguably also have a poor reputation. Not just that: Should a new firm decide to start producing baby powder, it also would be likely to inherit a bad reputation because the public would anticipate that it has an interest in cutting corners, and also because of an adverse selection mechanism at play—only firms willing to cut corners are expected to be profitable in a badly regulated market.[7] The reputation of one or more public organizations (the regulators of the market), which in turns stems from the signals conveyed by the poor-quality output of one or more producers, justifies that the public extends their negative perceptions of those particular firms to all firms in the market. The bad reputations of the firms, and of their regulators, feed into each other. To conclude, the organizational reputation of both private and public organizations are mutually linked by richly textured and externality-ridden interdependencies, complicating the prospects of single public organizations desiring to improve their reputation by their own means.

THE BUREAUCRATIC REPUTATION GAME

We may now consider which strategies, aimed at modifying the reputation of a public organization, are available to the different actors. We consider the public organization's managers, its political principals, and its several audiences. We begin by considering a question that only apparently has an obvious affirmative answer: whether the relevant actors prefer public organizations to have a good reputation, in one or more of its relevant dimensions. I argue that, in fact, the presence of such a desire is dubious.

To fix ideas, I focus on the reputation as a producer of a high-quality output. Much literature on the reputation of public organizations has justified the quest for a good reputation on two main grounds, well summarized in Carpenter and Krause (2012, 26): "public administrators at all levels of an organization spend much of their time in attempting to cultivate a reputation that will allow them not only to accrue autonomy . . . but also to offer a protective shield in the presence of opposition in the form of hostile external audiences." Implicit in this view is that (a) a good organizational reputation leads to more autonomy, (b) autonomy is deemed desirable by public organizations, and (c) a good reputation is also useful as a protective shield against attacks from hostile audiences, possibly through its effects on autonomy, or through some other channels. These assertions have been accepted rather uncritically in the literature, when in fact they should be subject to careful scrutiny.

With respect to the first assertion, several studies did show that a good organizational reputation leads to more autonomy (see Carpenter 2001; MacDonald and Franko 2007; MacDonald 2010). However, there may be doubts on the external validity of their conclusions. For the most part, these studies focused on regulatory agencies, which are characterized by the presence of strong professional bureaucracies. Their pronounced intrinsic motivations, and the presence of strong links with external reference groups of similar professionals (Wilson 1989, 149 ff.), are likely to make their members particularly sensitive to their individual and collective reputation. In this respect, regulatory agencies are not representative of public organizations in general. Most research, moreover, analyzes U.S. organizations.[8] The United States scores very highly on most quality-of-governance indicators, suggesting that its public organizations are not representative at the world level. It is still an open question whether a good reputation commands more autonomy where professional bureaucracies are not so prominent, and where the overall quality of governance is not as high as in the United States.

When it comes to the assertion that public organizations are fond of autonomy, there are reasons to believe that this may not always be the case. In fact, casual observation suggests that public organizations desiring to fend off attacks from unfriendly audiences often prefer the advantages conferred by the presence of cozy relationships with supportive political patrons. As much of the literature has correctly pointed out, a key question that a public organization has to confront is how to keep a sufficient amount of consensus among its different audiences. These audiences may have different reputational beliefs on a given public organization, but also, and more importantly, they often have widely divergent interests, and consequently preferences, vis-à-vis the public organization and the course of action that

46   *Lucio Picci*

it should choose.[9] Consider a law enforcement agency in a country where organized crime is powerful. There, an overzealous law enforcer may not last very long in his position, either because organized crime has the political clout to get him removed or demoted, or worse. In such a predicament, a public administrator would be well advised to be prudent, and to strike a balance when choosing the desired reputation for its organization. The same dilemma is likely to be present in less extreme situations. Consider young and not well-established regulatory agencies. Their support from the general public, which prefers markets to be effectively regulated, materializes with difficulty because of a daunting collective action problem. On the other hand, regulated firms, which often have compelling reasons to dislike regulators, may be more effective in promoting their partisan interests. In navigating in such perilous seas, a regulatory agency would be well advised to exercise prudence.

These examples suggest that a good reputation is not necessarily a useful protective shield against attacks, and that it may actually attract hostility. In these cases, organizations would be well advised to be content with a 'satisficing' reputation: one that is good enough to escape excessive criticisms from its favorable audiences, so as to avoid falling prey to one of those bureaucratic "vicious circles" described by Crozier (1963, 258), but that is not so good as to trigger a determined opposition from those audiences whose vested interests are at odds with the organization's charter.[10]

These considerations also allow us to assess the third assertion mentioned above, namely, that a good reputation is useful as a protective shield against attacks from hostile audiences. Indeed, in many cases a good reputation may take away ammunition from potential attackers. For example, after the outstanding success of its Mars Exploration Rover mission, it would feel awkward to affirm that NASA has not done its homework in robotics. In other situations, as discussed above, a good reputation may in fact *generate* attacks, to the point that the best course of action for a well-meaning public organization may be to choose a low profile while cultivating strong political allies. Patronage, exchange of favors, and outright corruption between public organizations and their political patrons can also be interpreted in this light, because the presence and the visibility of these ties make it clear that, if attacked, the organization will be defended.

Partly for similar reasons, the political principal may be ambivalent about the reputation of those public organizations over which it has some jurisdiction. On the one hand, better organizational reputations may command an electoral reward from a grateful citizenry. However, the political principal may be weary of the loss of control that a good reputation may entail, because public organizations command resources that may be summoned to build electoral success and personal wealth.

If the preferences of both public organizations and political principals with respect to organizational reputation may be ambivalent, we may be more confident that the general public unambiguously likes well-meaning public organizations to enjoy a good reputation.[11] Such benevolence, however, may be difficult to turn into active support because of the presence of a challenging collective action problem. To summarize, whereas the general public unambiguously prefers well-meaning public organizations to have a good overall reputation, both their administrators and their political principals may be ambivalent in their preferences, to the point that they may be content with a level of organizational reputation that is as low as the minimum needed to not incur the ire of the public.

We now turn to the analysis of the strategies available to the relevant actors who, whatever their motives, decide to improve the reputation of a public organization. I'll consider two main strategies: The first one, apparently commonsensical, aims at improving reputational beliefs through the improvement of what those beliefs are about—i.e., the organizational reality—and the second elaborates on the concept of 'legibility,' to be explained below.

As obvious as the recommendation may sound, because reputation derives from beliefs about organizational characteristics, the most direct way to improve reputation is to modify those characteristics for the better. A general discussion on how a public organization may be improved is outside the scope of the present chapter. Here, we restrict ourselves to a discussion of the role that reputational incentives may play in this respect. In the private sector, strong reputational incentives are often at play, and there is empirical evidence that a good reputation is advantageous for firms—for example, sellers with a better reputation tend to command a higher price for their products.[12] On the other hand, I argued that a good reputation is not unambiguously good for a public organization. One way to improve the quality of a public organization's output, and consequently its reputation, is to make it more desirable. A political principal with this objective in mind could, first of all, increase rewards of various types to public managers. One way would be to strengthen career concern motivations, thus adding relevance to those incentives discussed in Fama (1980) for managers of the private sector. A political principal may also have the means to modify incentives for employees of public organizations other than their managers. Modifying laws and regulations in order to make hiring and career advancements more meritocratic, and in general exercising self-restraint and avoiding seeing public organizations as instruments of patronage, would strengthen reputational incentives at all levels, better align them, increase the quality of the organizational output, and consequently improve reputation. The extent to which these actions would succeed depends in part on the credibility of the political principal's commitment to such reforms and promises of self-restraint. Reforms supporting stronger reputational incentives may, and as I argue in Picci (2011) should, be enabled by contemporary information and communication technologies.

A second route to improve reputational incentives is to address the 'legibility problem,' an issue that I discuss in Picci (2011, chapter 4) and Picci

(2012), and that here I briefly summarize. Reputational beliefs are formed by making sense of signals provided by public organizations, in a context where there is a plethora of both public organizations and signals. This amounts to a challenging cognitive problem. Any effort aimed at making the overall action of the public sector better discernible and interpretable to members of the different audiences would be helpful in this respect. Many current efforts to render most data owned by public organizations easily accessible, by making them 'open' and semantically valuable, may be seen under this light.

The idea of legibility resonates with that of transparency, which has attracted much attention both in academia and among practitioners. Of late, its salience has further increased, thanks to the possibilities offered by so-called open data. Increasing transparency, moreover, has been seen as one way in which organizations may improve their reputations (see Fombrun and Rindova 2000; Fombrun and van Riel 2004; van Riel and Fombrun 2007; Fombrun 2010). Researchers on transparency have generally been aware of the fact that individuals are boundedly rational and are "prone to a host of cognitive distortions that may lead them to make decisions different from those predicted in a world of perfect rationality" (Fung, Graham, and Weil 2007, 33). Fung et al. (2007, chapter 4), in particular, correctly stress that one of the preconditions for the success of disclosure policies is the effectiveness and *comprehensibility* of the information provided. This preoccupation is certainly present when we invoke legibility. However, there is an important difference of emphasis between the concept of transparency and that of legibility. Within the former, *comprehensibility* is a characteristic that information may or may not have. Legibility, on the other hand, describes a characteristic of a *system of governance,* which may or may not be suitable to generate information that is comprehensible. A system of governance that is not *legible* may hardly generate *comprehensible* information and as such is bound to be nontransparent.

The administrators of a public organization wishing to strengthen reputational incentives also have at their disposal those two main routes—strengthening reputational incentive and increasing legibility—but only within the confines of their jurisdictions. Whereas political principals may aim at systemic changes, administrators at most may lobby for them, and for the rest may only modify the public organization to which they belong. Again, these changes may be aimed at strengthening reputational incentives by prizing a good reputation at the subunit and individual levels, and also at increasing the organization's legibility from the outside. Obviously, to pursue their ends, administrators may also strengthen non-reputational incentives so as to align them better.

Improving legibility may be seen as a broadly defined communication strategy, as its objective is to modify the characteristics and quantity of the organizational information available to the public. Except for this mention, so far I have paid no attention to the role of communication strategies, which appear prominently in much of the literature on 'reputation management.' According to Wæraas and Byrkjeflot (2012, 190), public organizations should actively engage their audiences by communicating what they do within a "step-wise approach that involves bridging the gap between a desired and an actual image of the organization." Of late, there has been important progress in understanding how, in practice, such communication may be carried out. For example, Maor (this volume) stresses the issue of "decision timing and public observability" in the strategic use of communication, and communication is seen to be both 'signal' and silence, where silence is more likely to be used in those areas where the reputation of a public organization is perceived to be strong—see Maor, Gilad, and Pazit Ben-Nun Bloom (2012). Also, we've come to appreciate that a public organization's communication strategy may exhibit degrees of asymmetry with respect to the type of allegations that it has to confront (Gilad, Maor, and Ben-Nun Bloom 2013).

If I have deemphasized the role of communication, it is because I am convinced that, when thinking about organizational reputation, we should not lose sight of the simple reality that reputational beliefs are about *real* organizational characteristics, and that the main venue to modify such beliefs is to act on them. However, I recognize the importance of communication, and if I have somehow overlooked the issue, it is because I'm convinced that it is overemphasized in the literature. I acknowledge that differences in perceptions of organizational characteristics among different audiences could arise from information asymmetries that may be alleviated by the adoption of appropriate communication initiatives. Also, communication may be effective in lowering expectations about the organizational output by convincing an overly optimistic public of that simple truth, well known to every student of public administration, that public organizations lead no easy life, navigating as they do in perilous political seas and pursuing multiple and often contradictory objectives.

It is important to realize that each communication act has an explicit and an implicit component. The explicit one is what the organization communicates. The implicit message is the information that *there was a decision to communicate:* this signal blends with the others that the organization produces within its daily strategic interactions with its political principals, its audiences, and its subunits and employees. Such a realization may eventually lead to reassessing of the role of communication strategies within the bureaucratic reputation game. An organization may decide to invest resources not only to communicate but also to signal its resolve. This, after all, is one of the rationales for the particular form of communication that is product advertising, this being a sunk cost, also signaling to (potential) competitors the advertiser's resolve to stay in a particular market. Likewise, public organizations that are indeed determined to reform and improve themselves may want to signal their commitment in ways that make it more costly for them to renege. Publicly and loudly promising new higher standards may precisely achieve this end.

50   *Lucio Picci*

Declarations of commitments, however, may be more or less credible. Public organizations, without the constant pressure of the 'bottom line,' are intrinsically less credible than established firms. Communication campaigns always run the risk of being perceived by the public as mere attempts at 'spin,' in this way effectively modifying a reputation of the public organization as a trustworthy communicator, and for the worse. Much care, then, should be exercised in choosing what and how to communicate as part of a reputation management strategy.

CONCLUSIONS

The current literature on reputation in the public sector has correctly insisted on the presence of multiple audiences that may attempt to push public organizations in different directions. Audiences may differ in their perceptions of organizational characteristics and, most importantly, in their preferences concerning those characteristics. As a consequence, I argued that public organizations may rationally opt for a reputation that is 'satisficing'—that is, just good enough to get by. After all, as Wæraas and Maor (this volume, 1) aptly begin the introductory chapter of this book, "When the term *reputation* is used about public sector organizations, the connotation that most likely comes to mind is 'bad.'" If there really were compelling reasons for public organizations to seek better reputations for themselves, maybe their average reputation would not be as bad as it is today.

Asserting that public organizations may be reputation-satisficers should not be seen as a concession to cynicism. A well-meaning public organization could rationally constrain the quality of its output, and consequently its reputation, if such a choice significantly helped its chances of survival in an uncertain and potentially hostile environment. Survival, in turn, could allow advantage to be taken of any future windows of opportunity—such as a period of weakness of its unfriendly audiences and of strength of its political patrons—to consolidate and progress. As the French say, at times it is advisable to *reculer pour mieux sauter,* that is, to take a step backward to prepare a better jump forward. A public organization attempting to improve its reputation at all times may in fact decrease social welfare if such a strategy, by generating opposition, undermines its viability.

For those audiences, public administrators, and political principals desiring to improve the reputation of public organizations, the main route to success is to do what is in their power to improve themselves. With this aim in mind, we limited our attention to the role of reputational incentives and concluded that they can be strengthened in various ways, possibly with the help of information and communication technologies, and with attention to the overall 'legibility problem.' Narrowly defined communication strategies should be employed with care, while paying the utmost attention to the credibility of what is communicated.

Actors and Strategies 51

The emerging picture is a composite one. The bureaucratic reputation game is a complex one: Improving the reputation of a public administration may or may not be desirable; it is an objective fraught with problems, and simplistic strategies overly dependent on communication activities may backfire.

NOTES

1 I would like to thank Moshe Maor, Arild Wæraas, and an anonymous referee for their valuable comments on a previous version of this chapter. Charles Hindley provided valuable editorial assistance.
2 See also Walker (2010).
3 Doubts about the real intentions of a public organization—or of parts thereof—also clearly impact the organization's perceived legitimacy, an issue that I do not consider.
4 It may be argued that defining the very attributes of reputation may also depend on preferences. I acknowledge this fact but argue that such an issue is of second-order relevance when compared to contrasts in preferences deriving from divergences in vested interests. For example, there may be disagreement over what should qualify as high-quality law enforcement, but any difference in this respect falls away when we consider the difference in preferences about quality, however defined, that exists between the honest citizenry and criminals.
5 Hardin (2002) writes about "encapsulation of interests."
6 However, there could be situations where strong reputational incentives are detrimental to the quality of the organizational output. Leaver (2009, 572) considers a case where "a desire to avoid criticisms prompts otherwise public-spirited bureaucrats to behave inefficiently." In Picci (2011, 148–155), I consider a model where the presence of strong reputational incentives may induce the choice of excessively prudent policies.
7 That is, organizational reputations may arise even in the absence of a past history, in contrast with received wisdom. Consider for example the often-cited definition of organizational reputation by Fombrun (1996, 36), according to whom it is a "collective representation of . . . *past actions and results*" (italics mine).
8 In a similar tone, Maor (this volume, 31) notes that "considerable scholarship deals solely with one agency, mainly the FDA" and that "scholars should also analyze how the reputational considerations of one agency are similar or different from agencies entrusted with similar regulatory missions in other countries."
9 See also the discussion in Maor (this volume).
10 The concept of satisficing reputation resonates with that of 'neutral' reputation in Luoma-aho (2007). There, the point is made that public organizations are well advised to seek a reputation that is neither good nor bad because, for them, "facing cuts in funding and constant political interference, the maintenance of an excellent reputation may become a burden" and a "risk," in part because "the law" [may be] "changed or funding be altered" (ibid., 129). On the other hand, to explain the quest for a satisficing reputation in the public sector, I stress the implications of the presence of conflicting preferences among the different audiences that are relevant to the public organization's survival.
11 By 'well-meaning,' I intend those public organizations whose charter is coherent with the public good, as opposed to those—for example, a secret police serving a dictator—that arguably are not.

52 *Lucio Picci*

12 On the benefits of a good reputation for firms, see the discussion in Fombrun and Rindova (2000 79) and in Lange, Lee, and Dai (2011), which also reviews the scant literature pointing out possible negative effects of organizational reputation.

REFERENCES

Carpenter, Daniel P. 2001. *The Forging of Bureaucratic Autonomy: Reputations, Networks, and Policy Innovation in Executive Agencies, 1862–1928.* Princeton: Princeton University Press.

Carpenter, Daniel P., and George A. Krause. 2012. "Reputation and Public Administration." *Public Administration Review* 72:26–32.

Crozier, Michel. 1963. *Le phénomène bureaucratique.* Paris: Editions du Seuil.

Dewatripont, Mathias, Ian Jewitt, and Jean Tirole. 1999a. "The Economics of Career Concerns. Part I: Comparing Information Structures." *Review of Economic Studies* 66:183–198.

Dewatripont, Mathias, Ian Jewitt, and Jean Tirole. 1999b. "The Economics of Career Concerns. Part II: Application to Missions and Accountability of Government Agencies." *Review of Economic Studies* 66:199–217.

Fama, Eugene F. 1980. "Agency Problems and the Theory of the Firm." *Journal of Political Economy* 88:288–307.

Fombrun, Charles J. 1996. *Reputation: Realizing Value from the Corporate Image.* Boston: Harvard Business School Press.

Fombrun, Charles J., and Violina Rindova. 2000. "The Road to Transparency: Reputation Management at Royal Dutch/Shell." In *The Expressive Organization. Linking Identity, Reputation, and the Corporate Brand,* edited by Majken Schultz, Mary Jo Hatch, and Mogens Holten Larsen, 77–96. Oxford: Oxford University Press.

Fombrun, Charles J., and Cees B.M. van Riel. 2004. *Fame and Fortune: How Successful Companies Build Winning Reputations.* Upper Saddle River, NJ: Prentice Hall.

Fombrun, Charles J. 2010. "A Systematic Review of the Corporate Reputation Literature: Definition, Measurement, and Theory." *Corporate Reputation Review* 12:357–387.

Fung, Archon, Mary Graham, and David Weil. 2007. *Full Disclosure: The Perils and Promise of Transparency.* Cambridge, UK: Cambridge University Press.

Gellman, Barton. 2013. "NSA Broke Privacy Rules Thousands of Times per Year, Audit Finds." *The Washington Post,* August 15, 2013. http://www.washingtonpost.com/world/national-security/nsa-broke-privacy-rules-thousands-of-times-per-year-audit-finds/2013/08/15/3310e554-05ca-11e3-a07f-49ddc7417125_story.html.

Gilad, Sharon, Moshe Maor, and Pazit Ben-Nun Bloom. 2013. "Organizational Reputation, the Content of Public Allegations and Regulatory Communication." *Journal of Public Administration Research and Theory.* doi: 10.1093/jopart/mut041.

Hardin, Russell. 2002. *Trust and Trustworthiness.* New York: Russell Sage Foundation.

Lange, Donald, Peggy M. Lee, and Ye Dai. 2011. "Organizational Reputation: A Review." *Journal of Management* 37:153–184.

Leaver, Clare. 2009. "Bureaucratic Minimal Squawk Behavior: Theory and Evidence from Regulatory Agency." *American Economic Review* 99:572–607.

Luoma-aho, Vilma. 2007. "Neutral Reputation and Public Sector Organizations." *Corporate Reputation Review* 10:124–143.

MacDonald, Jason A. 2010. "Limitation Riders and Congressional Influence over Bureaucratic Policy Decisions." *American Political Science Review* 104:766–82.

MacDonald, Jason A., and William W. Franko, Jr. 2007. "Bureaucratic Capacity and Bureaucratic Discretion: Does Congress Tie Policy Authority to Performance?" *American Politics Research* 35:790–807.

Maor, Moshe, Sharon Gilad, and Pazit Ben-Nun Bloom. 2012. "Organizational Reputation, Regulatory Talk and Strategic Silence." *Journal of Public Administration Research and Theory* 23:581–608.

Meyer, John W., and Brian Rowan. 1977. "Institutionalized Organizations: Formal Structure as Myth and Ceremony." *American Journal of Sociology* 83:340– 363.

Noe, Thomas. 2012. "A Survey of the Economic Theory of Reputation: Its Logic and Limits." In *The Oxford Handbook of Corporate Reputation,* edited by Michael L. Barnett and Timothy G. Pollock, 114–139. Oxford: Oxford University Press.

Picci, Lucio. 2011. *Reputation-Based Governance.* Stanford, CA: Stanford University Press.

Picci, Lucio. 2012. "Reputation-Based Governance and Making States 'Legible' to Their Citizens." In *The Reputation Society,* edited by Hassan Masum and Mark Tovey, 141–150. Cambridge, MA: The MIT Press.

van Riel, Cees B.M., and Charles J. Fombrun. 2007. *Essentials of Corporate Communication. Implementing Practices for Effective Reputation Management.* New York: Routledge.

Wæraas, Arild, and Haldor Byrkjeflot. 2012. "Public Sector Organizations and Reputation Management: Five Problems." *International Public Management Journal* 15:186–206.

Wilson, James Q. 1989. *Bureaucracy: What Government Agencies Do and Why They Do It.* New York: Basic Books.

Wong, Edward. 2013. "Chinese Search for Infant Formula Goes Global." *The New York Times,* July 25, 2013. http://www.nytimes.com/2013/07/26/world/asia/chinas-search-for-infant-formula-goes-global.html?pagewanted=all&_r=0.

4 Driving Forces, Critiques, and Paradoxes of Reputation Management in Public Organizations[1]

Haldor Byrkjeflot

INTRODUCTION

The question of how one should protect and improve one's reputation has undoubtedly been important for public agencies, universities, and private firms throughout history. In political science, Daniel Carpenter and Moshe Maor, among others, have provided an argument about how executive agencies have constructed and, in the process, enhanced their reputation and gained policy-making autonomy (Carpenter and Krause 2012; Maor in this volume). As they have pointed out, a number of public sector organizations manage their reputation, but this does not necessarily mean that they have adopted the reputation management recipe from the private sector context. In other words, there is a difference between reputation management and the reputation management recipe as will be discussed in this chapter. Regarding universities, Wernick has pointed out something new in respect of reputation management:

> [It] is neither the mere fact of rivalry and competition, nor the importance of reputation. These were part and parcel of the university from its classical and medieval origins. It is, rather, the self-consciousness with which a university's corporate image has come to be managed, the administrative prominence this task assumes, and the objectification, and indeed monetization, of academic reputation itself as Brand.
>
> (Wernick 2006, 566)

Accordingly, the focus in this chapter is not on the historical antecedents to reputation management or the emergence and development of reputational networks in the public sector, but rather on the recent buildup of administrative capacities centered on the managerial concepts of reputation management and branding. Such administrative capacities and recipes have become increasingly important, for both private and public institutions (Kornberger 2010). In many ways, it seems like branding and reputation management have now become what Røvik (2002) calls a super-standard for

Driving Forces, Critiques, and Paradoxes   55

organizing, given that individuals, organizations, agencies, municipalities, and nations have all become preoccupied with managing their reputations. People pursuing careers in management are expected to develop their own brand. Cities and municipalities do 'place branding.' Finally, reputation monitoring has become important for foreign policy, as nations seek to improve the way they are viewed by the international community.

In this chapter, I seek to draw attention to the driving forces, critiques, and paradoxes of reputation management in a public sector setting.

At the outset, let me be clear that I do not question the argument that public sector agencies have historically been pursuing strategies to improve their reputation, if, by *reputation*, one means the symbolic beliefs about an organization that are embedded in a network of multiple audiences (Carpenter 2001). My definition and investigation of reputation management is more specifically related to the management ideas that circulate and the expertise and measurement practices that are being developed in contemporary organizations.

In the chapter's first section, I present the reputation management concept as it comes to expression through *recipes*. This term is stipulated to point to the dominant thinking in the reputation management industry, as embodied in various managerial doctrines used as guidelines for action in a business setting. When referring to reputation recipes, I specifically point to an international trend in advising, teaching, and research on reputation management that can be traced back to Fombrun (1996), Argenti (1998), Fombrun and van Riel (2004), and van Riel and Fombrun (2007).

Section two discusses why such recipes have become so important and applicable in public sector agencies. I highlight two driving forces for why all kinds of organizations, also those within the public sector, now find it important to use these recipes: the expansion of the private business model and organizational model, and the increased significance of so-called intangible value in today's organizations, to the suppression of real economic value.

In section three, I discuss critiques launched against reputation management, especially regarding the use of managerial recipes in the public sector. According to these recipes, public sector agencies must now decide 'what kind of business' they are in. This is unrealistic because public sector agencies are accountable to elected officials who must "ensure that agencies do not drift from the goals set by elected authorities" (Maor in this volume). However, as also observed by Maor, a public agency may face diverse expectations and consequently develop multifaceted reputations, which in turn enable them to gain a certain autonomy.

Part four presents and discusses paradoxes that emerge when reputation-management recipes are used. It may be that the arguments for using the recipes can be turned about-face and become arguments for not using them. Instead of generating trust, reputation recipes may generate mistrust. To conclude, I summarize 10 such dilemmas or paradoxes.

56 Haldor Byrkjeflot

FROM BRANDING PRODUCTS TO ORGANIZATIONS AND REPUTATION MANAGEMENT

In the following, I outline some of the ideas behind reputation management (e.g., Fombrun 1996; Argenti 1998; Gray and Balmer 1998; Brown et al. 2006). These ideas are based on a managerial, strategic, and rational perspective on communication in business organizations and emerge from the economics perspective on reputation (see Wæraas and Maor in this volume). Because it is recommended that a reputation be developed and managed step by step, this is akin to following a recipe (Byrkjeflot 2010). There have been few attempts to compare this theoretical and recipe-like approach to managing a reputation with what has taken place historically and in current practices of organizational reform, so my aim is to present examples that can show how the actual practice may differ from the theory.[2]

In step 1 of what I shall call the 'basic reputation-management recipe,' the aim is to evaluate the current situation with a view to formulating a strategy that includes a vision, mission, and set of values for the organization (Bordum and Hansen 2005). The point is for all these elements to form a coherent whole and ensure differentiation from other organizations. However, as I will argue, the leaders and employees in public organizations may not be in a position to choose a strategy or identity freely.

Step 1 is also about integration between the strategy and the organization culture. The goal is to have employees fully embrace the strategy, thus narrowing the gap between the organization's official values and the employees' values, beliefs, and basic assumptions. It is often recommended that before developing a strategy, one should do an identity-defining project that focuses on the employees and a record of previous history. In practice, however, a top-down approach predominates. Often ignored in such processes are the possible contradictions between policy development and implementation, as well as the different interests of management, employees, and audiences.

In step 2, the main task for a reputation-seeking organization is to communicate with its environment, to proclaim who it is or wants to be. This means that logos and graphic profiles must give a coherent, unified outward representation (Riel and Fombrun 2007). But rather than creating a durable reputation, this could end up being a superficial and temporary way to improve the environment's impressions of the organization.

Step 3 requires the organization to conduct measurements of stakeholder perceptions, both of the immediate kind (image) and the more resilient perceptions that develop over time, as stakeholders compare the organization's performance and status with that of other organizations (reputation). A whole range of indexes for measuring image has developed (see, for example, Aaker 1997). The idea is to use the results as background for further interventions that may reduce the gap between vision, identity, and image (Hatch and Schultz 2003, 2008). Data are also collected that give the organization information about its general reputation—that is, stakeholders' shared perceptions of the organization, both in terms of how well they know it and whether they view it positively or negatively (Lange, Lee, and Dai 2011).

All organizations of significance now do their own measurement or collaborate with others in reputation monitoring. Fombrun (2007) found 183 reputation rankings in 38 countries. Nowadays one finds rankings of everything from the best employers, the best hotels, and the best leaders to the best academic subjects at universities, and so forth. Organizations report that they evaluate their reputation on a regular basis. Accordingly, in textbooks, reputations are treated like objective phenomena, out there for surveys to capture (Brønn and Ihlen 2008, 169). A divergent view, one that accords with the social construction and institutional perspectives on reputation (see Wæraas and Maor in this volume), is put forward by Michael Power, who asserts that organizations' reputations are socially constructed, often by specialist organizations that monitor, evaluate, and measure (Power 2007, 129). In realizing that reputations do not exist independently of these measurements, one can spot the performative aspect: When an organization is told that it has a reputation to take care of, it is likely that the demand for advice on what to do increases accordingly. If these measurements did not exist, then other notions of what is important for the organization to preoccupy itself with would gain attention.

The reputation-management recipe's recommendation is to follow a stepwise procedure, but it may be difficult in practice to follow the steps, especially because public organizations do not have the same kind of leverage as private organizations to develop their own strategies and establish coalitions with favored stakeholders in their environment. Nevertheless, public organizations are influenced by the emerging global reputation industry, which presumes that the same recipes should be followed in both the public and private sectors. In the next section, I outline some of the driving forces for the spread of the reputation-management recipes in the public and private sectors worldwide.

DRIVING FORCES

The Organizational Model and the 'Free Market'

The organizational model's spread throughout the public sector is a central research theme of neo-institutionalists. Meyer and Bromley (2013, 367), for instance, who outline the reasons for and consequences of a global reform trend, argue that "passive state bureaucracies are pressed by the 'New Public Management' and 'reinventing government' movements to become accountable, purposive, decision-making organizations." A central premise for this argument is that 'the organization,' originally modeled after the private

58 Haldor Byrkjeflot

business firm, has become the norm for how to structure public service activities as well. In order to become 'complete' organizations, public units that previously had been subordinate to the central state now must become autonomous actors with identity, rationality, and hierarchy (Brunsson and Sahlin-Andersson 2000).

Whereas the neo-institutionalists perceive the driving forces to be public sector reforms and the endeavor to create complete organizations, Kornberger (2010) believes branding is also connected to the increased influence of neoliberalism. To his mind, the free market is a precondition for other types of freedom, such as democracy and personal freedom:

> The brand plays an important role in the defense of free market principles: brands create accountability, loyalty and wealth for everybody. In other words, brands liberate.
>
> (Kornberger 2010, 205)

But even before the economic downturn in 2008–10, 'the free market' was seen as a somewhat old-fashioned concept, despite social constructivism having furnished it with new, less controversial content ('the market as dialogue,' cultural markets, etc.). According to Alvesson (1990), the most important impetus for the reputation-management idea's spread lies in several trends that, when taken together, drive the development "from substance to image." For instance, service provision and cultural consumption have become much more important than they used to be. There are also cultural changes toward less fixed identities and individualization, increased complexity, and the increased influence of the mass media. Since Alvesson wrote his article in 2000, the financialization of a whole range of industries and mundane fields of action has become more obvious; in a steadily increasing number of areas, the focus has turned toward earning money on investments and loans rather than on what is produced (Davis 2009; Willmott 2010).

An additional explanation for the expansion of reputation-management recipes is to point to changes in people's understanding of what constitutes a democratic society. Whereas democratic ideals used to emphasize citizenship, representative government, and the political governance of public agencies, there has been a shift toward emphasizing enterprise, freedom to choose, individual rights, and consumer needs. This means that citizens now should expect to be consulted about service quality, to make choices, and to respond directly to the service-providing public organizations, also conceived as the output side of the public sector. Policy implementation and the role of government are thus less emphasized. When considered together, financialization, the movement toward expansion in services, and the associated changes in people's understanding of democracy indicate that there has been a transition from material to so-called intangible values.

Intangible Values

In accordance with the shift toward intangible values, the World Economic Forum, in 2004, claimed that "corporate brand reputation outranks financial performance as the most important measure of corporate success" (Power 2007, 129). The notion of intangible value is still somewhat mysterious, but in the new value regime it is assumed that brand value is accounting for about 30 percent of the market capitalization of the stock market index S&P 500 (Arvidsson and Peitersen 2013, loc 673, 473 Kindle). For a selection of large global companies in 1975, 83 percent of the value of the companies could be explained through financial and physical ownership, whereas only 20 percent could be related to such factors in 2009 (Financial Management 2013).

The increasing belief in reputation management underlies the current suggestion that communications managers should be in charge of intangible assets (Fombrun 1996, 197; Brønn and Ihlen 2009). This coincides with the view of former U.S. Federal Reserve Board Chairman Alan Greenspan (1999):

> In today's world, where ideas are increasingly displacing the physical in the production of economic value, competition for reputation becomes a significant driving force, propelling our economy forward.

Before the economic crisis started in the fall of 2008, Greenspan had for several years enthusiastically communicated a strong belief in reputation management:

> In a market system based on trust, reputation has a significant economic value. . . . I am therefore distressed at how far we have let concerns for reputation slip in recent years.
>
> (Greenspan 2008)

The crisis, for Greenspan, did not concern the lacking regulation of financial industries, but that the banks and financial industries had not understood the significance of protecting their reputations.

Consequences: The Reputation Recipe's Hegemony

Amongst politicians, it has been conservatives, especially those in the neo-liberal (*laissez faire*) tradition, who have had as their foremost concern that all institutions ought to be autonomous and free of state intervention. Like Greenspan, they see reputation self-management as a means for developing this kind of society. An example from Norwegian politics, however, will show that even politicians who place themselves on the left and in a socialistic tradition have become concerned about individuals' and businesses' self-regulation through reputation management. The Norwegian so-called red-green government's crisis package for banks, which was a response to

60   Haldor Byrkjeflot

the financial crisis that began in the fall of 2008, was administered by Kristin Halvorsen, leader of the Socialist Left Party and then-Minister of Finance. After she had pushed top bank executives to freeze their own salaries, they unwillingly accepted, after voicing standard arguments against government intervention in financial affairs. This incited Halvorsen to exclaim that the banks had not "understood how poorly they appear . . . they were dependent on a positive reputation. Most people cannot respect banks that give the impression of being more concerned about the conditions for their own salaries than to handle a crisis" (*Aftenposten*, January 3, 2009, 4). Thus, rather than pointing to higher wages and bonuses as threats to solidarity with the wider society and as evidence of the unfortunate effect of market forces, the minister of finance pointed to the risk of reputational loss and her trust in the merits of self-regulation. This, along with the increased use of the reputation concept in the daily news media (Byrkjeflot 2010), illustrates how the reputation recipes' impact now cuts across party lines and serves as a general frame in the mass media's interpretation of current problems, as well as in politics, bureaucracy, and business.

Similarly, one sees politicians, bureaucrats, and business leaders heavily emphasizing corporate social responsibility (CSR), a form of corporate self-regulation formulated as a business model, whereby a business monitors and ensures its active compliance with the law, ethical standards, and international norms. Like reputation management, CSR can be described as an expanding concept with a particular content expressed in numerous guidelines, principles, and codes (Jutterström and Norberg 2013). However, the U.S. former Minister of Labor, Robert Reich (2007) speaks for several critics when he questions whether the focus on CSR means businesses truly take more social responsibility, or whether their efforts in this direction are for the sake of PR and out of reputational concerns. Social responsibility becomes an alternative to public and super-national regulation. It is not a given, says Reich, that from the perspective of society, such public regulations are unnecessary or less effective. Simultaneously, as companies' PR departments communicate the message of social responsibility, the large companies are exerting greater influence over politics than ever before; they block regulations aimed at safeguarding social responsibility (Reich 2007).

The raison d'être for many public agencies, however, is to safeguard social responsibility through public regulations. One should therefore assume that it is less necessary for such organizations to legitimate their existence through CSR. There is now a strong pressure on such institutions to use the same language and recipes as private institutions, and this may symbolize a privatization of public responsibility parallel to the type of activity Greenspan has suggested.

Thus far I have introduced the reputation-management recipes, discussed two driving forces for the increased demand for them, and elucidated the mechanisms through which they spread. While doing so, I have implicitly criticized the reputation recipes in two key ways. Now it is time to be explicit.

CRITIQUES

Reputation Management: A Recipe also for the Public Sector?

First, as a managerial recipe, reputation management builds on a neoliberal ideology that recommends the least possible amount of regulation while excessively trusting in market actors' self-regulation. Second, it promotes inauthentic behavior, thus contradicting the ethics of public office and the strong elements of a "logic of appropriateness" (March and Olsen 2006), which, according to some authors, lies at the root of the development of the modern welfare state (Vike et al. 2002).

As an extension to this, one can ask: Could reputation management have unfortunate effects on the values and democratic principles undergirding the public sector? According to a centrally situated Norwegian reputation assessor (Hind 2008), all studies, in Norway and internationally, show that municipalities score 20–30 percent lower on reputation than do private businesses. One finds similar results for other public organizations. The explanation for this could be that public organizations often deal with so-called wicked issues—that is, problems that cannot be solved or that, when solved, result in new problems. They lack easy solutions and are couched in complex environments with a diverse set of audiences. Some public services, moreover, are provided by so-called natural monopolies (e.g., tax collection and policing), and among the current antibureaucratic public, there is a great deal of skepticism to such monopolies. The public sector is also more open and vulnerable to mass-media coverage than is the private sector. When a psychiatric patient with a criminal record escapes from a psychiatric ward, for example, this is deemed newsworthy for mass media and of interest to politicians, particularly those who have argued for more closed psychiatric wards. But this is a very complex issue, in part because the politicians and the experts dealing with psychiatric problems have diverging views on how to deal with risks associated with such patients. It will thus be difficult for public psychiatric institutions to enlist their employees as ambassadors for reputation campaigns and achieve top rankings in reputation surveys, if that was desired. It may also prove difficult to uphold professional secrecy, maintain rule of law, and respect the principle of representative democracy if one must also satisfy the reputation recipes' demands for visibility, transparency, and uniqueness.

Citizens' expectations for the public sector are often higher than what can be achieved, and this, in turn, must be seen in light of the fact that politics largely concerns making promises about the future, thereby influencing people's expectations. Reputation-management recipes may clash with this state of affairs because they prescribe that the political lines of conflict leading to exaggerated expectations should preferably not exist. The desire to close the gap between expectations and what is actually on offer could thus indicate a desire to transfer power from the political to the administrative

62   Haldor Byrkjeflot

system in society, eventually rendering public institutions as self-governed rather than units in the service of representative democracy.

Presuming that the ideal of equality and the ambition to care for each other's welfare constitute the normative foundation for the welfare state, one can question the reputation recipes' emphasis on developing excellent organizations. Such organizations are developed through competition and by individuals who use them to increase their own status at the expense of others—a 'zero-sum game' (Alvesson 2013).

Public institutions, which must often legitimate their existence through being neutral and impartial, can have problems promoting their image publically in the way a reputation-management recipe recommends (Luoma-aho 2007; see also Picci in this volume). As Rothstein (2011) argues, if neutrality and impartiality are crucial for maintaining trust on the more general level, for instance in dealing with clients in a tax collection agency, it would be counterproductive for such institutions to curry favor with dominant interest groups in the environment.

Reputation Management and Democracy

The reputation recipes emphasize an organization's relation to customers and stakeholders in its environment. When applied to public institutions and organizations, this could be called an output model for democracy because it presents an alternative to the representative, so-called input democracy, where citizens and political parties set the direction for the policies that are to be developed and implemented (Scharpf 1999; Marsh and Fawcett 2011).

In the New Public Management (NPM) movement, as in the reputation movement, autonomous and responsive organizations—that is, output-oriented organizations with their own identities, hierarchy, clear boundaries, and resources—are preferred over those that follow traditional principles for government institutions (Brunsson and Sahlin-Andersson 2000). So it is hardly surprising that what I above characterize as a movement for reputation management has problems relating to municipal councils, political parties and other political institutions that cannot easily adapt to the recipe of becoming complete organizations. It is as if the ugly stepsisters are trying to fit into Cinderella's shoe. Recently, a controversy was sparked over Norway's Municipal Reputation School. This was established by the government in 2008, and thus far 77 out of 428 municipalities have participated (Elgvin 2013; see also Bjørnå in this volume).[3] The controversy began when a local politician criticized the reputation movement and the school that orchestrates it for undermining democracy and creating authoritarian municipalities. In response to this critique, the school's previous instructor argued that "politicians who quarrel and forget their role as employers by demoralizing the organization make the citizens demotivated and drag down the reputation" (Berglund 2008, 22). Similarly, in the official compendium

Driving Forces, Critiques, and Paradoxes 63

used for teaching, he described municipalities as inherently at odds with themselves:

> In reputation building, municipalities are more handicapped than private organizations. Municipalities have a (municipal) government that is embroiled in an eternal and professional battle with itself. A significant part of politics is to emphasize what is negative, and this presents municipal reputation building with a somewhat special challenge.
>
> (Berglund 2006, 6)

If a reputation-management recipe finds it contradictory to act according to norms of local democracy, then even the word *municipality* may conjure negative associations; hence it may be better to try to get rid of it. To exemplify: during a reputation-building project in Lom Municipality, it was deemed best to cut municipality from the name and just to say "Lom." This was because, according a survey, 85 percent of Norway's population thinks of Lom as a travel destination—at the same time as Lom's politicians found the word *municipality* somewhat 'burdened' (*Ukeavisen* newspaper editorial "Kutter kommune" February 13, 2009, 37).

According to the reputation recipes, public organizations should make use of the opportunities and resources provided by external audiences and adapt to those audiences' needs and desires in order to gain their support. Put bluntly: even heads of public agencies must now decide what kind of business they are in. Yet this type of attitude potentially conflicts with the established distinction between politics and bureaucracy, as bureaucrats have a mandate to loyally implement decisions made within the political system. According to the view of representative democracy—where citizens, and not just customers, are the center of attention—it is the case that public agencies and institutions cannot be rendered autonomous or independent to such an extent where they can choose their identities. They cannot adapt sufficiently to users as citizens by coming to understand them better through user surveys and reputation measurements. Because public institutions are politically governed and must deal with important, prioritized, and legal problems, in order to retain legitimacy, they must also relate to laws and policies and thus also to citizens as voters and in a capacity as generators of public opinion.

As outlined by Weber (1922/1978), a bureaucratic agency combines principles of organization such as technical competence, public ethos, and legal-rational procedures, and since Weber wrote this in the early 1920s, performance has also become increasingly central (Scharpf 1999). The Weberian bureaucratic values and the more neo-bureaucratic value of performance all relate to the types of reputation—procedural, technical, moral, and performative—as presented by Carpenter and Krause (2011). But in research on corruption and public reforms (Pierre and Rothstein 2011), it is particularly emphasized that Weberian values are fundamental for building

64 *Haldor Byrkjeflot*

and maintaining trust in public institutions. A morally trustworthy institution builds on four core values: truthfulness, keeping promises, justice, and solidarity (Grimen 2009).

Building trust is also a leitmotif in reputation-building literature, and one even finds the claim that reputation is trust (Brønn and Ihlen 2008, 87). This statement provides the springboard for pointing out a few paradoxes in the reason normally given for why organizations should carry out reputation management: For starters, it can just as easily be claimed that reputation management, due to its emphasis on expressivity and performance, creates mistrust.

PARADOXES

Reputation Management and Trust

Studies show that those who are least trusted are politicians, journalists, and consultants, whereas the classic professions, doctors for instance, enjoy a high degree of trust (Edelman 2013; MORI 2014). Particularly within the public sector, modern reformers aim to make the professions speak to their organizational environment with one unified voice. For this to happen, the professions' loyalty to their organization must increase. Instead of the organization speaking with many voices, a communications manager functions as the organization's external voice. The question, however, is whether this undermines trust in the organization, because communications managers have less trust than the professionals for whom they speak. In general, trust in business ethics, which leaders of private organizations use to achieve loyalty to their organizations, is lower than trust in profession ethics. Part of the reason why doctors and other professionals enjoy extensive trust is that they have restricted possibilities of appearing as anything other than what they are. For instance, in some countries there are restrictions on marketing legal and medical services and so forth. Seen from this angle, the notion that reputation management concerns building trust appears at best to be a truth with modifications. Actually, it can be claimed that reputation management may promote transient goodwill more than enduring community relations because, through user surveys and rights guarantees, more contract-like relations emerge between the institutions and the local community, to the detriment of relations of trust.

Here, however, one could counter-argue that it is a misunderstanding to think that introducing mechanisms for control and mistrust contributes to undermining trust. Such mechanisms could be precisely what enable people to trust that the given institutions act predictably and honestly. Indeed, there are good reasons for this assumption, and they underlie Grimen's argument (above), yet it is uncertain whether reputation management and communications managers can be reckoned to create more trustworthy public organizations. This is because communications managers, like top executives of a given organized unit, may want to promote certain aspects at the expense of others, even hiding certain information about the organization. This leads to us question the relation between reputation management and transparency.

Reputation and Transparency

Like reputations, transparency has become a goal in itself. By showing openness and generosity toward those who want to know more, even going the extra mile and offering more information than transparency laws and rules prescribe, organizations can build good reputations. This is how the Norwegian Meteorological Institute's top ranking in national surveys has been explained; the institute has developed open portals that the public can use to read weather reports whenever they want (Øvrebø 2009). In other cases, organizations have proactively informed the public of their plans, strategies, and deviations from such, and this is reckoned to be the reason for their good reputation.

Studying these success stories, however, one can question how transparent the respective organizations are, and whether there really is reason to trust apparently open and transparent organizations more than those that are more closed and dominated by, for instance, professions and collegial relations. The idea of transparency presupposes opaqueness, just as the idea of a public sphere in political theory presupposes the idea of a private sphere (Arendt 1958). Yet this does not mean that the state of being public involves full openness; it is most likely characterized by strategic communication. According to the reputation recipes, it is important to meet one's surroundings through a coherent, consistent communications strategy. This entails stronger control of the streams of information both within and from the organization. It is not merely an organization's profile and logo that should be consistent with each other; reputation management can also be a matter of disciplining employees' values and voices to harmonize with the message the organization wants to spread to its surroundings (Christensen, Morsing, and Cheney 2008). In practice, therefore, campaigns for openness and transparency can in some cases lead to organizations being more closed. Empirical research shows that increased transparency does not necessarily mean that public organizations gain more trust. The effect on trust is limited at best, and it varies in relation to the task area (de Fine Licht 2014) and national culture (Grimmelikhuijsen et al. 2013).

Reputation and Risk

The reputation recipes are claimed to be means for reducing risk, but campaigns for maintaining or developing a good reputation can also create new challenges in terms of risk. One example of this was when a former general secretary of the Norwegian Association of Local and Regional Authorities

66   *Haldor Byrkjeflot*

(Kommunenes Sentralforbund, KS) claimed that Norway's municipalities were mired in a "reputation crisis" (*Ukeavisen Ledelse* 2006). This was because he had received and responded to an inquiry about the results of a survey, conducted among business leaders, where the respondents almost unanimously answered that they did not want to apply for leadership positions in municipalities. But from previous surveys and experience, it was already known that business leaders do not want to work in municipal administration, so the survey results could hardly be called news, nor was it accurate to describe the situation as a reputation crisis. Is it possible that KS's leader just used a formula he had learned through reputation management, and that the 'script' for the so-called crisis was provided by the reputation recipe itself? It was the comment from the public manager that was newsworthy, not the survey results.

This exemplifies how advice from the communications profession, on how to handle situations where one risks losing face (prostrate yourself and call it a crisis), gave the very grounds for defining the situation as a crisis. Another problem can be that exaggerating for the sake of self-promotion may create a false appearance. Exaggerated promises ("We shall be the top-ranking public institution by 2015") also may provoke a negative attitude in the environment and lead to a worse reputation. Reputation management in itself can therefore be a risky project.

Integrated Communication

As Røvik (2007, 217–222) has pointed out, modern organizations have a 'multi-standard' character, which means they are 'sediments' of different types of expertise and experience. Public organizations, moreover, usually have several hierarchical levels. Because both the organizations and their environments are complex, it is extremely difficult to achieve the integrated communication ideal that the reputation recipes foresee. The necessary preconditions for coordinating divergent areas of expertise—between executives, communications staff, and others—seem rather unrealistic, given the past experiences of trying to coordinate functional areas of organizations in other fields and in earlier epochs. Operational research during the 1960s was one such attempt deemed post-factum to have had little success, as is the case with human resources management today (Guest and King 2004). Studies also show that top managers and communications professionals have divergent visions about the chief communications officer's role in organizations (Zerfass et al. 2014). And neither do reports from the reputation-management industry itself indicate that it is easy to create an integrated top-management function of communication, as has been presumed in the idea of corporate communication. In a summary of a research project on communications managers, one can read that "[p]articularly great is the disagreement on who should have the everyday responsibility for integrated communication" (Bjornå 2000).

Reputation and Diversity

Reputation management is claimed to help a diversity of organizational voices to be heard, and that the world of organizations becomes more differentiated as a consequence, yet one could just as easily argue that homogenization is the outcome. For instance, when a group of local farmers wants to have a local agricultural product established as a 'terroir' or Protected Designation of Origin (PDO), they must go through a procedure of documenting that the production processes are hygienic, certified, and so forth. This ultimately means that the PDO product must become more similar to rival products (Hegnes 2012). This paradox is summed up by the Norwegian social anthropologist Thomas Hylland Eriksen (2007, 146): "The more different we try to be, the more similar we become—since most of us try to be different in roughly the same way worldwide."

DISCUSSION AND CONCLUSION

Organizations in general, but perhaps especially government agencies and institutions, are expected to be morally trustworthy, not just appear to be so; they must be truthful, keep promises, and ensure fairness and solidarity (Grimen 2009). These expectations have developed through time, as part of democratic processes and social mobilization. According to reputation recipes, however, instrumental rationality is ranked highest, along with efforts to appear visible, relevant, transparent, and unique (Fombrun and van Riel 2004). The recipes maintain that organizations should see their environment as a set of stakeholders, not "faith-holders" (Luoma-aho 2005). This "reputation gaze" creates a myopic situation where the significance of intervening institutions, all of which help maintain general relations of trust between the given organization and its environment, fall beyond the scope of vision. Furthermore, the measuring instruments and managerial techniques for reputation management partly presuppose relations of mistrust. In the immediate enthusiasm of prioritizing and attracting particular stakeholders, one may risk undermining relations of trust and values that have taken years to develop.

These reflections on the limitation and possibilities of the reputation gaze come as an extension to Brunsson and Sahlin-Andersson's observations about the effects of reform on the public sector: By necessitating the development of complete organizations with separate identities, reforms contribute to homogenizing organizations across all sectors. These observations, however, were made during a period marked by New Public Management (NPM). Nowadays most scholars who do research on public sector reforms perceive the onset of a post-NPM phase. They argue that the trend today is toward reforms aimed at creating a more unified, coherent public sector, so-called whole-of-government reforms (Christensen and Lægreid 2007). If this is the case, reputation-management recipes may actually be better adapted to the previous NPM phase because they seek to establish autonomous

68 Haldor Byrkjeflot

organization units. Yet such units have resulted in problems of fragmentation that the new post-NPM reforms are supposed to correct. One may thus assume that the reputation-management recipes need adjusting also in order to cope with problems identified by the post-NPM movement and that there might be something to learn from the historical studies mentioned above (Carpenter and Krause 2012).

The spread of reputation recipes needs explaining, and I have outlined two possible explanations: (1) the private business model's expansion, and (2) the development from substance to image in society in general, which has increased the significance of immaterial values that legitimate indexes, which in turn replace or stand in for real economic value. The research on trends, however, shows that the first organizations to implement a recipe can have good reasons for doing so and can experience clear benefits, yet those implementing the recipes later on do so mostly because they must adapt to competitors within the field in order to be perceived as legitimate (Tolbert and Zucker 1983). The recipes then conserve the status quo rather than provide new solutions to existing problems.

Reputation recipes are ambitious and demand consistency between actions and words, between the present and the future. Despite this, or perhaps because of it, they have thus far not shown themselves suited to increasing people's trust in the communications profession, or in the leaders who administer reputation-management businesses. This can be a weakness, because the communications function has thus far been unable to professionalize in the sense of establishing itself as a separate, trusted expertise with its own associations, education institutions, etc. One reason for the problems communications professionals have encountered in trying to establish themselves as a respected profession in the public mind may be the mutual distrust between journalists and communication professionals (Røvik 2011).

The trend toward standardization and formalization of such activities may also make it easier for managers and other professions to do the communication work themselves, which means that the communication professionals may be pushed out of the strategic positions they are reported to have established in top management teams.

As pointed out in the introduction, a number of public sector organizations manage their reputations, but this does not necessarily mean that they have adopted the reputation-management recipe as it has been outlined in this chapter. In order to develop an understanding of reputation management as it has been practiced in public organizations, further research into real cases from the history of public administration in various contexts may be needed. In such research it may be useful to take into account the paradoxes and dilemmas that can arise when reputation-management recipes are used, and with a particular emphasis on the public sector:

1. According to the reputation-management recipe presented above, the first step should be to 'find yourself,' which means that an organization

must dig into its past and consult its employees in order to identify and develop an identity. Proponents of reputation-management recipes claim that an institution should start seeking its identity by pinpointing its enduring, distinctive, and unique characteristics. Given the demand to respond to immediate problems and achieve results for the organization here and now, however, it may seem more realistic to assume that reputation management is about making a self-presentation tailored to political demands, as well as the more immediate expectations and 'needs' of external audiences.

2. It is claimed that private and public organizations have no principal differences as far as reputation management goes. This claim presupposes a particular understanding of society that emphasizes output democracy, where the relationship between the public sector as service producer and citizens as users and consumers are at the center of attention. If using a different approach—one that sees a more fundamental distinction between public and private spheres, and that sees representative democracy as a condition for other democratic benefits—the conclusion would be different. The aim of reputation management for public organizations should be to uphold public values like impartiality, neutrality, and expertise rather than to aim for 'efficiency' in service provision as the one and only goal.

3. Reputation management is claimed to be about creating trust, but one could just as easily claim that the consequence may be to create mistrust. Mistrust can in some cases be a precondition for general trust, of course. However, because the communications professionals and the managers are not among the most trusted in society, it may nonetheless be better to leave the communication to other professionals or those who are actually doing the work, because they may speak better to the expectations of the public. This may also go for the language of the organization, that a too managerialist or media-adapted language may not be the right way to improve reputation. The claim that reputation management generally helps develop relations of trust in society is doubtful.

4. It is claimed that organizations must follow reputation recipes to prepare themselves for responding to crises and reputational loss. In some cases, however, and perhaps especially in a public sector setting, reputation management itself may generate the risk it is supposed to ward against.

5. Integrated communication is claimed to be an ideal situation where several disciplines and functions collaborate and an organization's central leadership manages all communication. In practice, however, leaders may either not want to integrate the various specialties of communication, or at least find it extremely difficult to do so because it is a contested area of expertise and a potential challenge to the role of the top manager.

70   Haldor Byrkjeflot

6. The recipes present openness and transparency as preconditions for trust from the environment. The assumption is that if government organizations open up and show the public how and what decisions are made and what the results are, people will automatically have more trust in government. But research on the relationship between transparency and trust does not show that there is such an effect. The effect of transparency on trust might instead be negative, and it will at least depend on the task area and culture.

7. Reputation management is claimed to help create diversity, but one could just as easily claim the opposite: that it contributes to homogenization. When everyone seeks to be unique but follows the same recipe for creating uniqueness, the outcome may be that they all become more similar. This may happen when unique local products go through a certification process in order to be branded as 'terroir,' or when TV stations seek to develop unique programming in a competitive market. Bruce Springsteen sings: "There was [*sic*] fifty-seven channels and nothing on."

8. In order for a reputation-management recipe to have lasting significance, it is claimed, those who administer it—those who plan and take care of the communication function—must gain increased status through professionalization. Yet it is uncertain whether this is the case, because the movement toward standardization and routinization allows for other professionals, and not the least managers, to take over tasks related to communication.

NOTES

1 This chapter is a substantially revised version of an article published in *Scandinavian Journal of Public Administration* (Byrkjeflot 2010). I have received permission from the publisher to translate parts of that text.
2 Regarding historical comparison, Carpenter and Krause (2012) and the literature referred to by Maor in this volume are exceptions, and as regards a comparative analysis of current practices, Bjørnå in this volume represents an exception.
3 In Norway, local governments have strong standing. Development activities and service provisions are organized under democratically elected municipal organizations, so place names are often the same as municipality names.

REFERENCES

Aaker, Jennifer L. 1997. "Dimensions of Brand Personality." *Journal of Marketing Research* 34:347–356.
Alvesson, Mats. 1990. "Organization: From Substance to Image." *Organization Studies* 11:173–194.
Alvesson, Mats. 2013. *The Triumph of Emptiness*. Oxford: Oxford University Press.

Driving Forces, Critiques, and Paradoxes   71

Arendt, Hannah. 1958. *The Human Condition*. Chicago: University of Chicago Press.

Argenti, Paul A. 1998. *Corporate Communication*. New York: Irwin McGraw-Hill.

Arvidsson, Adam, and Nicolai Peitersen. 2013. *The Ethical Economy: Rebuilding Value after the Crisis*. New York: Columbia University Press.

Berglund, Børre. 2006. *Omdømmebygging i omstillingskommuner*. Oslo: Innovasjon Norge.

Berglund, Børre. 2008. "Omdømmebygging—hvorfor bruke tid på dette?" Power-Point presentation, Hasvik municipality, April 22, 2008.

Bjornå, H. 2000. "Integrert Kommunikasjon: Strid om organiseringen." *Kommunikasjon.info*, June 30, 2000.

Bordum, Anders, and Jacob H. Hansen. 2005. *Strategisk ledelseskommunikation—er hvervslivets ledelse med visioner, missioner og værdier*. Copenhagen: DJØF.

Brønn, Peggy S., and Øyvind Ihlen. 2009. *Åpen eller innadvendt—Omdømmebygging for organisasjoner*. Oslo: Gyldendal.

Brown, Tom, Peter Dacin, Michael Pratt, and David Whetten. 2006. "Identity, Intended Image, Construed Image, and Reputation: An Interdisciplinary Framework and Suggested Terminology." *Journal of the Academy of Marketing Science* 34:99–106.

Brunsson, Nils, and Kerstin Sahlin Andersson. 2000. "Constructing Organizations: The Example of Public Sector Reform." *Organization Studies* 21:721–746.

Byrkjeflot, Haldor. 2010. "Omdømmebygging—drivkrefter, kritikk og paradokser." *Scandinavian Journal of Public Administration* 12:3–24.

Carpenter, Daniel P. 2001. *The Forging of Bureaucratic Autonomy: Reputations, Networks and Policy Innovation in Executive Agencies, 1862–1928*. Princeton, NJ: Princeton University Press.

Carpenter, Daniel P., and George A. Krause. 2012. "Reputation and Public Administration." *Public Administration Review* 72:26–32.

Christensen, Lars. T., Mette Morsing, and George Cheney. 2008. *Challenging Corporate Communication: Convention, Complexity and Critique*. London: Sage.

Christensen, Tom, and Per Lægreid, editors. 2007. *Transcending New Public Management: The Transformation of Public Sector Reforms*. Aldershot: Ashgate.

Davis, Gerald F. 2009. *Managed by the Markets: How Finance Reshaped America*. New York: Oxford University Press.

de Fine Licht, Jenny. 2014. "Policy Area as a Potential Moderator of Transparency Effects: An Experiment." *Public Administration Review* 74:361–371.

Edelman. 2013. "Edelman Trust Barometer 2013." http://trust.edelman.com/.

Elgvin, Olav. 2013. "Saman om et bedre omdømme—en kunnskapsstatus." Fafo Institute for Applied International Studies, April.

Eriksen, Thomas Hylland. 2007. *Globalization—The Key Concepts*. Cambridge, UK: Cambridge University Press.

Financial Management. 2013. "The Data: The Increasing Value of Intangible Assets." *Financial Management* July 16. http://www.fm-magazine.com/infographic/data/increasing-value-intangible-assets.

Fombrun, Charles J. 1996. *Reputation: Realizing Value from the Corporate Image*. Boston: Harvard Business School Press.

Fombrun, Charles J. 2007. "List of Lists: A Compilation of International Corporate Reputation Ratings." *Corporate Reputation Review* 10:144–153.

Fombrun, Charles J., and Cees B.M. van Riel. 2004. *Fame and Fortune: How Successful Companies Build Winning Reputations*. Upper Saddle River, NJ: Prentice Hall.

Gray, Edmund R., and John M.T. Balmer. 1998. "Managing Corporate Image and Corporate Reputation." *Long Range Planning* 31:695–702.

72 Haldor Byrkjeflot

Grimmelikhuijsen, Stephan, Gregory Porumbescu, Boram Hong, and Tobin Im. 2013. "The Effect of Transparency on Trust in Government: A Cross-National Comparative Experiment." *Public Administration Review* 73:575–586.

Greenspan, Alan. 1999. "Maintaining Economic Vitality" Millennium Lecture Series, sponsored by the Gerald R. Ford Foundation and Grand Valley State University, Grand Rapids, Michigan, September 8.

Greenspan, Alan. 2008. "Markets and the Judiciary" speech at Sandra Day O'Connor Project Conference, Washington, DC, October 2.

Grimen, Harald. 2009. *Hva er tillit?* Oslo: Universitetsforlaget.

Guest, David, and Zella King. 2004. "Power, Innovation and Problem-Solving: The Personnel Managers' Three Steps to Heaven?" *Journal of Management Studies* 41:401–423.

Hatch, Mary Jo, and Majken Schultz. 2003. "Bringing the Corporation into Corporate Branding." *European Journal of Marketing* 37:1041–1064.

Hatch, Mary Jo, and Majken Schultz. 2008. *Taking Brand Initiative: How Companies Can Align Strategy, Culture and Identity through Corporate Branding.* San Francisco: Jossey-Bass.

Hegnes, Atle Wehn. 2012. "Introducing and Practicing PDO and PGI in Norway: Turning to Protected Quality through Translations of Meaning and Transformations of Materiality." *Anthropology of Food,* special issue 7.

Hind, Roar. 2008. "Hvorfor har kommunene så dårlig omdømme—eller har de det?" http://www.distriktssenteret.no/Godeeksempel/Artikkel/tabid/7364/smid/15674/ArticleID/104/Default.aspx.

Jutterström, Mats, and Peter Norberg, eds. 2013. *CSR as a Management Idea: Ethics in Action.* Cheltenham: Edward Elgar Publishing.

Kornberger, Martin. 2010. *Brand Society: How Brands Transform Management and Lifestyle.* Cambridge, UK: Cambridge University Press.

Lange, Donald, Peggy M. Lee, and Ye Dai. 2011. "Organizational Reputation: A Review." *Journal of Management* 37:153–184.

Luoma-aho, Vilma. 2005. "Faith-holders as Social Capital of Finnish Public Organisations." *Jyväskylä Studies in Humanities* 42. Ph.D. dissertation, University of Jyväskylä.

Luoma-aho, Vilma. 2007. "Neutral Reputation and Public Sector Organizations." *Corporate Reputation Review* 10:124–143.

March, James G., and Johan P. Olsen. 2006. "The Logic of Appropriateness." In *The Oxford Handbook of Public Policy,* edited by Michael Moran, Martin Rein, and Robert E. Goodin, 689–708. Oxford: Oxford University Press.

Marsh, David, and Paul Fawcett. 2011. "Branding, Politics and Democracy." *Policy Studies* 32:515–530.

Meyer, John W., and Patricia Bromley. 2013. "The Worldwide Expansion of 'Organization.'" *Sociological Theory* 31:366–389.

MORI. 2014. "Trust in Professions Archive." http://www.ipsos-mori.com.

Øvrebø, Olav Anders. 2009. "Bedre omdømme med åpne data?" *Vox Publica,* October 2009.

Pierre, Jon and Bo Rothstein. 2011. "Contending Models of Administrative Reform. The New Public Management Versus the New Weberianism?" In *Administrative Reforms and Democratic Governance,* edited by Jean-Michel Eymeri-Douzans and Jon Pierre, 121–131. New York: Routledge.

Power, Michael. 2007. *Organized Uncertainty: Designing a World of Risk Management.* London: Oxford University Press.

Reich, Robert B. 2007. *Supercapitalism: The Transformation of Business, Democracy, and Everyday Life.* New York: Alfred A. Knopf.

Rothstein, Bo. 2011. *The Quality of Government: Corruption, Social Trust, and Inequality in International Perspective.* Chicago: University of Chicago Press.

Driving Forces, Critiques, and Paradoxes 73

Røvik, Kjell Arne. 2002. "The Secrets of the Winner: Management Ideas that Flow." In *The Expansion of Management Knowledge: Carriers, Flows, and Sources,* edited by Kerstin Sahlin-Andersson and Lars Engwall, 113–144. Stanford: Stanford University Press.

Røvik, Kjell Arne. 2007. *Trender og Translasjoner: Ideer som former det 21. århundrets organisasjon.* Oslo: Universitetsforlaget.

Røvik, Kjell Arne. 2011. "Analyse av kommunikatorenes innmarsj i offentlig sektor." In *Substans og framtreden: Omdømmehåndtering i offentlig sektor,* edited by Arild Wæraas, Haldor Byrkjeflot, and Svein Ivar Angell, 71–83. Oslo: Universitetsforlaget.

Scharpf, Fritz W. 1999. *Governing in Europe: Effective and Democratic?* Oxford: Oxford University Press.

Tolbert, Pamela S., and Lynne G. Zucker. 1983. "Institutional Sources of Change in the Formal Structure of Organizations: The Diffusion of Civil Service Reform, 1880–1935." *Administrative Science Quarterly* 28:22–39.

Ukeavisen Ledelse. 2006. "Toppledere skyr kommunejobber." *Ukeavisen Ledelse,* June 11, 2006.

van Riel, Cees B.M., and Charles J. Fombrun. 2007. *Essentials of Corporate Communication: Implementing Practices for Effective Reputation Management.* London: Routledge.

Vike, Halvard, Runar Bakken, Arne Brinchmann, Randi Kroken, and Heidi Haukelien. 2002. *Maktens samvittighet. Om politikk, styring og dilemmaer i velferdsstaten.* Oslo: Gyldendal Akademisk.

Weber, Max. 1922/1978. *Economy and Society.* Edited by Guenther Roth and Claus Wittich. Berkeley: University of California Press.

Wernick, Andrew. 2006. "Rebranding Harvard." *Theory, Culture & Society* 23:566–567.

Willmott, Hugh. 2010. "Creating 'Value' beyond the Point of Production: Branding, Financialization and Market Capitalization." *Organization* 17:517–542.

Zerfass, Ansgar, Joachim Schwalbach, Günter Bentele, and Muschda Sherzada. 2014. "Corporate Communications from the Top and from the Center: Comparing Experiences and Expectations of CEOs and Communicators." *International Journal of Strategic Communication* 8:61–78.

Part II

Reputation Management in Central Government Agencies

5 The Relationship between an Irish Government Department and Its Newly Established Agency

A Reputational Perspective

Ciara O'Dwyer

> *Regulatory reputations take time to build up and can be quickly lost—regulators are only as good as their last decisions.*
>
> (Stern 1997, 73)

INTRODUCTION

A wide literature has developed over the last 30 or so years, outlining how private sector companies can develop and maintain a strong reputation. In contrast, research on public sector reputation is limited, even though negative stereotypes of the public sector have placed increasing pressure on individual organizations to present themselves in a better light, often by demonstrating that they are transparent, accessible, and responsive (Wæraas 2010). Understanding how and why public sector reputation is developed is particularly important given that the public sector has increased in size throughout the OECD over the last 20 years. This is largely due to the wealth of independent governmental agencies that are established every year to fulfill a range of increasingly specialized tasks. Although such agencies typically operate under the aegis of a federal executive department, legislation allows them to make decisions autonomously.

Of the research carried out on this important topic to date, much has focused on the characteristics of a strong public sector reputation and the strategies used by long-established public sector organizations to maintain a strong reputation (see Maor in this volume). However, significant gaps in our understanding of this important topic remain. Limited research has examined the strategies available to newly established organizations to develop a strong reputation. In addition, the extent to which governmental agencies have the autonomy to develop their reputations remains unclear, given that key decisions about how the organization conducts its work are often made by superordinate political bodies (Carpenter and Krause 2012; Wæraas and Byrkjeflot 2012). Finally, scholarship on public sector reputation has to date not meaningfully explored why a strong reputation has become such an important issue throughout the sector as a whole.

78   Ciara O'Dwyer

This chapter seeks to develop our understanding of these issues on the basis of a qualitative case study of a newly established health care regulator in Ireland. Relying on a political science approach to reputation (see Wæraas and Maor in this volume), it seeks to document the strategies used by newly established governmental agencies in establishing a strong reputation among their key stakeholders. Second, it investigates the extent to which governmental agencies have sufficient autonomy to control their reputation (see Maor in this volume), and moreover, whether a strong reputation facilitates agencies to "claim a measure of autonomy" (Carpenter 2010, 53; see also Carpenter 2001). Finally, it seeks to theorize about why public sector organizations seek to protect their reputations, and the myriad of challenges they face in doing so.

BACKGROUND

Organizational Reputation

There has long been significant interest in the reputations of private (for-profit) organizations, defined broadly as how the organization is judged by its observers (Lange, Lee, and Dai 2011). There is now a wide consensus that a strong reputation is generally of huge benefit to such firms, allowing them to attract and retain high-quality staff and increase profit margins (Burke 2011). In contrast, researchers have only recently begun to recognize that many governmental agencies also make significant efforts to develop and maintain a strong reputation (Carpenter 2001; see also Maor in this volume). Indeed, developing and maintaining both a strong reputation and public support is important in order to be able to successfully operate and can even be "vital for their survival" (Luoma-aho 2007, 124). For example, if the public does not trust messages coming from a regulatory agency (e.g., a public health warning), and so ignores them, public safety itself may become undermined, in turn further damaging the reputation of the agency in question (Walls et al. 2004). Furthermore, governmental agencies must seek to overcome the negative stereotype of the public sector more generally: being overly bureaucratic and inefficient, opaque, and inflexible (Wæraas and Byrkjeflot 2012).

According to Carpenter (2010), agencies seek to demonstrate their uniqueness by emphasizing one or two of the four facets of organizational reputation: performance (competency and efficiency), morality (transparency, humanity), procedure (consistency in following the rules), and technical capacity (expertise and skill). Agencies with a highly specialized function will endeavor to build a reputation around their technical skills, whereas administrative agencies are more likely to market their procedural reputation for following guidelines (Carpenter and Krause 2012). Agencies use relevant communication strategies to portray themselves in a positive light and manage public expectations of their remit, a refocusing of activities and a restructuring and investment in quality (Gilad and Yogev 2012; Maor in this volume; Maor, Gilad, and Ben-Nun Bloom 2013; Wæraas 2010). Furthermore, they can also develop their reputation simply by demonstrating that they consistently act to protect the public interest (Stern 1997). Finally, they can use ambiguity or delaying tactics in order to minimize the risk of alienating an important group of stakeholders (Carpenter 2010).

However, public sector organizations face a number of constraints in developing a strong reputation. First, public sector agencies have multiple audiences, often with competing demands, and so "satisfying some audience subset often means upsetting others" (Carpenter and Krause 2012, 29). In turn, this can undermine the ability of the agency to carry out its functions effectively, as it may refrain from taking important actions that can damage important relationships. Yet, a bigger constraint facing public sector agencies in developing their reputation is the limited autonomy they have over their actions. Although governmental agencies usually theoretically have a formal independent status, allowing them the freedom to pursue their own goals and policy preferences, including making unpalatable decisions when required (Stern 1997), their autonomy can be limited in practice. In theory at least, the mission of the organization and the rules governing how it can conduct its work are usually decided by superordinate political bodies (Carpenter and Krause 2012; Wæraas and Byrkjeflot 2012). As a strong reputation depends on how its actions are perceived by those who interact with it, agencies with limited autonomy thus have limited ability to shape their reputations. Furthermore, there are a number of more subtle ways politicians or government authorities can try to control or influence the decisions made by governmental agencies, such as by limiting access to information, reducing their budget and staff, and making key appointments within the organization. Such tactics can often put state bodies under significant pressure to make decisions that promote the government's agenda, even if they do not necessarily protect the public interest, and may thus damage their reputation in the long term.

According to Carpenter (2002, 491), a strong reputation is a valuable political asset for public sector organizations—"used to generate public support, to achieve delegated autonomy and discretion from politicians, to protect the agency from political attack, and to recruit and retain valued employees." As an agency's reputation is such a strong asset, Carpenter suggests that its focus inevitably turns to avoiding reputational damage, and thus avoiding risk taking and controversy, focusing instead on less contentious tasks, and can even create a reluctance to challenge political superordinates to a great extent (Carpenter 2010). However, somewhat counterintuitively, Carpenter (2010, 11) also suggests that agencies that manage to develop a strong reputation and become trusted by the public usually have a higher level of autonomy. This is in part because agencies with a reputation for making effective policy decisions (consistent with lawmakers' own priorities) can be trusted to continue this work (MacDonald and Franko 2007), but also because political superordinates try to use the strong reputations of their

80 *Ciara O'Dwyer*

agencies to advance their policy objectives (and in turn enhance their own reputations) (Carpenter 2010). Thus, they may claim credit for establishing the agency in the first place, or demonstrate its commitment to an area of concern to the public by endeavoring to implement any recommendations made by the agency. Consequently, they offer greater support to the agency.

This suggests that the shaping of a governmental agency's reputation is reliant on its relationship with its parent department, particularly when it is first established (Gilardi 2008); this is when agencies have the opportunity to develop a strong reputation that can dictate the level of support they can command from their parent departments. However, it is possible that Carpenter underestimates the extent to which governmental agencies can promote their own reputation independently. Maor argues that

> reputation-sensitive agencies are adaptive, strategic and sometimes even opportunistic actors. . . . They have a repository of ideas, values, and strategies that they may combine in various ways, deploy them politically, and redeploy them between different audiences, thereby redefining relations with these audiences.
>
> (Maor, this volume, 24)

In other words, well-established organizations have the capacity to act creatively and astutely in order to remain free from excessive political control. Yet it is unclear whether newly established organizations have the same resources to react strategically to challenges created by their stakeholders, particularly their parent department, in order to gain a degree of autonomy and thus build a strong reputation.

Related research by governance theorists suggests that state agencies were established with the purpose of enhancing the reputations of central governments, whose own reputations will always take precedence. According to governance theorists, trust in governments throughout the Western world began to decline within almost all advanced industrial democracies in the 1980s and 1990s (Dalton 2005; Fukuyama 1995; Putnam 1993), and it has been suggested that this decline was because the public felt that governments were prioritizing the interests of powerful groups over those of wider society (Dalton 2005; Jordana and Levi-Faur 2004; Majone 1994). This mistrust led many governments to attempt to improve their reputations and demonstrate their responsiveness to the concerns of the public. Often, they did so by establishing governmental agencies with an oversight function to respond to a crisis or issue of concern to the public. Indeed, there has been such a sharp increase in the number of regulatory agencies established across most OECD member states since the 1980s that we are now said to be living in the era of the Regulatory State. The introduction of such agencies has led to a tension whereby governments are meant to relinquish control to these new agencies while at the same time demanding greater accountability (Christensen and Lægreid 2007). In practice, this tension has led to instability and disintegration within the political and administrative functions of the state, as well as only limited additional autonomy for newly established agencies (Christensen and Lægreid 2007; Verhoest et al. 2010). Indeed, it has been suggested that governments establish governmental agencies to purport to be acting in the public interest without actually changing the status quo: "When governments are short of cash or unwilling to spend it, the creation of (regulatory) agencies provides a low cost symbolic commitment to action" (Loughlin and Scott 1997, 205). Thus, whereas political superordinates often try to rely on the reputations of the agencies under their aegis to enhance their own reputations, the failure to give them adequate support in the first place may in fact result in their own reputations being even further damaged; at least, the public often appears to trust governmental agencies to a greater extent than central governments (Carpenter 2010; Lang and Hallman 2005; Poortinga and Pidgeon 2003). Indeed, it appears that two broad public sector reputations have developed in the minds of the public in recent years, one of bureaucratic and self-interested central government departments, which have less direct contact with the public, and that of governmental agencies, responsible for carrying out the directives of central government, whose strong, unique reputation comes from their ability to act in the public interest and carry out their functions effectively (Luoma-aho 2008). It is thus possible that central governments may have become more reluctant to grant autonomy to their governmental agencies for fear that it will further damage their own reputation.

Overall, it is clear that the study of public sector reputation is important but that it is currently underdeveloped, and significant gaps in our knowledge of the area remain. This chapter seeks to contribute to our understanding of the topic by exploring the strategies used by a newly established Irish health care regulator, the Health Information and Quality Authority (HIQA). It set out to formulate standards for residential care settings for older people in Ireland, and, by doing that, it developed its reputation while negotiating its relationship and status with its parent department and other stakeholders. The case is particularly illuminating, as successive Irish governments have been criticized for disrespecting the statutory independence of governmental agencies (Economist Intelligence Unit 2009), ultimately limiting their potential to build and maintain a strong reputation. The case also allows an exploration of why superordinate political bodies deliberately undermine the autonomy, and the reputation, of agencies that they themselves set up.

IRISH CONTEXT

Ireland has a highly centralized administrative system, often described as both insular and clientelist, wherein "the central government is captured by provincial interests" (Collins and O'Shea 2003, 94). The focus on appeasing key voters has meant that successive Irish governments have adopted

82   Ciara O'Dwyer

a style of 'pragmatic' policy making, cherry picking tools and ideas from other jurisdictions, particularly the U.K. (Dellepiane and Hardiman 2011; MacCarthaigh and Hardiman 2010). As a result, policy making in Ireland has been described as "a political project that . . . contain[s] a confusing and contrasting myriad of inconsistent ideological arguments to support a particular trajectory" (Taylor 2005, 190–191). Moreover, whereas Ireland (and Fianna Fáil) has always been praised for having transparent and consultative policy-making processes, commentators have questioned the extent to which they are truly consultative (Hardiman 2006; Taylor 2005). This may highlight a key skill of Irish politicians, whereby they appear to consult while continuing to develop their own policies intent on appeasing key voters (Weeks 2009). This approach has led to a growing mistrust in Irish politics, increasingly seen as corrupt and self-interested (Transparency International 2009).

There has been a particular lack of confidence in the Irish health care system (Wren 2002), prompting major reform in 2001, including of the regulation of residential care settings for older people through the establishment of a new health care regulator, the HIQA (Department of Health and Children 2001). However, after four years, the Department made little progress in establishing HIQA. In 2005, the course of action was speeded up considerably following the broadcasting on national television of an investigative documentary, *Home Truths,* which showed 'unbearable' hidden footage (Hegarty 2005) of day-to-day life in a private nursing home, Leas Cross. It showed both the extensive physical and emotional abuse to which residents of the home were subjected and also the poor care practices of the home. The program led to public outrage, particularly once it emerged that inspectors had raised concerns about the home since 1998 (O'Donovan 2009). A review of the home suggested that inadequate regulation was partly to blame (O'Neill 2006).

In response, the government began to speed up the lengthy process of establishing HIQA, which prioritized the establishment of minimum quality standards against which it would eventually inspect residential care settings for older people. In order "to ensure a shared vision across all stakeholders as to what should be contained in the National Quality Standards" (HIQA 2009, 6), HIQA set up a large Working Group made up of representatives of HIQA, the Department of Health and Children (DOHC), older peoples' representatives groups, and public (statutory) and private providers. The *National Quality Standards for Residential Care Settings for Older People* were published in February 2009 (HIQA 2009), following approval from the Minister for Health. Since the July 1, 2009, all care homes—public, private, and voluntary—have been subject to inspection by HIQA.

However, the legislative framework underpinning the regulation of the sector, and the functions of HIQA, was somewhat unusual, largely because the legislation to formally establish HIQA and set out its functions was only passed in May 2007 (Government of Ireland 2007), five months after HIQA's Working Group began its deliberations. Furthermore, the Act did not set out the regulations governing residential care settings, but gave the Minister the power to develop regulations at a later date. Thus, from early on in the process, there was a lack of clarity about the status of the Standards being written by HIQA to govern the residential care sector, as well as the relationship between the Standards and the subsequent regulations coming from the Minister for Health, an issue that created significant challenges for HIQA, as described below.

METHODOLOGY

This research is based on a larger study that aimed to explore the standard-setting process in the residential care sector in Ireland. The study took the form of a qualitative, exploratory case study. A total of 44 in-depth interviews were conducted with members of HIQA's Working Group, HIQA staff members, officials from the Department of Health and Children, and other stakeholders from the residential care sector. These interviews aimed to explore *inter alia* respondents' attitudes toward HIQA and how it carried out its work. Interviews lasted 45 minutes on average. All were audio-recorded. The majority of interviews were transcribed verbatim the day of or in the days immediately following the interview. In addition, a number of key documents were analyzed in order to triangulate the findings, including the Standards developed by HIQA and the Working Group (HIQA 2009); the 2007 Health Act (Government of Ireland 2007), which formally established HIQA and set out its functions; the 2009 Care and Welfare Regulations (Government of Ireland 2009), which sought to give legal effect to HIQA's Standards; and, finally, the minutes of the meetings of the Working Group established by HIQA to write the Standards.

Data Analysis

A process-tracing approach was used to guide data analysis (George and Bennett 2005). The first stage of the analysis explored how HIQA first established its reputation, the second explored the subsequent actions of the Department of Health that threatened to undermine this reputation, and the third explored the strategy used by HIQA to maintain its reputation in light of this threat. The interview data were analyzed thematically and focused on HIQA's role in facilitating and managing its Working Group; attitudes by various stakeholders on HIQA and its management of the process; how decisions were made and HIQA's relationships with the Department of Health and care providers; and its views of care recipients and their families. The software program NVivo 8 (QSR International, Doncaster Australia) was used to aid analysis. A comparative content analysis (Krippendorf 2004)

84 Ciara O'Dwyer

was used to compare the content of HIQA's Standards and the 2009 Care and Welfare regulations underpinning them. This involved a simple cross-check and count of the differences between the two documents. Microsoft Excel was used to facilitate this analysis.

FINDINGS

The Development of HIQA's Reputation

As noted earlier, HIQA established a Working Group made up of various stakeholders from the residential care sector to formulate the new standards that would be used to regulate the quality of care provided to older residents. In order to create a collaborative, trusting atmosphere on the Working Group, HIQA staff deliberately did not set formal rules about membership. Instead, staff used an open, inclusive process to ensure that all relevant stakeholders were represented on the Working Group. Many members of the Working Group felt that this approach helped to engender an atmosphere of trust, which encouraged all the different actors to work together:

> [M]y initial impression was . . . I remember you know being struck by the range of different professions, interests, vested interests, you know around the table and I remember how expertly how I felt it was chaired. Everyone was heard and listened to.
>
> (Member of the Working Group, private sector)

Setting standards using this collaborative approach can be a challenging process, as without broad consensus on the measures developed, there is a risk that high levels of noncompliance will develop (Walshe 2003). Different stakeholder groups often have different agendas and views on what the appropriate standard should be, what is affordable for the regulated sector, and what will lead to safe working practices. Indeed, conflict developed between the various members of the Working Group, requiring significant compromises, particularly on costly issues (e.g., the ratio of single to shared bedrooms). However, HIQA managed to consolidate its reputation in resolving these conflicts, largely by illustrating that its primary focus was on reaching consensus, and aimed to meet the needs of older people living in residential care, its core 'client':

> Once HIQA took over, I really had a lot of confidence in the process because I actually think they are probably about the most professional public body I have seen in Irish public life thus far. HIQA were inclusive. This is really atypical in Ireland.
>
> (Member of the Working Group, private sector)

What was really important was the facilitation of the group, "have other people got views on that," you know, "let's look at that," "let's think about that" . . . There was a lot of that.

(Member of the Working Group, public sector)

This was in stark contrast to the approach taken by the Department of Health and Children, which was regarded by many Group members as non-inclusive:

I do feel HIQA kind of invested time, resources. . . . It was clear this was very important to them. And I think there was there political will behind it from the Department. Because of the public outcry [about Leas Cross]. At least until the cancer [scandal] came more to the forefront.

(Member of the Working Group, public sector)

Once the Working Group had finished drafting the Standards (March 2008), HIQA issued a press release to publicize their relevance for the residential care sector and to inform the public about the likely changes that would take place in the sector. It emphasized the key role of HIQA in inspecting all providers "to ensure that they are delivering care in accordance with the new quality standards":

This is a significant and important day for older people in Ireland. For the first time, we have quality standards that clearly set down . . . what a resident, their family, carer or the public can expect to receive in residential care settings. As has been demonstrated in the past, the most vulnerable of older people must be protected and supported to live a quality life in a safe, caring and respectful environment and . . . these are at the heart of these standards.

(HIQA Press Release 2008)

Thus, from the outset, HIQA was demonstrating its awareness of the need to develop quality standards and to maintain a positive working relationship with regulated homes, but also to prioritize acting in the public interest (Feintuck 2004; Kagan 2004; Stern 1997).

The Undermining of HIQA's Reputation

The Minister for Health publicly expressed approval for HIQA's Standards, thus signaling the government's respect for HIQA's autonomy and independence within the regulatory process. Furthermore, as Poortinga and Pidgeon (2003) note, public trust in the regulator is an important element in determining the effectiveness of a regulatory system. However, before writing the regulations to make it mandatory for regulated firms to comply with HIQA's Standards, the Minister for Health commissioned a cost analysis of the Standards, which showed that, for private (for-profit) providers, the cost of meeting the Standards would be relatively small (€4 million in total), largely because most private homes were built recently, so standards relating to the physical environment of the home (e.g., room sizes, wheelchair accessibility) would not affect them. However, as many public care homes were built in old, unsuitable settings, the cost would reach approximately €1.2 billion, plus extra costs for staff training. It appears that the potential cost influenced the Department of Health's decision to alter HIQA's Standards, which coincided with the start of the 2008 economic crash. A comparative analysis highlights a significant number of differences between them and the 2009 Care and Welfare Regulations (Government of Ireland 2009), and many of the Standards that would have led residential care settings to incur significant costs are not referenced in the regulations.

An interview with an official from the Department corroborated this interpretation:

> There were financial constraints associated with higher standards. Within the Department, you are more aware that money is an issue; the Secretary General is even more aware of the money! But it's not surprising that HIQA was not as concerned with the costs; their job was to try and get the standards to be as high as possible and not worry about where the funding came from.
> (DOHC staff member, not on the Working Group)

With its decision not to underpin the Standards, the Department was not only undermining HIQA's reputation by insinuating that it was not competent enough to write realistic and implementable standards, one of the organization's key functions. But, by altering the Standards, the Department was compromising the independence of the regulator. Indeed, comments made by civil servants indicate that there was some disquiet over the assumptions being made by HIQA about its level of independence from the Minister and her Department:

> HIQA have their job to do but ultimately, the authority rests with the Minister.
> (DOHC staff member, not on Working Group)

These findings indicate that the Department prioritized the maintenance of its own reputation over that of HIQA—seeking to avoid stating publicly that it would not be financially investing in residential care settings. This supports the argument that central governments attempt to control the reputation of governmental agencies in order to protect their own reputation, even if it has the potential to compromise trust in the agencies set up with the very intention of enhancing their reputation in the first place (Loughlin and Scott 1997). However, when providers perceive that the government

The Irish Gov. and Its Newly Established Agency   87

is not supportive of the regulator's actions, they are less likely to comply (Parker 2006). This meant that HIQA was faced with a dilemma at an early stage in its development: either to challenge the government's decision on the basis that it potentially undermined the well-being of older people living in residential care, or to accept the government's decision and face the prospect of its reputation being tarnished.

Maintaining Regulatory Reputation: HIQA's 'Middle Ground' Strategy

HIQA privately acknowledged that it had made a significant mistake in failing to understand both its relationship with the Department and the legal status of the Standards it had developed, mistakes it sought to correct in similar exercises carried out subsequently:

> It was a huge learning process. . . . The learning was setting out a time-frame for ourselves, having clearer membership rules, setting out the terms of reference.
>
> (HIQA Staff member on the Working Group)

Yet as a newly established regulator, the publication of the Standards was an important milestone for HIQA, as it represented the culmination of the organization's first project. Indeed, HIQA staff appeared to have used the process as a way to develop a strong reputation from the outset:

> One of our primary functions under the Health Act is the development of Standards. So before we put our stamp on them, we had to have a sense of ownership over them. We had to believe that they reflect . . . what HIQA wants to achieve, HIQA's key function. And it was . . . the first set of Standards that we developed, so it was a very important exercise for us. And the collaboration. . . . There is no question of ever developing standards without consultation. It's part of our framework.
>
> (HIQA staff member on the Working Group)

> I think part of what went on in the older people's standards was that people felt they could trust individuals, because they weren't sure about HIQA as an organization yet. They felt we were reasonable and listening and that. In a sense I think the organization has its own reputation now. . . . I think people see it as an organization that gets things done, that has pushed for change.
>
> (HIQA staff member on the Working Group)

Although HIQA had been welcomed by its various key stakeholders, staff were aware that it was still a new and as-yet-unproven organization, and

88   Ciara O'Dwyer

so its reputation was still under development. As a result, they became concerned about the extent to which the challenge by the Department of Health could undermine its fledgling reputation:

> It would have been more helpful if regulations had been available earlier. It was the cart driving the horse when we were asked to develop the Standards first and through that process the Department was able to test the waters to see what would rise or sink as it was. So these things get worked out and obviously part of the Department's role, they have to cost it. And cost was the big issue, and by then we didn't have any money anymore!
>
> (HIQA staff member on the Working Group)

> Well the regulations were never going to look like Standards. They don't. . . . What it will come down to is whether people's needs can be met within those homes in a dignified way, respectful way. . . . We won't be ignoring anything that's of any risk in the first instance, but at the same, we have to live within the world we're in.
>
> (HIQA staff member on the Working Group)

HIQA was faced with a choice of challenging the Department or accepting its decision in order to maintain positive working relations. In order to not damage its reputation with its key stakeholders at a critical, early stage in its development, HIQA developed an alternative 'middle ground' strategy, effectively denying its mistake and suggesting that, even though many of the Standards it had carefully developed were no longer mandatory requirements, it could use its own power to coerce homes to take them into account. It issued a press release implying that the regulations underpinned the Standards, and that it thus had the full support of the government:

> Nursing homes will be inspected against the National Quality Standards for Residential Care Settings for Older People in Ireland and regulated under the Health Act 2007 to see if they are safe and whether the residents are cared for properly.
>
> (HIQA 2009)

At the same time, it issued guidance more discreetly within the sector stating that the Standards themselves had no legal powers and that those not covered within the 2009 regulations had simply become guidance for providers:

> If the provider is not in compliance with the regulations, registration may be refused or he/she may lose the registration status. In the case of those standards which are not regulatory standards, nor linked to

regulations, failure to comply will not lead to refusal to be registered or loss of registration, but they are designed to encourage continuous improvement.

(HIQA 2009)

Many members of the Working Group failed to understand the difference between the two documents because they worked at a policy level, rather than in care homes. They simply trusted HIQA's word, as the organization had proved so trustworthy in the past:

Just about the regulations underpinning the standards, I don't know if you have looked at them? [Researcher's question]

Well I suppose you need to make everything enforceable. And there is kind of a statutory obligation now to implement as well . . . I mean the regulations came from the standards and I think that the message has gone out . . .

(Member of the Working Group, public sector)

In contrast, the weakened standards made providers happy, largely because the costs of adhering to the new regulations had been significantly reduced:

Most of what we are now putting our efforts into is ticking the boxes of the regulations. . . . If you look at the reports that are up, it is the regulations they are following, not the Standards.

(Member of the Working Group, private sector)

However, rather than losing respect for HIQA, most providers remained positive toward the regulator. Any concerns about the differences between the Standards and the regulations were blamed on the Department and interpreted as a prioritization of saving money over resident care. For the most part, this was because care providers were aware of the reputational damage the sector had incurred, but also because HIQA had worked hard throughout the process of developing the Standards to show that, regardless of the rules, its primary goal was to promote the interests of residents, its key client group. Furthermore, it has advocated on behalf of the sector overall to encourage the State to invest financially in residential care:

At the end of the day, we inspect and regulate residential care services against the regulations and the Standards. But the other side of it is that we have a policy role too, in the sense that, if 70% of homes are having difficulty meeting a standard, we will try and bring information about that to the relevant authority and say this is a common issue that needs to be addressed.

(HIQA staff member on the Working Group)

90   *Ciara O'Dwyer*

These findings support Carpenter's (2001) and Carpenter and Krause's (2012) assertion that a poor reputation, or at least mistakes that threaten the reputation of a governmental agency, may limit its autonomy and may weaken its relationship with its parent department. However, it is equally clear that HIQA was able "to act adaptively, strategically, and opportunistically in developing [a] good reputation" (Maor, this volume, 17). It did so by focusing on *appearing* competent and balancing the various competing interests of its key stakeholders (Gilad and Yogev 2012), and adopting a blame-avoidance strategy (Hood and Rothstein 2001). This may indicate that even newly established agencies have the capacity to retain their autonomy in ways that acknowledge the myriad of constraints they face. In contrast, the lack of initiative by the Department of Health to do its part in improving the quality of residential care may suggest that governmental agencies often have a greater capacity to develop and maintain a more trustworthy reputation than central government departments, as they are less bureaucratic and more responsive to the needs of the public—promoting the idea that two public sector reputations are developing simultaneously (Luoma-aho 2008). This appears to support the belief proposed by governance scholars that the failure by central governments to offer consistent support to the agencies they establish will simply result in greater mistrust in government itself (Loughlin and Scott 1997).

DISCUSSION

This chapter set out to document the strategies used by newly established governmental agencies to establish strong reputations among their key stakeholders, to investigate the extent to which governmental agencies have sufficient autonomy to control their reputation, to theorize about why public sector organizations seek to protect their reputations, and to explore the myriad of challenges they face in doing so. The strategies used by HIQA to develop its reputation included developing positive working relations with all of the key stakeholders with whom it would interact regularly; demonstrating that it was willing to work collaboratively and transparently; highlighting its competence and technical skills in writing standards for a specialized area; highlighting its key achievements and strengths to the public via mass communication strategies; and making clear that its primary objective was to protect the public interest, in this case, older people living in residential care settings. These strategies broadly mirror those strategies used by long-established organizations (Gilad and Yogev 2012; Maor, this volume; Maor, Gilad, and Ben-Nun Bloom 2013; Stern 1997; Wæraas 2010), although the approach taken by HIQA may indicate that governmental agencies learn from experience to become more cautious about the decisions and actions they take that may compromise their reputations (Carpenter and Krause 2012). In this case, HIQA did not try to avoid tasks that had the potential to damage its reputation, nor did it try to manage public expectations about its ability to carry out its role (Gilad and Yogev 2012; Hood and Rothstein 2001). On the contrary, it welcomed the opportunity to carry out challenging and highly politicized work in order to build its reputation as a protector of the public interest. However, in doing so, it may have failed to fully understand the importance of its relationship with its parent government department, thus threatening its independence and its ability to manage its reputation effectively. Indeed, as Luoma-aho (2007, 129) notes, a neutral reputation "is the ideal level of reputation for public sector organizations: one that does not aim to high or too low." In other words, organizations may do well to develop a reputation of being trusted by stakeholders and capable of autonomy without attracting too much positive or negative attention, and so avoid the risk of disappointing a highly expectant public.

To some extent, the findings from this study offer support to Carpenter's (2001) argument that agencies with a poor reputation can fail to maintain high levels of political discretion and autonomy. In this case, HIQA's attempt to assert its autonomy was thwarted by its parent department, which did not approve of the actions taken by HIQA and so prioritized the enhancement of its own reputation over that of respecting the expertise of the agency it had only recently established. This mirrors a significant body of evidence that has already found that central governments often fail to respect the independence of government agencies (Bertolotti et al. 2011; Edwards and Waverman 2006; Gilardi 2008; Stern and Holder 1999) and, furthermore, highlights the tension and uncertainty that can be created by the expectation that governments are meant to relinquish control to these new agencies while at the same time demanding accountability (Christensen and Lægreid 2007). However, as Maor (this volume) argues, autonomy can be obtained in many ways. In this case, HIQA managed to maintain a strong reputation with the public and industry insiders by acting strategically and by demonstrating that its key priority was to protect the best interests of the public. Indeed, HIQA arguably boosted its own reputation by acting strategically; it is now a large, high-profile and widely respected agency that has significant capacity to challenge government's actions, and inactions, in the health care sector. Although this does lend some support to Carpenter's (2001) assertion that a strong reputation can in turn create greater autonomy, the findings also illustrate how an agency's reputation is heavily reliant on its (often ambiguous) relationship with its parent department, indicating that endogenous processing may almost be a necessity for newly established organizations as they seek to build their reputations and assert their independence (Maor, this volume).

This in turn highlights the need to better understand the relationship between central governments and government agencies and, in particular, why reputation has become so important for all public sector organizations—both central governments and government agencies.

92 Ciara O'Dwyer

CONCLUSION

Newly established government agencies face a range of challenges—they must demonstrate their capacity and expertise to carry out their functions, gain the trust of key stakeholders, and decide on their key priorities, without the benefit of established institutional resources. Although it is not possible to generalize from the findings of one case study alone, the findings presented in this chapter indicate that it is possible for agencies to develop a strong reputation, provided that they are fully aware of the constraints they face, particularly the extent to which central government can exert control over its operations. Not only does this emphasize that agencies need to act flexibly and strategically to protect their reputation, it also highlights the level of ambiguity and tension between agencies and central governments, particularly as the aims and objectives of each can clash. Although central governments may, in practice, have greater capacity to control the agencies under their aegis, they themselves may be at a greater loss in the long run as their own reputations suffer.

REFERENCES

Bertolotti, Barnardo, Carlo Cambini, Laura Rondi, and Yossi Spiegel. 2011. "Capital Structure and Regulation: Do Ownership and Regulatory Independence Matter?" *Journal of Economics and Management Strategy* 20:517–564.

Burke, Ronald. 2011. "Corporate Reputations: Development, Maintenance, Change and Repair." In *Corporate Reputation: Managing Opportunities and Threats,* edited by Ronald Burke, Graeme Martin, and Cary Cooper, 3–44. Farnham, Surrey: Gower Publishing.

Carpenter, Daniel P. 2001. *The Forging of Bureaucratic Autonomy: Reputations, Networks, and Policy Innovation in Executive Agencies, 1862–1928.* Princeton: Princeton University Press.

Carpenter, Daniel P. 2002. "Groups, the Media, Agency Waiting Costs, and FDA Drug Approval." *American Journal of Political Science* 46:490–505.

Carpenter, Daniel P. 2010. *Reputation and Power: Organizational Image and Pharmaceutical Regulation at the FDA.* Princeton: Princeton University Press.

Carpenter, Daniel P., and George Krause. 2012. "Reputation and Public Administration." *Public Administration Review* 72:26–32.

Christensen, Tom, and Per Lægreid. 2007. "Regulatory Agencies—The Challenges of Balancing Agency Autonomy and Political Control." *Governance* 30:499–520.

Collins, Neil, and Mary O'Shea. 2003. "Clientelism: Facilitating Rights and Favours." In *Public Administration and Public Policy in Ireland,* edited by Maura Adshead and Michelle Millar, 82–100. London: Routledge.

Dalton, Russell J. 2005. "The Social Transformation of Trust in Government." *International Review of Sociology: Revue Internationale de Sociologie* 15:133—154.

Dellepiane, Sebastian, and Niamh Hardiman. 2011. "Governing the Irish Economy: From Boom to Bust." ECPR Standing Group on Regulatory Governance Biennial Conference *Regulation in the Age of Crisis,* 1–31.

Department of Health and Children (DOHC). 2001. *Quality and Fairness—A Health System for You.* Dublin: Stationery Office.

Economist Intelligence Unit. 2009. *Review of the Regulatory Environment in Ireland.* Dublin: Department of the Taoiseach.

The Irish Gov. and Its Newly Established Agency 93

Edwards, Geoff, and Leonard Waverman. 2006. "The Effects of Public Ownership and Regulatory Independence on Regulatory Outcomes." *Journal of Regulatory Economics* 29:23–67.

Fukuyama, Francis. 1995. *Trust: The Social Virtues and the Creation of Prosperity.* New York: Free Press.

George, Alexander L., and Andrew Bennett. 2005. *Case Studies and Theory Development in the Social Sciences.* Cambridge, MA: MIT Press.

Gilad, Sharon, and Tamar Yogev. 2012. "How Reputation Regulates Regulators: Illustrations from the Regulation of Retail Finance." In *The Oxford Handbook of Corporate Reputation,* edited by Michael Barnett and Timothy G. Pollock, 320–340. Oxford: Oxford University Press.

Gilardi, Fabrizio. 2008. *Delegation in the Regulatory State: Independent Regulatory Agencies in Western Europe.* Cheltenham, UK/Northampton, MA: Edward Elgar.

Government of Ireland. 2007. *Health Act 2007.* Dublin: Stationery Office.

Government of Ireland 2009. *Health Act 2007 (Care and Welfare of Residents in Designated Centres for Older People) Regulations 2009.* Dublin: Stationery Office.

Hardiman, Niamh. 2006. "Politics and Social Partnership: Flexible Network Governance." *The Economic and Social Review* 37:343–374.

Hegarty, Shane, "Prime Mover," *The Irish Times,* June 4, 2005.

Hood, Christopher, and Henry Rothstein. 2001. "Risk Regulation under Pressure: Problem Solving or Blame Shifting?" *Administration & Society* 33:21–53.

HIQA. 2009. *National Quality Standards for Residential Care Settings for Older People in Ireland.* Dublin: Health Information and Quality Authority.

Jordana, Jacint, and David Levi-Faur. 2004. "The Politics of Regulation in the Age of Governance." In *The Politics of Regulation: Institutions and Regulatory Reforms for the Age of Governance,* edited by Jacint Jordana and David Levi-Faur, 1–27. Cheltenham, UK/Northampton, MA: Edward Elgar.

Kagan, Robert A. 2004. "Regulators and Regulatory Processes." In *The Blackwell Companion to Law and Society,* edited by Austin Sarat. Malden, MA/Oxford/ Victoria: Blackwell.

Krippendorf, Klaus. 2004. *Content Analysis: An Introduction to Its Methodology.* London/Thousand Oaks/New Delhi: Sage.

Lang, John T., and William K. Hallman. 2005. "Who Does the Public Trust? The Case of Genetically Modified Food in the United States." *Risk Analysis* 25:1241–1252.

Lange, Donald, Peggy M. Lee, and Ye Dai. 2011. "Organizational Reputation: A Review." *Journal of Management* 37:153–184.

Loughlin, Mike, and Colin Scott. 1997. "The Regulatory State." In *Developments in British Politics,* edited by Patrick Dunleavy, Ian Holliday, Andrew Gamble, and Gilian Peele, 205–219. Basingstoke: MacMillan.

Luoma-aho, Vilma. 2007. "Neutral Reputation and Public Sector Organisations." *Corporate Reputation Review* 10:124–143.

Luoma-aho, Vilma. 2008. "Sector Reputation and Public Organisations." *International Journal of Public Sector Management* 21:446—467.

MacCarthaigh, Muiris, and Niamh Hardiman. 2010. "The Unpolitics of New Public Management in Ireland." In *Administrative Reforms and Democratic Governance,* edited by Jean-Michel Eymeri-Douzans and Jon Pierre, 55–67. London: Routledge.

MacDonald, Jason A., and William S. Franko. 2007. "Bureaucratic Capacity and Bureaucratic Discretion: Does Congress Tie Policy Authority to Performance?" *American Politics Research,* 35:790–807.

Majone, Giandomenico. 1994. "The Rise of the Regulatory State in Europe." *West European Politics* 17:77–101.

94 *Ciara O'Dwyer*

Maor, Moshe, Sharon Gilad, and Pazit Ben-Nun Bloom. 2013. "Organizational Reputation, Regulatory Talk and Strategic Silence." *Journal of Public Administration Research and Theory,* 23:581–608.

O'Donovan, Diarmuid. 2009. *The Commission of Investigation (Leas Cross Nursing Home) Final Report.* Dublin: Department of Health and Children.

O'Neill, Des. 2006. *Leas Cross Review.* Naas: Health Service Executive.

Parker, Christine. 2006. "The Compliance Trap: The Moral Message in Responsive Regulatory Enforcement." *Law and Society Review* 40:591–622.

Poortinga, Wouter, and Nick F. Pidgeon. 2003. "Exploring the Dimensionality of Trust in Risk Regulation." *Risk Analysis* 23:961–972.

Putnam, Robert. 1993. *Making Democracy Work: Civic Traditions in Modern Italy.* Princeton: Princeton University Press.

Stern, Jon. 1997. "What Makes an Independent Regulator Independent?" *Business Strategy Review* 8:67–74.

Stern, Jon, and Stuart Holder. 1999. "Regulatory Governance: Criteria for Assessing the Performance of Regulatory Systems." *Utilities Policy* 8:33–50.

Taylor, George. 2005. *Negotiated Governance and Public Policy in Ireland.* Manchester: Manchester University Press.

Transparency International. 2009. *Transparency International Country Study: Ireland 2009.* Berlin: Transparency International.

Verhoest, Koen, Paul Gerhard Roness, Bram Verschuere, Kristin Rubecksen, and Muiris MacCarthaigh, eds. 2010. *Autonomy and Control of State Agencies: Comparing States and Agencies.* New York: Palgrave MacMillan.

Wæraas, Arild. 2010. "Communicating Identity: The Use of Core Value Statements in Regulative Institutions." *Administration & Society* 42:526–549.

Wæraas, Arild, and Haldor Byrkjeflot. 2012. "Public Sector Organizations and Reputation Management: Five Problems." *International Public Management Journal* 15:186–206.

Walls, John, Nick Pidgeon, Andrew Weyman, and Tom Horlick-Jones. 2004. "Critical Trust: Understanding Lay Perceptions of Health and Safety Risk Regulation." *Health, Risk & Society* 6:133–150.

Walshe, Kieran. 2003. *Regulating Healthcare: A Prescription for Improvement.* Berkshire/Philadelphia: Open University Press.

Weeks, Liam. 2009. "Parties and the Party System." In *Politics in the Republic of Ireland,* edited by J. Coakely and M. Gallagher, 137–167. London/New York: Routledge.

Wren, Maev-Ann. 2002. *Unhealthy State: Anatomy of a Sick Society.* Dublin: New Island Press.

6 Reputation Management in Times of Crisis
How the Police Handled the Norwegian Terrorist Attack in 2011

Tom Christensen and Per Lægreid

INTRODUCTION

The literature on reputation has focused mainly on private sector organizations, where the emphasis is on corporate reputation (Barnett and Pollock 2010), but there has also been an increasing focus on reputation in public sector organizations (Carpenter 2002, 2010; Carpenter and Krause 2012; Wæraas, Byrkjeflot, and Angell 2011; Maor 2010; Maor, Gilad, and Ben-Nun Bloom 2013; Salomonsen 2013). As public organizations have become increasingly preoccupied with their reputations and reputation management, they have adopted various positive values and identities to present themselves to the different stakeholders in the environment (Wæraas and Byrkjeflot 2012). This phenomenon is not new, however, and has been identified by various social science theorists over a long period of time. It appears in Goffman's (1959) work on the distinction between front-stage and back-stage in an organization; in Edelman's (1964) work on the importance of symbols in organizations; in Meyer and Rowan's (1977) work on myths and institutional environment; in Brunsson's (1989) theory of double-talk in organizations; and in research on organizational prescriptions or recipes (Czarniawska and Sevón 1996; Røvik 2002).

On a general level, organizational reputation can be understood as a collective perception of an organization's past actions and achievements and its ability to deliver valuable results to multiple stakeholders (Petkova 2012; Fombrun 1996). It is a set of beliefs about an organization's capacity, intentions, history, and mission that is embedded in a network of multiple audiences (Carpenter and Krause 2012). Reputation arises out of judgments and assessments by external stakeholders of an organization's quality and attractiveness, reflecting considerations that have accumulated over time (Schultz, Hatch, and Adams 2012). These may be citizens' collective perception of an organization's behavior or its position within a social system (Rhee and Kim 2012). Reputation evolves as an interaction between the organization and its users, its stakeholders, or the general public. Organizational reputation is a multifaceted concept, especially within a multidimensional and complex public administration. Carpenter (2010) distinguishes between

96 *Tom Christensen and Per Lægreid*

performative, moral, procedural, and technical reputation, and normally there is a trade-off between them.

Reputation management can be seen as an organization's overall strategy for intervening in reputation-creating and maintenance processes via external communications (Wittington and Yakis-Douglas 2012). It involves deliberate actions by managers designed to influence the beliefs, attitudes, and expectations about an organization and to improve, protect, or repair perceptions of the organization's quality and character (Elsbach 2012). Such a communication strategy can take many forms, including managing media relations and influencing judgments by significant third parties via inquiry reports and other initiatives. Reputation management is especially crucial after a crisis or a collapse (Rhee and Kim 2012). When an organization faces a scandal or a crisis that might produce negative reactions among stakeholders and damage the organization's reputation, the organization often responds by engaging in reputation-repairing activities.

Thus, the purpose of reputation management is often said to be external. It is designed to enhance the image and public legitimacy of an organization (cf. Brunsson 1989). However, there are many challenges involved in reputation management denoted by keywords like *consistency, excellence, uniqueness,* and *context* (Wæraas and Byrkjeflot 2012). 't Hart (1993) coined the term 'masking' to describe impression management and the selective external communications strategies crisis stakeholders adopt to reduce impact. One may ask how rational reputation management is and whether it is not also based on cultural factors, which follow a different kind of logic. Reputation management can be seen as a consciously furthered, professionalized practice that is more or less coupled to the instrumental activities of a public organization engaged in regulation or service provision.

Organizations with a good reputation are normally better equipped for successful crisis management (Watson 2007). Crises normally represent a threat to an organization's reputation, and one goal of crisis management is to protect or repair the reputation of an organization in crisis. One can distinguish between different reputation-management strategies (Coombs 1998). Responses can be seen as either accommodative or defensive. Accommodative strategies, such as apology, corrective actions, and ingratiation, emphasize reputation repair and might be more common when there is a strong perception of responsibility for the crisis and personal control. Defensive strategies, such as attacking the accuser, denial, playing down the crisis, or making excuses, might be more common when there are weak perceptions of responsibility for the crisis, and they become less effective the more organizations are viewed as responsible for the crisis.

The focus in this chapter is on reputation management under unusual conditions—namely, in the wake of the terrorist attack in Norway on July 22, 2011. After the attack, the police were initially praised for their actions, but they subsequently came in for increasing criticism, both for how they had actually handled the crisis and for how they presented their handling of the crisis. They were accused of being too self-congratulatory and lacking in empathy, meaning being defensive rather than accommodative. The background to reputation management in this case was thus both a serious crisis and strong criticism of how the police handled it.

We will focus on the following research questions:

- How can we explain the police's reputation management in this crisis? Can we see it primarily from an instrumental perspective, with leaders consciously using certain symbolic elements to further a certain image, or should we see it more as an expression of traditional cultural norms and values in the police organization?
- What seems to be the effect of the police's reputation management in this crisis on the citizens' trust in the police? Is the 'reputation threat' aspect of the crisis important for strategies and eventual trust, or is generalized trust more typical in our case?

We will first describe what characterized the way the police presented and defended their actions and the reactions they got, and then look briefly into the effects of reputation management on the popular legitimacy of the police and citizens' trust in the police. The empirical focus in this study will primarily comprise a content analysis of two public documents, the first being the police's own evaluation of its response to the crisis and the second, the report by the official enquiry commission. But we will also use other sources, such as newspaper articles and other reports. The theoretical point of departure will be instrumental and cultural perspectives from organization theory, in the Scandinavian tradition of integrating political science theory and organization theory (Christensen et al. 2007).

THEORETICAL PERSPECTIVES

According to an *instrumental perspective,* when a public organization engages in reputation management, leaders and specialists will seek to control the processes whereby certain symbols, values, and identities are used consciously to further the instrumental goals of the organization (cf. March and Olsen 1983). This perspective comes in both a typical 'bounded rationality' and an 'economics' oriented version (cf. Christensen et al. 2007). In accordance with the political science approach to reputation (see Wæraas and Maor in this volume), the assumption is that reputation is affected by deliberate actions by the organization. Self-presentation strategies may take different forms and may involve trade-offs between different values (Wæraas 2010). First, reputation management may involve symbolizing in different ways what the leaders see as the strong instrumental aspects of the organization, such as efficiency or service orientation, whereby action and symbols are closely aligned. The more consistent the message, the better (Fombrun

98 *Tom Christensen and Per Lægreid*

and van Riel 2004). Second, leaders may deliberately engage in 'double-talk'—that is, present visions or intentions without actually following them up, in which case reputation management is loosely coupled with instrumental activities (Brunsson 1989). Third, reputation management may involve different parts of the organization presenting a hybrid mixture of changing norms and values to different audiences (Christensen et al. 2007). Loose coupling, double-talk, and hybridity in reputation management may have the advantage of allowing leaders and organizations to be flexible and to please different stakeholders at the same time, but the downside is potential conflicts, ambiguities, and lack of direction (Cyert and March 1963).

Reputation repairing might be seen as a process of problem solving that triggers a simple-minded search for solutions to the problems at hand (Rhee and Kim 2012). The search is normally problem oriented, leading the organization to rely on short-term superficial solutions that might temporarily hide the causes of the problem. The search is also often based on a simple model of causality, which looks for new solutions that resemble old solutions and is biased by the expectations of the participants in the organization (Cyert and March 1963). Thus substantive reputation-repairing activities are inevitably supplemented by superficial activities.

A *cultural perspective,* which largely reflects the organizational approach to reputation (see Wæraas and Maor in this volume), will see reputation management less as an instrumental act and more as a cultural-institutional process. The focus will be more on how public organizations gradually adapt to internal and external pressure and develop a set of informal norms and values that characterize their identity or 'soul' (Selznick 1957). The agency's predominant basis for its reputation is important (Maor 2011). If it starts out with a high level of trust and confidence, then the reputation capital is strong and the conditions for reputation management will be different than for an agency that enjoys little public trust. According to this perspective, reputation management is more a reflection of a natural, path-dependent process than something an organization can freely and instrumentally decide. The point of departure for reputation management from a cultural perspective is the historical-cultural path the organization has followed. Important factors will therefore be which leadership traditions this path has fostered, which professions dominate the organization, what its main tasks are, and which target groups it caters to. Thus deliberate reputation management is constrained by organizational traditions and culture. Reputation management is hence more about what is culturally appropriate than about what is rational or effective (Brunsson and Olsen 1993; March and Olsen 1989). This perspective is closely aligned to another institutional perspective—a more neo-institutional perspective focusing on social constructivism, myths, and symbols (Røvik 2002). What is seen as culturally appropriate in reputation management may reflect what is taken for granted in the institutional environment, for example.

Reputation Management in Times of Crisis 99

Seen from an instrumental perspective, reputation management may be accommodative, because the leadership has more freedom to choose symbolic measures that are rather loosely coupled to the actual performance, in a 'double-talk' way (cf. Brunsson 1989). This may therefore give the strategies more of a moral flavor. According to the cultural perspective, the leaders will have less freedom of action in a crisis situation. They will probably react to defend traditional cultural norms and values, meaning doing what they normally do. The argument will often be "we have always done it in these ways, so why not do it again," which will appear often as a defensive strategy if preconditions are changing and new measures are necessary in a crisis situation. Instead of confronting the instrumental and moral challenges of a situation, leaders may hide behind traditions, procedures, and rules. This will be more problematic to withhold than an accommodative strategy that is more flexible, if it is made clear that the performance of the leadership and organization as such is rather questionable or outright bad.

What are the important features of reputation management in our case—that is, in a crisis situation? According to 't Hart (1993), three core features of symbolic action are central in a crisis: *framing,* which concerns the ability to define what the crisis is all about; *rituals,* which concern symbolic behavior that is socially standardized and repetitive, such as setting up inquiry commissions and evaluation committees; and *masking,* which concerns impression management and the external communications strategies crisis stakeholders adopt to reduce impacts by selective communication. In the aftermath of crises, the administrative leadership has to cope with public inquiries, public criticism, and political verdicts (Boin, Busuioc, and Groenleer 2010). What may be typical for reputation management by a police organization? As emphasized in the literature, regulatory organizations like the police have certain characteristics that will distinguish them from more typical service-delivering organizations (Wæraas 2010). They have the public authority to control, scrutinize, and take action and, in the case of the police, also a monopoly on using physical force in certain situations. The police are, however, not only a regulatory but also a service-oriented organization, with an increasing need to emphasize the service aspect. These features have become more important in the last decade, as seen in Norway in the discussion after the Police Reform of 2000 about reduced public access to the police following the merging of police districts (Abrahamsen 2006). The modern police organization is thus characterized by a balance between authority and service and by partly contradictory identities and symbols (cf. Aberbach and Christensen 2007; Goodsell 1988).

Police reputation management has to balance possible conflicts between three core sets of administrative values (Hood 1991). First, the police are expected to be *lean and purposeful,* focusing on matching resources with defined tasks and emphasizing performance, efficiency, economy, and parsimony. Second, the police are supposed to be *honest and fair,* espousing values such as mutuality, impartiality, neutrality, and trust, and using standard

100   *Tom Christensen and Per Lægreid*

operating procedures and process control. Third, the police are supposed to be *robust and resilient,* focusing on security, reliability, survival, adaptivity, and redundancy. It will be hard to satisfy all three sets of values using the same administrative design, making the police vulnerable to criticism, and reputation management hence a tricky task. A strong focus on economy and frugality, for instance, might undermine the values of honesty and resilience. A crisis situation will probably be rather different from a routine situation for the police, and the severity and scope of the crisis will also be important.

A terrorist act like the one we focus on here, which was unprecedented in the history of Norway, is an extreme case that potentially affects all Norwegians. It will be unpredictable and potentially characterized by a lack of control by leaders and a need for flexibility. A crisis situation may evoke two different reactions from the police concerning what Wæraas and Byrkjeflot (2012, 193–194) label the "politics problem" in reputation management. The police may either be very limited by political frames and guidelines, because their actions potentially have serious political implications, or else a crisis may give the police more autonomy to decide how to act and more scope for reputation management. In facing a crisis there is a need both for centralization (strong leadership, hierarchical control, and command) and for decentralization (flexibility and an ability to improvise by those handling the situation on the ground) (Kettl 2003).

A serious crisis situation like the terrorist attack also highlights the emotional aspect of reputation management (Wæraas and Byrkjeflot 2012, 196–197). In this case reputation management was potentially a challenging task that needed to take into account the strong reactions from the victims' families, the political-administrative apparatus, the general public, and the media. The police needed to strike a balance between showing strength and control and being open and showing empathy. In addition, modern reputation management often has an excellence problem (Wæraas and Byrkjeflot 2012, 199). This may be relevant in our case because the police actions during and after the crisis were heavily criticized, evoking a potential need for the police to engage in 'retrospective rationalization' of their actions as part of reputation management.

Seen from an instrumental perspective, what might have been a rational approach for the police to take to reputation management during and after the crisis? Taking into consideration the extreme seriousness of the terrorist attack, one would expect the police to emphasize control on the one hand and the empathy required in such a tragic situation on the other, which would have entailed showing firmness and reaching out at the same time. One would also expect a tight coupling between reputation management and citizens' trust in the police, meaning that the use of inappropriate symbols would probably undermine public support for the police.

Seen from a cultural perspective, one would expect a firmer reaction, with the police stressing that they had made a great effort and done everything they could. This would reflect the path-dependent, macho culture traditionally associated with the police, where they would seek to project a strong image and to calm down the public, showing strong cultural features. Regarding relations with the public, one might expect path dependency to enhance robustness, leaving trust in the police more or less unaffected by reputation management in this specific crisis. The traditionally high level of trust in the police will probably survive the specific failures revealed in their handling of the terrorist attack (cf. Easton 1965).

CONTEXT

Norway is a society characterized by a high level of trust (Rothstein and Stolle 2003), and surveys of public support for political institutions accord Norway a leading position (Catterberg and Moreno 2006). This applies to both interpersonal and institutional trust (Wollebæk et al. 2012a). Indeed, trust is frequently regarded as a fundamental and characteristic value of Norwegian society (Selle 1993; Wollebæk and Segaard 2012a, 2012b). Trust in government institutions is generally high, and the police are among the most trusted institutions. A general survey of citizens before the terrorist attack (April 2011) revealed that 77 percent of the population had a high level of trust in the police (Wollebæk et al. 2012a). So the terrorist attack took place in an environment in which the police enjoyed a high level of trust and a very good reputation.

Integrity and accountability of the police is essential to public trust in law enforcement (UNODC 2006). But police managers often find themselves caught between their responsibility to maintain public trust in policing and to protect the reputation of the police, their responsibility to discipline individual police officers who display problematic behavior, and their duty to protect citizens (Gottschalk 2011). Generally, police culture is known for stressing the importance of presenting a favorable picture of what is going on within the organization. It has a reputation for strong group pressure to keep silent regarding misconduct, making whistle-blowing difficult (Prenzler 2009; Johnson 2005). But in spite of this, there has been a certain amount of whistle-blowing in the Norwegian police (Gottschalk and Holgersson 2011).

Historically, the police organization in Norway has been characterized by centralization on the one hand and small local units on the other. After a 40-year-long process and debate, the police organization was finally reformed in 2000 (Christensen et al. 2010). The main elements of the reform were the establishment of a Police Directorate (PD) and the merging of police districts to reduce the total number from 54 to 27. The new PD was organized along what we might call traditional lines of authority, reporting to the Ministry of Justice and Police. This implied a rather strong potential for political control, even though the overall tendency in the last two decades has been to give agencies more autonomy. This reflects the political importance of the police and the need for democratic control.

102   *Tom Christensen and Per Lægreid*

The terrorist attacks on July 22, 2011, consisted of two events: the bomb attack on the government complex in central Oslo in which eight people were killed, and the shooting of 69 young people attending a Labor Party youth organization camp on the island of Utøya, near Oslo. All of the public authorities involved during or after the attacks produced their own internal reports the following year. These included a report by the Police Directorate (PD 2012). The report of the 22 July Commission published in August 2012 was very critical of how the attacks had been handled (NOU 2012: 14). Two of its main critical points primarily concerned faulty police work (Christensen, Lægreid, and Rykkja 2013). The first point concerned the police delay in following up information on the escape car reported early on by a witness. The second concerned an undue delay in the time taken to respond to the Utøya attack caused by miscommunication and a misunderstanding about where to board the police boat. These two points of criticism closely reflected the main criticism from the victims' families, politicians, and the media during the year after the attacks. The media early on took a very critical attitude both to the police response and to the strategy chosen by the police to explain and defend their actions.

The main reactions from the police leadership were somewhat mixed. Before publication of the commission's report, it did not accept much criticism. Its internal report evaluated the police effort as rather good and gave 'tactical' reasons for some police decisions that were later heavily criticized. The Director General of the PD, who was new in his job at the time of the attack and was on leave half a year after the attack, tried in a press conference on March 15, 2012, to counter the impression of a police force that was self-congratulatory and lacking in empathy. However, his attempts were undermined by the reluctance of other police leaders to apologize. After the report from the commission was published, the Director General's main strategy was to stress that the commission's findings were quite similar to the police's own evaluation and to try to close ranks, but this made him vulnerable to continued criticism both from the media and from politicians (Christensen, Lægreid, and Rykkja 2013). Eventually, the Director General resigned, citing lack of support from the political leadership as the main reason for his resignation.

SELF-EVALUATION AND REPUTATION MANAGEMENT

On August 18, 2011, the Director General of the PD appointed an internal committee to evaluate the police's handling of the two terrorist attacks. The head of the committee, a former police chief, presented the report on March 15, 2012. As already mentioned, the committee was charged with drawing up the report amid an atmosphere of heavy criticism of the police, particularly by the victims' families and by the media. The committee's report started on an empathetic and accommodative note:

Primarily, many have lost loved ones in their immediate family, colleagues, and friends, and they will carry their grief and loss for the rest of their lives. Many young people have experienced extreme fear of death and must be given help to continue their lives. Many people have seen their workplace destroyed and feel insecurity and fear in such a situation.

(PD 2012, 18)

But it soon turned more defensive than accommodative. The report stated that it was difficult for professional-collegial reasons to make such an evaluation. The committee's mandate was to produce an evaluation that would enable the police to learn as much as possible from what had happened and that would help them to develop the competence to handle such crucial tasks in the future. It was explicitly stated that the evaluation was not primarily intended to reveal failures or identify scapegoats. The committee was also tasked with evaluating the effectiveness, capacity, and competence of the police to handle serious, encompassing, and complex crisis events and with proposing measures to strengthen these. The five main areas covered by the evaluation were: (1) warning and situational reporting; (2) organization, formal planning, leadership, and coordination; (3) evacuees and affected groups; (4) handling information and the media; and (5) health, environment, and security. Overall, the mandate indicated a rather defensive strategy with a technical-formalistic focus. Because of the difficulties mentioned, it sought to avoid self-criticism and to stress learning, according to more or less formal criteria. The main potential problem with the evaluation was that public opinion was critical and wanted answers about the reasons why several aspects of the police operation had gone so very wrong. Being abstract and defensive was a challenge.

The report started by discussing the framework and preconditions for police handling of crises, including formal structure, directives, instructions, routines, plans, reporting, etc. One theme that runs all the way through the report is the scarcity of resources, reflecting a defensive strategy. The report stressed that the availability of resources had had consequences for the decisions made on July 22 and the days after and had affected what kind of measures were possible and what the effects were for the different stakeholder groups.

The first area evaluated—warning and alarm systems—starts with a long discussion about formalities and ideals. It admits that the national alarm system did not function properly and that this should be improved. A crucial point in the external criticism was that it took 71 minutes before the license number of the bomb car, reported by a witness who saw the terrorist walking away from it, was circulated to the police or the public. However, although the evaluation states this fact, it does not delve into why it took so long, nor does it discuss the consequences, creating the impression that the police do not consider the delay important or a reason for self-criticism. Concerning situational reporting, the report states that this did not function well overall, partly because of problems of communication.

104 Tom Christensen and Per Lægreid

The second area evaluated—organization, leadership, and coordination—is again characterized by a lot of discussion of formalities and cites a lack of capacity (i.e., resources and competence). The immediate mobilization of police and medical emergency services after the bomb attack is evaluated as relatively good, but the report cites problems of communication related to the enormous extra pressure on the personnel. With respect to another critical point, the failure to mobilize a helicopter, the report traces the timeline but is not in any way particularly critical. A second point in the criticism of how the Utøya attack was handled was that the two policemen who arrived on the mainland across from Utøya should have gone by boat to the island immediately and risked their lives trying to catch the terrorist, instead of directing the traffic and hiding behind a container. The report is also defensive on this point:

> The view of the committee is that the police carried out their duties as quickly as the situation and other conditions (the information they had at that time) allowed. Police actions accorded with the procedures for immediate action and were in line with the police duty to help and the special instructions for "ongoing shootings."
>
> (PD 2012, 98)

A third, and maybe the most critical, point was that the response time for catching the terrorist was far too long. This was generally attributed to miscommunication, leading the Delta Force to launch the rescue boat from a departure point too far away from the island and to overload the boat, thus further increasing the delay. While admitting that there had been some problems, the report was not willing to draw a very critical conclusion on this point either:

> Based on a realistic evaluation of what was practically feasible with the available resources, the committee thinks that the response time to the shooting on Utøya was what the police were able to achieve on July 22. The police boat was overloaded when the Delta Force boarded it. This contributed to a delay in reaching the island.
>
> (PD 2012, 100)

Concerning information and media handling, the report was again rather technical and formal, describing the formal setup and existing plans but again alluding to a lack of resources and problems in providing reliable information. But for the performance of the Director General of the PD, the accommodating element of the strategy was clear:

> Because of the character and seriousness of the terrorist attacks, the Police Directorate saw it as important that the Director General participated in

Reputation Management in Times of Crisis 105

creating a greater feeling of security by showing a firm handling towards the population and also empathy with those affected.

(PD 2012, 143)

The report also stressed the importance of being aware of the media in handling the attack, which mainly can be seen as defensive:

The media participate in shaping public perceptions of how an event is handled. Rumors and misinformation can easily arise if there is a lack of information, and this can influence how the police handle the situation. It is therefore important for the police to follow the media portrayal closely and to correct wrong information. Scrutinizing the media is also important for keeping the police leadership up to date on how the media present an event and on how our own messages are presented and understood.

(PD 2012, 150)

The week after the terrorist attacks, a media scrutiny bureau produced a broad quantitative evaluation for the PD of coverage of the main messages in 113 different media. The PD identified five main messages and evaluated the one about response time, the most critical issue for the police, as follows:

Message 3: We chose the quickest way to reach Utøya. It took one hour, not an hour and a half. The corrected time-line was mentioned in 300 news reports in 68 media. This message was the one that received the most attention during this period. Few media commented on the fact that the police chose the fastest solution. The use of time was questioned, as was the issue of why a helicopter was not used, and it was reported that the police boat capsized.

(PD 2012, 154)

The report admits that it was necessary to hold a press conference a month after the terrorist attacks to defend police actions, which for a while reduced criticism. But it later increased again, and the media kept up the pressure on the police.

Summing up, the police's reputation management, as evidenced by the police's own evaluation of its handling of the terrorist attack, was mainly defensive, with some accommodative elements. First, the report focused on formalities and technicalities, and its mandate was to learn from the experience and to try to make improvements rather than to be very self-critical. Second, even though the report admitted that a lot of things had gone wrong with planning and communications systems, it sought to attribute this mainly to a lack of resources. Third, the report did not signal much self-criticism on the most critical points in the police handling of the attacks. The message

106 *Tom Christensen and Per Lægreid*

it sought to convey was that the police had done as much as possible under the extreme circumstances and that delays and other problems had probably had little impact on the outcome.

It is also fair to say that, after the report was published, the police continued to be criticized for not being self-critical or empathetic enough. Even the police trade union said the report should have been more self-critical.[1] The media portrayed the handling of criticism in the report as a PR disaster (Christensen, Lægreid, and Rykkja 2013).

THE OFFICIAL COMMISSION'S REPORT

The official enquiry commission—the Gjørv Commission—published its report on August 15, 2012 (NOU 2012: 14). Overall, it was even more critical than expected, especially with respect to the police, and eventually led to the resignation of the leader of the Police Directorate. Here we will concentrate on those aspects of the report of direct significance for the police's self-evaluation and reputation management. This is primarily addressed in one of the report's main conclusions:

> The authorities' ability to protect the people on Utøya failed. A faster police reaction would in reality have been possible. The perpetrator could have been stopped earlier on July 22.
>
> (NOU 2012: 14, 5)

The commission managed to obtain and publish much more detailed data on personnel and timelines than the police self-evaluation committee did. After a thorough discussion of the police operation in Oslo after the bomb attack, it concluded:

> Despite the competence and efforts of the police, the commission sees a lot of weaknesses. . . . The same goes for the failure of the police to utilize the helpful witness observations about the perpetrator. . . . Many obvious measures that could have been used to warn the public and other members of the police about the alleged perpetrator and the car he was driving were not implemented. We can only speculate about whether such measures would have stopped him. But in the actual circumstances it could have increased public awareness and the ability of the police to find him.
>
> (NOU 2012: 14, 30)

So the commission was far more critical of how the police had handled the observations of witnesses than the police self-evaluation report was, and also considered this a significant failure overall. The commission attributed the failure to lack of capacity and of a good system for sharing written information.

Reputation Management in Times of Crisis   107

Concerning the police operation on Utøya, the commission underscored that the capacity in this police district was low and the plans for such events nonexistent, meaning that the police were unprepared. Three main types of criticism had emerged in the media: the two policemen who were the first to reach the quay closest to Utøya were too passive and should have tried to go out to the island to catch the terrorist; the Delta Force should have gone to the same quay and not to one farther away, which delayed the response time; and the 12 members of the Delta Force made a mistake in boarding a boat that seemed about to sink, delaying the capture of the terrorist. Overall, the commission remarked the following:

> The commission's analysis of the police operation on Utøya shows that the police quickly mobilized a rather large action force on the mainland close to Utøya. Police communication was not good enough, however, and the police didn't manage to utilize the available civilian boat resources early enough. This led to the police arriving later at Utøya than they could have.
>
> (NOU 2012: 14, 110)

The commission criticized the two policemen who arrived at the scene first for being too passive to get onto a boat. It stopped short of more severe criticism, however, citing that they would have risked their lives going out to Utøya, that they had orders to remain passive, and that there were communication problems.

On the second point—namely, why the Delta Force took a detour and did not start from the nearest quay—the commission was very critical and completely rejected the arguments of the police self-evaluation:

> The commission analysis shows that this change did not stem from tactical considerations, but occurred as a result of a misunderstanding in a telephone conversation between a member of the Delta Force and the local operational center.
>
> (NOU 2012: 14, 126)

The commission was also very critical of the loading of the Delta Force into the boat and showed through a detailed timeline that this had delayed their arrival on Utøya by potentially critical minutes:

> The commission's analysis shows that in loading the police boat the police didn't think about the need for fire power versus the need to reach the island fast enough. The force boarded the boat without any planning or control, with only the size of the boat as a limit. No one thought about the implications for the speed of the boat. At that time the police boat was the only known boat resource. Overloading the boat damaged the ability of the police to respond and represented a danger to the

108 Tom Christensen and Per Lægreid

> safety of the policemen. They would have endangered their lives if they had fallen into the water with the heavy equipment they had. . . . The overload represents a critical failure that documents faulty judgment.
>
> (NOU 2012: 14, 140)

Overall, the commission's evaluation and report had a devastating impact on the police's reputation management. Even though the police recognized the need to balance control and empathy and hired communications specialists for this purpose, the end result was in many ways disastrous for the police. First, their arguments related to instrumental control—their main strategy of self-representation—fell flat. The arguments contained in the police self-evaluation that, even though the police had made some mistakes, these had not been crucial and they had basically done a good job given the circumstances, were effectively undermined by the commission. The commission showed that most of the media criticism had turned out to be right—namely, that the police operation had been characterized by a lack of coordination and communication, by misjudgments and misunderstandings, and by 'false' arguments.

Second, given the lack of instrumental self-criticism, the way the police presented themselves made police leaders vulnerable to external accusations of being self-congratulatory and showing little empathy. Whereas the leader of the PD (a trained psychiatrist) attempted to correct this message when the self-evaluation was presented, this was undermined by the three other police leaders present. He had a second opportunity to present the police in a better light when the commission's report was presented, but this attempt failed too. The leader of the self-evaluation committee and the director of the PD both claimed that their evaluation had been rather similar to the conclusions of the commission, which infuriated many actors and media who considered this to be plainly wrong.

LEGITIMACY: CITIZENS' TRUST IN THE POLICE

In the weeks after the terror attacks in 2011, institutional trust toward the government, the parliament, and the public administration increased (Wollebæk et al. 2012a, 34–35). The findings from a similar survey in 2012, however, show a return to the situation before the terrorist attacks in 2011 (Wollebæk et al. 2012a). Interpersonal trust and trust in central institutions were roughly at the same level as before. The terror attacks led neither to a collapse of public confidence nor to a lasting sense of cohesion and unity. Nor do the attacks seem to have had any major impact on the overall sense of security. General institutional trust probably provides an important clue to an explanation, i.e., what Easton (1965) labels "diffuse support." Trust in the political and administrative authorities seems particularly important and seems to be deeply rooted in Norway (Wollebæk et al. 2012a, 2012b).

Reputation Management in Times of Crisis   109

In the nine months after the terrorist attack, trust in the police remained high and even increased to 82 percent in May 2012, despite an increasingly critical debate about how the police handled the terrorist attack. But by August 2012 trust in the police had fallen to 69 percent (Wollebæk et al. 2012a). The same tendency was revealed by a survey conducted by the leading national newspaper *VG*. This must be seen in relation to the Gjørv Commission's critical report, which was presented in August 2012. The more closely citizens followed the public debate in the aftermath of the report, the greater the decrease in their trust in the police. The more information citizens got, the more they lost trust in the police.

However, trust in the police varies. Trust in street-level and local police is still pretty high and apparently not influenced by the Gjørv Commission. In contrast, the police chiefs and management have experienced a bigger loss in trust—only 48 percent still have a high level of trust in them. In 2012, 80 percent still thought the police would probably or definitely be able to implement effective means to enhance security measures against terror (Wollebæk et al. 2012a).

In Norway, levels of support for police counterterrorism measures—such as holding people in custody indefinitely without putting them on trial, telephone tapping, and randomly stopping and searching people on the street—declined immediately after the terrorist attacks (Fimreite et al. 2013). But by 2012, support for counterterrorism measures in Norway had returned to the rather high pre-2011 levels. This is related to a change in the discourse following publication of the Gjørv Commission's report. Attitudes toward counterterrorism measures therefore seem stable and robust.

The combination of two fundamental features—trust and state friendliness—probably explain the comparatively high level of acceptance of counterterrorism measures *and* the simultaneously low level of fear of another terrorist attack directly after July 22 (Fimreite et al. 2013). High levels of trust combined with tolerance for strong prevention measures seem to reflect confidence in government more generally and in the police more specifically, and a corresponding trust in the 'virtuousness of the state.'

ANALYSIS

Why Did the Police Leadership Have Severe Problems in Reputation Management?

The commission discussed what determined the handling of the terrorist attacks and the crisis, of which the police operation was a crucial part:

> The main factors explaining failure were primarily: the ability to realize risk and learn from exercises was too weak. The ability to implement decisions and to use existing plans was too weak. The ability to

110 *Tom Christensen and Per Lægreid*

coordinate and interact was lacking. Information and communications technology potential was not utilized enough. The leadership's ability and will to clarify accountability, establish goals and take measures was not strong enough. The commission thinks that the lessons to be learned concerned leadership, interaction, culture and attitudes rather than lack of resources, the need for new laws, organization or major value choices.

(NOU 2012: 14, 16)

The latter conclusion—that the shortcomings were more due to police culture than to organization—was later debated (Fimreite et al. 2012), and a new public commission (the police analysis) pointed to the need for a structural reform and a quality reform (NOU 2013: 9). Thus, the police's reputation is multidimensional, and what aspects were addressed varied over time and across actors and stakeholders. One aspect was performance and whether the police had handled the terrorist attack in a competent and efficient manner; another was the moral aspect (i.e., whether the police were compassionate and protected the interests of citizens and the police corps); a third aspect was procedural, asking whether the police had followed plans, standard operation procedures, and accepted rules and norms; and the final aspect addressed was technical issues and whether the police had had the necessary capacity and skills required to handle the terrorist attack. These different dimensions made reputation management a challenging and demanding task.

We have revealed that the reputation of the police was strong before the attack, but differentiated and weakened for a while after the attack, with most of the criticism directed at the leadership, but eventually it regained its strength. The reputation management was, as stressed, mainly defensive with some accommodative elements, which may indicate that the reputation-management strategy deployed actually worsened the police's reputation.

Seen from an instrumental perspective, we would expect it to be rational for the police to balance showing control on the one hand and showing openness and empathy on the other. But our main empirical conclusion is that alleged control, reflecting a defensive strategy, overshadowed empathy and an accommodative attitude by a long way. So what could be the explanation for this? First of all, police leaders apparently firmly believed that the police had done a good job and that it was important to acknowledge this. They thought that the terrorist attacks were so serious and the background so unusual that the public would understand and forgive. If this was the case, the police were completely wide off the mark in their reputation management, and their strategy backfired.

Second, at the beginning of the crisis, when the situation was unclear and information about events uncertain, it was important for the police— primarily the top officials of the Oslo Police—to give the impression that they were in control and to calm people down, i.e., an instrumental message. It was not a time for sitting down and thinking about communications

Reputation Management in Times of Crisis 111

strategies, but for enacting their formal roles. And because the message was control and the police were supposedly doing the best they could in this respect, it was difficult to change that message later on.

Third, the mainly defensive strategy was an example of blame avoidance (Hood 2002). They realized that their performance in and after the crisis was not good, and they tried to mask it in different ways ('t Hart 1993). The problem with this strategy was that the political leadership succeeded in the first phase with their reputation management (Christensen, Lægreid, and Rykkja 2013), which made the police strategy look extra bad. When the official report came, making the performance of the police look even worse, the police leadership was having even larger trouble with their strategy. They were outmaneuvered by the top political leadership, which also took a large beating, by the fact that the director of the police agency was pushed out, adding to the resignation of the director of the secret police service, making it look like the police was mainly to blame. This strategy from the top political executive was, however, made easier because the government was a majority coalition government, where the PM could protect most of his involved ministers.

Fourth, there were disagreements within the police leadership about how to handle the situation, indicating heterogeneity and compromise (Christensen et al. 2007). The new leader of the PD, who had a non-police background and long experience as a politician in the justice sector, seemed to prefer a more balanced strategy, being more accommodative, but he had to contend with 'old school' police leaders who were reluctant to admit problems and failures in police operations. Because he was also on leave after the attack, his influence on the decisions taken during that period were rather limited. So the reputation-management strategy to be pursued ended up being defensive and was decided mainly by a majority of top officials at Oslo Police and in the Police Directorate—hence the selection of the 'hawkish' leader of the evaluation committee. The Director General returned to the scene when the self-evaluation committee presented its report on March 15, 2012. The contrast between his empathetic style and the 'stand-firm' style of the other three police leaders was striking and commented on in the media, but he did manage, at least for a while, to tilt the reputation-management strategy toward the empathy side. His dilemma was that, if he wished to make changes in the police organization to reflect criticism of police handling of the crisis, he could not afford to be too critical of his colleagues. His attitude, therefore, seemed to change somewhat in a defensive direction following publication of the commission's report in August 2012. While accepting much of the criticism, he said the two reports had had different mandates and different data and claimed that their conclusions had not been that different. This made him popular within the police, and the police chiefs united behind him, but this strategy backfired with the public and led to his resignation. This was something of a paradox given that he had had very little responsibility for police operations during the crisis.

112   Tom Christensen and Per Lægreid

According to a cultural perspective, we would expect the more traditional 'macho' culture in the police to produce 'stand-firm' reputation management. Having not analyzed police culture as such, we can take as a point of departure what seems to characterize the 'self-presentation' of the police in public (cf. Goffman 1959). Our main take on this is that the police's alleged lack of empathy and inability to admit failures—a reflection of their macho culture—backfired because of problems in their relationship with stakeholders in the environment. The media was full of the grief and anger of the families of the victims and that of politicians like the prime minister, who managed fully to play the symbolic empathy role (Christensen, Lægreid, and Rykkja 2013). The media was also full of information that contradicted police accounts of the number of dead, witness information, and response time, so when the police stood firm and declined to admit that they had made any major mistakes, this was received as a provocation. The lack of cultural compatibility and sensitivity in the police's reputation management thus proved to be devastating. Citing Easton (1965), we can say that the generally high level of public trust in the police was consigned to the background in the face of a more specific mistrust in the police leadership's handling of the crisis, which severely undermined the public legitimacy of the police, at least for some time. This is also underlined in surveys of citizens, who tend to point a finger at the police leadership, believing that it has attempted to mask failure and mislead the public ('t Hart 1993). Selective labeling, displacement of crisis perceptions, and obscuring operational details were all elements of this strategy.

The managerial executives in the police had, first, to cope with the public inquiry. The inquiry process and the immediate response to the commission's report revealed cooperation and acceptance of the critical assessments on the part of the police. During the hearings, however, some actors, especially the police, stonewalled in their responses and primarily dug into technicalities and procedures, which enraged the critics even more. Second, the responsible authorities had to face public criticism. Whereas the main strategy was to acknowledge rather than to deny accountability, the relationship between political and administrative accountability was blurred, and accountability relations were multidimensional and ambiguous. Third, the responsible authorities faced a political verdict. The police managers who eventually left their positions also gave vicarious reasons for their resignation, but the media saw them as 'sacrifices' made by the political leadership.

Summing up, the police leaders continued to adhere to a failing symbolic strategy and seemed constrained by difficult structural-instrumental conditions and an apparent cultural resistance to admitting failure or wanting change. The defensive reputation management became more problematic to maintain when the commission's report came, but being more accommodative was seen as rather shallow against the background of a long denial of wrongdoing. So the police leadership ended up in rather a 'double-bind' situation.

Did Reputation Management Matter?

The question of whether the failure of reputation management mattered for police legitimacy is rather easy to answer from the point of view of public debate and the media. Attempts by the police leadership to engage in reputation management were continually attacked by the relatives' families, by the media, and by some politicians. However, the impact of this on public trust is trickier to gauge. We face a problem of causal relationships, meaning that it is not easy to link changes in citizens' trust in the police directly to the police's reputation management. There are many other factors that might increase or decrease trust in the police, such as the handling of the crisis by political executives. Trust relations may change either despite or because of the police's reputation management. We have observed that the level of trust in the police is rather robust and does not seem to have been strongly affected by the terrorist attack, something that we would expect from a cultural perspective. Failed reputation management related to the handling of a terrorist attack by the police would, according to an instrumental perspective, lead to a major reduction in people's trust in the police. This is not the case. This perspective does, however, get some support, because trust in police chiefs and management has been falling for some time, especially among the well-informed public. The main picture is, however, that reputation seems to be durable rather than volatile, given that the citizens' trust in the long run did not change very much.

If we come back to Easton's distinction between diffuse (general) and specific support in a political-administrative system, comparable to general and specific trust, our case seems mainly to show that diffuse support trumps specific support, meaning that the citizens' trust in the police mainly stays strong even though the police failed both instrumentally and in their reputation management. But it is important to point to the time factor, i.e., the longer after the crisis, the more diffuse the support rebound. This reflects that right after the terrorist attack the media managed to paint a picture of a poorly performing and clueless police, but this effect did not last. And citizens' reactions are differentiated—they blame more and trust less over time the police leaders, again a reflection of the media—but this time it stuck more, different from the rebound of general trust in the police. This is somewhat puzzling.

CONCLUSION

The overall focus of our analysis has been on the balance between symbols, culture, and instrumental actions in the police's reputation management after the July 22 attacks. The police encountered problems and lost legitimacy when they tried to balance symbols and action in their reputation management, both initially and in the aftermath of the commission's report.

114　*Tom Christensen and Per Lægreid*

This can be explained by different roles and by the dynamics between different constraining factors. The police did not handle operations on the ground well, and their top officials certainly mishandled the balancing of talk and action (cf. Brunsson 1989). They were considered overly self-righteous in their response to criticism. We find that their symbolic strategy was shaped by structural and cultural constraints. When severe operational problems were eventually revealed and turned out to be even more severe than thought, this aggravated criticism of the police. Thus, the findings confirm Maor's (this volume) view that public sector organizations behave opportunistically and strategically in their reputation management, but also underscore the consequences of having to deal with the socially constructed nature of reputation.

The overall conclusion is that police reputation management was a failure, but, in spite of this, citizens' trust in the police did not deteriorate significantly. This paradox might imply that reputation management in the public sector is a tricky business, and it is not always easy to see the effects of such efforts. But it also tells us that public institutions that traditionally enjoy a high level of trust will prevail because general trust and support are long term and strong (cf. Easton 1965).

What can we learn from our case in a broader perspective? First, having a strong reputation may help in overcoming failed reputation management. Second, having a strong reputation definitively is no guarantee against a weakening of reputation over time because of bad reputation management. Third, a severe crisis is a major challenge, both for reputation and reputation management, because it stirs emotions that will trump the reaction of the public at large, regardless of the difficult preconditions for action. Fourth, a crisis with a lot of open information and interpretations challenges the information monopoly normally enjoyed by the authorities in more routine situations and makes it difficult to engage in successful reputation management.

NOTE

1　TV2 reported this on May 30, 2012.

REFERENCES

Aberbach, Joel D., and Tom Christensen. 2007. "The Challenges of Modernizing Tax Administration Putting Customers First in Coercive Public Organizations." *Public Policy and Administration* 22:155–182.

Abrahamsen, S. N. 2006. "Politireform 2000: sammenslåing av politidistriktene—en organisasjonsteoretisk prosess- og effektanalyse." Master's thesis, University of Oslo.

Barnett, Michael T., and Timothy G. Pollock, eds. 2012. *The Oxford Handbook of Corporate Reputation.* Oxford: Oxford University Press.

Boin, Arjen, Madalina Busuioc, and Martijn Groenleer. 2011. "Building Joint Capacity: The Role of European Union Agencies in the Management of Transboundary Crises." In *Jerusalem Forum on Regulation & Governance*. Hebrew University of Jerusalem, oai: RANO:44019.

Brunsson, Nils. 1989. *The Organization of Hypocrisy. Talk, Decisions and Actions in Organizations*. Chichester: Wiley.

Brunsson, Nils, and Johan P. Olsen. 1993. *The Reforming Organization*. London: Routledge.

Carpenter, Daniel P. 2002. "Groups, the Media, Agency Waiting Costs, and the FDA Drug Approval." *American Journal of Political Science* 46 (July):490–505.

Carpenter, Daniel P. 2010. *Reputation and Power. Organizational Image and Pharmaceutical Regulation at FDA*. Princeton, NJ: Princeton University Press.

Carpenter, Daniel P., and George A. Krause. 2012. "Reputation and Public Administration." *Public Administration Review* 12:26–32.

Catterberg, Gabriela, and Alejandro Moreno. 2006. "The Individual Bases of Political Trust: Trends in New and Established Democracies." *International Journal of Public Opinion Research* 18:31–48.

Christensen, Tom, Morten Egeberg, Helge O. Larsen, Per Lægreid, and Paul G. Roness. 2010. *Forvaltning og politikk*. Oslo: Universitetsforlaget.

Christensen, Tom, Per Lægreid, and Lise H. Rykkja. 2013. "After a Terrorist Attack? Challenges to Political and Administrative Leadership in Norway." *Journal of Contingencies and Crisis Management* 24:167–177.

Christensen, Tom, Per Lægreid, Paul G. Roness, and Kjell A. Røvik. 2007. *Organization Theory and the Public Sector. Instrument, Culture and Myth*. London: Routledge.

Coombs, W. Timothy. 1998. "An Analytical Framework for Crisis Situations: Better Responses from a Better Understanding of the Situation." *Journal of Public Relations Research* 10:177–192.

Cyert, Richard M., and James G. March.1963. *A Behavioral Theory of the Firm*. Englewood Cliffs, NJ: Prentice-Hall.

Czarniawska, Barbara, and Guje Sevón, eds. 1996. *Translating Organizational Change*. Berlin: De Gruyter.

Easton, David. 1965. *A Systems Analysis of Political Life*. New York: Wiley.

Edelman, Murray. 1964. *The Symbolic Uses of Politics*. Urbana: University of Illinois Press.

Elsbach, Kimberly D. 2012. "A Framework for Reputation Management over the Course of Evolving Controversies." In *The Oxford Handbook of Corporate Reputation,* edited by Michael L. Barnett and Timothy G. Pollock, 466–486. Oxford: Oxford University Press.

Fimreite, Anne L., Peter Lango, Per Lægreid, and Lise H. Rykkja. 2012. "22. juli kommisjonen. Organisering, styring og ansvar." *Nordiske Organisasjonsstudier* 14:49–58.

Fimreite, Anne L., Peter Lango, Per Lægreid, and Lise H. Rykkja. 2013. "After Oslo and Utøya: A Shift in the Balance between Security and Liberties in Norway?" *Studies in Conflict & Terrorism* 36:839–856.

Fombrun, Charles J. 1996. *Reputation: Realizing Value from the Corporate Image*. Boston: Harvard Business School Press.

Fombrun, Charles J., and Cees van Riel. 2004. *Fame and Fortune: How Successful Companies Build Winning Reputations*. Upper Saddle River, NJ: Prentice Hall.

Goffmann, Erving. 1959. *The Presentation of Self in Everyday Life*. New York: Doubleday.

Goodsell, Charles T. 1988. *The Social Meaning of Civic Space*. Lawrence, KS: University Press of Kansas.

Gottschalk, Petter. 2011. "Public Leadership in Police Oversight." In *Public Leadership,* edited by Justin A. Ramirez, 21–38. Hauppauge, NY: Nova Science Publishers.

Gottschalk, Petter, and Stefan Holgersson. 2011. "Whistle-Blowing in the Police." *Police Practice and Research* 12:397–409.

Hood, Christopher. 1991. "A Public Management for All Seasons?" *Public Administration* 69:3–19.

Hood, Christopher. 2002. "The Risk Game and the Blame Game." *Government and Opposition* 37:15–37.

Johnson, Roberta A. 2005. "Whistleblowing and the Police." *Rutgers University Journal of Law and Urban Policy* 1(3):74–83.

Kettl, Donald. F. 2003. "Contingent Coordination: Practical and Theoretical Puzzles for Homeland Security." *American Review of Public Administration* 33:253–277.

Maor, Moshe. 2010. "Organizational Reputation and Jurisdictional Claims: The Case of the U.S. Food and Drug Administration." *Governance* 23:133–159.

Maor, Moshe. 2011. "Organizational Reputations and the Observability of Public Warnings in 10 Pharmaceutical Markets." *Governance: An International Journal of Policy, Administration, and Institutions* 24:557–582.

Maor, Moshe, Sharon Gilad, and Pazit Ben-Nun Bloom. 2013. "Organizational Reputation, Regulatory Talk, and Strategic Silence." *Journal of Public Administration Research and Theory* 23:581–608.

March, James G., and Johan P. Olsen. 1983. "Organizing Political Life. What Administrative Reorganization Tells Us About Government." *American Political Science Review* 77:281–297.

March, James G., and Johan P. Olsen. 1989. *Rediscovering Institutions : The Organizational Basis of Politics.* New York: Free Press.

Meyer, John W., and Brian Rowan. 1977. "Institutionalized Organizations: Formal Structure as Myth and Ceremony." *American Journal of Sociology* 83:340–363.

NOU (2012: 14). *Rapport fra 22. juli-kommisjonen.* Oslo: Government Administration Service.

NOU (2013: 9). *Ett politi—rustet til å møte fremtidens utfordringer.* Oslo: Government Administration Services.

PD (2012). *22. juli 2011. Evaluering av Politiets innsats.* Oslo: Police Directorate.

Petkova, Antoaneta. 2012. "From the Ground Up: Building Young Firms' Reputation." In *The Oxford Handbook of Corporate Reputation,* edited by Michael L. Barnett and Timothy G. Pollock, 383–401. Oxford: Oxford University Press.

Prenzler, T. 2009. *Police Corruption: Preventing Misconduct and Maintaining Integrity.* Boca Raton, FL: CRC Press.

Rhee, Mooweon, and Tohyun Kim. 2012. "After the Collapse: A Behavioral Theory of Reputation Repair." In *The Oxford Handbook of Corporate Reputation,* edited by Michael L. Barnett and Timothy G. Pollock, 446–465. Oxford: Oxford University Press.

Rothstein, Bo, and Dietlind Stolle. 2003. "Introduction: Social Capital in Scandinavia." *Scandinavian Political Studies* 26:1–26.

Røvik, Kjell A. 2002. "The Secrets of the Winners: Management Ideas That Flow." In *The Expansion of Management Knowledge —Carriers, Flows and Sources,* edited by Kerstin Sahlin-Andersson and Lars Engwall. Stanford. CA: Stanford University Press.

Salomonsen, Heidi H., ed. 2013. *Offentlig ledelse og strategisk kommunikation.* Copenhagen: Jurist- og økonomforbundets forlag.

Schultz, Majken, Mary J. Hatch, and Nick Adams. 2012. "Managing Corporate Reputation through Corporate Branding." In *The Oxford Handbook of Corporate Reputation,* edited by Michael L. Barnett and Timothy G. Pollock, 420–445. Oxford: Oxford University Press.

Reputation Management in Times of Crisis 117

Selle, Per. 1993. "Voluntary Organisations and the Welfare State: The Case of Norway." *Voluntas* 4:1–15.

Selznick, Phillip. 1957. *Leadership in Administration.* New York: Harper & Row.

't Hart, Paul. 1993. "Symbols, Rituals and Power. The Lost Dimensions of Crisis Management." *The Journal of Contingencies and Crises Management* 1:36–50.

UNODC 2006. *The Integrity and Accountability of the Police Criminal Assessment Tool-kit.* United National Office of Drugs and Crime (UNODC), Vienna: Vienna International Centre.

Wæraas, Arild. 2010. "Communicating Identity: The Use of Core Value Statements in Regulative Organizations." *Administration & Society* 42:526–549.

Wæraas, Arild, and Haldor Byrkjeflot. 2012. "Public Sector Organizations and Reputation Management: Five Problems." *International Public Management Journal* 15:186–206.

Wæraas, Arild, Haldor Byrkjeflot, and Svein I. Angell, eds. 2011. *Substans og framtreden. Omdømmehåndtering i offentlig sektor.* Oslo: Universitetsforlaget.

Watson, Tom. 2007. "Reputation and Ethical Behavior in a Crisis: Predicting Survival." *Journal of Communication Management* 11:317–384.

Wittington, Richard, and Basak Yakis-Douglas. 2012. "Strategic Disclosure: Strategy as a Form of Reputation Management." In *The Oxford Handbook of Corporate Reputation,* edited by Michael. L. Barnett and Timothy G. Pollock, 402–419. Oxford: Oxford University Press.

Wollebæk, Dag, Bernhard Enjolras, Kari Steen-Johnsen, and Guro Ødegaard. 2012a. *Ett år etter 22. juli. Har rosetoget gått?* Oslo: Senter for forskning på sivilsamfunn & frivillig sektor.

Wollebæk, Dag, Bernhard Enjolras, Kari Steen-Johnsen, and Guro Ødegaard. 2012b. "How a High Trust Society Reacts to Terror. Trust and Civil Engagement in the Aftermath of July 22." *Political Science and Politics* 45:32–37.

7 How Organizational Reputation and Trust May Affect the Autonomy of Independent Regulators
The Case of the Flemish Energy Regulator

Koen Verhoest, Jan Rommel, and Jan Boon

INTRODUCTION

This chapter explores how an independent regulatory agency can develop a reputation for being a trustworthy actor and how this reputation and the corresponding trust from the political principal can affect the autonomy of the agency.

The creation of independent regulators has been one of the most widespread features of the regulatory state (Jordana and Levi-Faur 2004). Many studies have found that the actual extent of autonomy from parent ministers may be very different from what is prescribed in formal-legal statutes (Christensen and Lægreid 2007; Groenleer 2009; Maggetti 2009).

In order to explain differences in formal and de facto autonomy, autonomy has been regarded as a relational concept. Autonomy is increased or reduced through the relations that agencies have with their principals. Assuming that actors can manage their relationships with others, they can also try to influence their autonomy vis-à-vis these actors. In the literature, both reputation and trust have been named as factors increasing the de facto autonomy of public organizations. Carpenter (2001) stated that bureaucratic autonomy is politically forged by agency leaders. Bureaucratic autonomy is said to be the result of agency efforts to gain bureaucratic legitimacy stemming from a unique reputation, which is grounded in diverse network coalitions (Carpenter 2001). The concept of trust has also been used to describe and explain de facto relationships between agencies and parent ministers (van Thiel and Yesilkagit 2011). When trust is high, ministers will enforce controls less rigidly and will allow for more autonomy for their agencies (Lægreid, Roness, and Rubecksen 2005; Verhoest 2002, 2005). However, the question arises how reputation building and trust building relate as explanations for the increase of de facto autonomy of regulatory agencies. This chapter aims to explore the link between (strategies to increase) reputation building and trustworthiness, and the effects on de facto autonomy. Whereas there is some private sector literature on the link between reputation and trust (see, e.g., Aqueveque and Ravasi 2006), this topic is largely unexplored in public administration literature.

EMPIRICAL PUZZLE

We draw from a case study of the Flemish Regulator for Electricity and Gas (VREG). VREG is a semi-autonomous regulatory agency, involved in the regulation of electricity and gas in one region of Belgium (Flanders). In Belgium, the authority to regulate energy markets is shared by two levels of government. The federal level is competent for production (i.e., generation of electricity in power plants or the pumping up of natural gas) and transmission networks (i.e., transport over long distances, via high-voltage power lines/high-pressure pipelines), whereas the regional level regulates distribution networks (transport via low-voltage/low-pressure lines) and supply markets (selling electricity or gas to end users, notably households and firms). The authority to set tariffs (i.e., taxes that energy suppliers must pay to network operators for transporting energy to end users) remains the exclusive competence of the federal level, even for distribution tariffs. This makes the regulation of distribution networks highly fragmented, as they are regulated by the federal level (for tariff setting) and by the regional regulator (for setting technical standards of networks).

As required by EU regulations (European Parliament and Council 2009), VREG has a high extent of policy autonomy for operational affairs. VREG is legally competent for making binding individual decisions. These decisions include economic regulation (e.g., imposing unbundling in case network operators also have supply undertakings), technical regulation (e.g., demanding more investments from network operators to increase network capacity), and social regulation (e.g., imposing public service obligations). For these affairs, the parent minister has no hierarchical authority and cannot simply reverse the decisions nor take the place of the agency. However, the policy autonomy for strategic affairs is more restricted by formal control instruments and legal provisions. At the time of the study, the legal statutes of VREG prescribed the appointment of two *commissaires du gouvernement* (Verhoest, Demuzere, and Rommel 2012). These are appointed by the minister and have the authority to appeal all decisions of the agency that they deem incompatible with the interests of the Flemish government. Their appeal would effectively suspend the decision taken by the regulator. Moreover, VREG is bound by a multi-annual performance contract, which is concluded with the Flemish government. This contract defines the strategic objectives of VREG for a period of five years. These control instruments formally restrict the strategic autonomy of VREG to a large extent. In addition, VREG is not formally competent for preparing new policy.

In practice, however, the de facto policy autonomy of VREG and its role in the policy process have developed to be much more extended than formally stipulated. For example, the *commissaires du gouvernement* have never been appointed. Furthermore, the involvement of VREG in regulatory policy making has been very substantial. This divergence between formal and de facto autonomy presents an empirical puzzle. Whereas regulatory

120   *Koen Verhoest et al.*

agencies are usually separated from policy (Scott 2004), and regulators have little contact with politicians due to the need for credible commitment, VREG maintains a close collaborative relationship with its parent minister.

In this chapter, we are interested in how the de facto autonomy of VREG is affected by its reputational strategies and the trustworthiness that stems from it. We argue that VREG has developed a specific reputation, composed of organizational characteristics such as technical expertise and behavioral traits like reliability, openness, and being sensitive to the needs of political principals. The agency built this reputation explicitly vis-à-vis the parent minister in order to be perceived as trustworthy. The recognition by the parent minister of this reputation and the trustworthiness that stems from it has led to trusting behavior by the minister, which has manifested itself in the increased de facto policy autonomy of VREG.

The chapter is structured as follows. We will first discuss the applied research design and research context. Next, we will present the results using the theoretical framework, presented in Figure 7.1, as a guide to structure our results, by (a) finding evidence for VREG rationally pursuing and cultivating a unique organizational reputation through several relational strategies that simultaneously signal VREG's trustworthiness, (b) finding evidence for the actual recognition of this reputation and trustworthiness by the political principal, and (c) finding evidence that this recognition by the political principal and the trust emerging from it has translated into a political asset (high policy-making autonomy and forms of collaboration).

THEORETICAL ARGUMENTS AND CENTRAL CONCEPTS

The Theoretical Framework: Connecting Reputation, Trust, and Autonomy

In order to explore how reputation serves as a means to achieve de facto autonomy through the mechanism of trust building, we use a theoretical model based on the framework of Carpenter (2001), complemented with insights from trust theory (see Figure 7.1). It starts from the assumption that regulators are generally rational and politically conscious organizations that cautiously construct and protect their unique reputations (Maor, Gilad, and Ben-Nun Bloom 2013). They choose agency traits as the basis to cultivate an organizational reputation. Next, relational strategies are developed to signal this reputation to other actors, such as stakeholders and principals, in order to foster social embeddedness of the organizational reputation and recognition by these actors (see phase 1 in Figure 7.1). When stakeholders and principals recognize and reassert the reputational signals of the agency, they will consider the agency as trustworthy regarding the traits that underlie the reputation. Multiple forms of trust by the political principal can arise grounded in the perceived competences, routines, or norms of the agency,

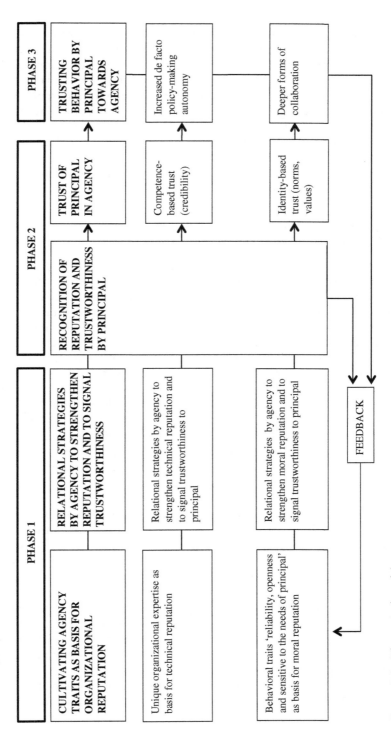

Figure 7.1 Theoretical model

122   *Koen Verhoest et al.*

enabling political principals to accept risks in dealing with the agency (see phase 2 in Figure 7.1). Finally, the political principal may reward the agency for its trustworthiness by granting a higher extent of autonomy to the agency, or by engaging in more strategic, 'deeper' forms of collaboration with the agency. Other forms of trusting behavior might be an expansion of tasks and remit of the regulatory agency or an increase of financial resources (phase 3 in Figure 7.1). In turn, these rewards motivate the agency to further strengthen its investments in building a strong organizational reputation toward principals (and stakeholders).

The following sections discuss the different parts and concepts underlying this theoretical model in more detail.

Cultivating Agency Traits as a Basis for Organizational Reputation

Public entities are increasingly aware of the benefits of having a favorable reputation and have implemented measures to nurture, maintain, and protect their reputation (Wæraas and Maor in this volume). This chapter subscribes to the political science approach of bureaucratic reputation (Carpenter 2002, 2010; Gilad, Maor, and Ben-Nun Bloom 2013; Maor, Gilad, and Ben-Nun Bloom 2013; Maor and Sulitzeanu-Kenan 2013; Maor 2007, 2011; Moffitt 2010). This literature has studied the behavior of regulatory agencies in relation to the multiple audiences they aim to address. Whereas research on independent agencies had traditionally focused on control by political principals based on principal-agent theory (Jensen and Meckling 1976), the literature on bureaucratic reputation puts the focus on the strategic behavior of agencies. The central argument of this literature is that agencies are no passive actors. Instead, they strategically craft and manage their organizational reputation (Gilad, Maor, and Ben-Nun Bloom 2013).

Organizational reputation refers to a set of symbolic beliefs about the unique or separable capacities, intentions, roles, obligations, history, and mission of an organization that are embedded in a network of multiple audiences (Carpenter 2010, 33, 45). As such, organizational reputations rely on external audiences' perceptions. When regulatory agencies are conscious about their reputation, concerns about these perceptions can trigger a regulatory agency's decision making and actions (Maor and Sulitzeanu-Kenan 2013; Wæraas and Maor in this volume). When a regulator succeeds in establishing a unique reputation that is recognized by its multiple audiences, this reputation becomes a valuable political asset used to generate public support, to achieve delegated autonomy and discretion from politicians, to protect the agency from political attack, and to recruit and retain valued employees (Carpenter 2001, 491).

Organizational reputation may have different bases residing in an organization: It might relate to an organization's performative, moral, procedural, and technical traits (Carpenter 2010). Performative reputation refers to

Organizational Reputation and Trust 123

whether an agency can execute its tasks competently and efficiently. Moral reputation means that an agency is sensitive, flexible, honest, and protective of the interests of its clients. Procedural reputation refers to following accepted rules and norms. Finally, technical reputation means an agency has the technical capacity and skill required to do its job (regardless of its actual performance). According to bureaucratic reputation theory, a full optimization of all these traits would be infeasible. Regulators must choose to which trait they give priority (Carpenter and Krause 2012).

However, a unique trait as the basis for reputation needs to be socially rooted in coalitions or networks benefiting from and supporting this organizational trait. Without relational strategies to build and maintain these networks, an organizational reputation is not likely to turn into a political asset (Carpenter 2001). These relational strategies might target multiple audiences to varying degrees (political parties, European networks, business groups, etc.). The recognition by the principals and stakeholders of a unique organizational reputation is of crucial importance (see phase 2 in Figure 7.1). Figure 7.1 shows that the process of recognition of reputation by the political principal builds upon signals of trustworthiness of the agency toward this political principal.

Organizational Trustworthiness

The strategic value of reputation for organizations is related to the concept of organizational trustworthiness (Aqueveque 2005; Aqueveque and Ravasi 2006), as it may increase the set of exchange opportunities for the involved organization. As it is difficult to observe trustworthiness and the organizational traits that bring forth trustworthiness, organizations send out signals of their trustworthiness, like organizational reputation. Organizational reputation can be treated as a mechanism for stakeholders to evaluate the risk of interacting with the organization (Aqueveque and Ravasi 2006; Davies and Chun 2003; Fombrun and van Riel 1998). Smaiziene and Jucevicius (2009, 96) even define reputation by referring to trustworthiness: "corporate reputation can be defined as socially transmissible company's (its characteristics', practice's, behavior's and results', etc.) evaluation settled over a period of time among stakeholders, that represents expectations for the company's actions, and level of trustworthiness, favorability and acknowledgement comparing to rivals." In a similar vein, Carpenter (2001, 20) mentions the interplay of accumulated expertise (technical reputation) of bureau chiefs through time and the resulting political trust in ensuring the unique durability and stability of the bureau chiefs.

In the literature on trust, the concept of trustworthiness has been defined as an antecedent of trust. Trust refers to the confidence of an actor that another actor will not behave opportunistically, despite uncertainty and risk (Gambetta 1988; Lyon 2006). As such, trusting behavior takes place when an actor is in a potentially vulnerable position and is driven by some knowledge

124 Koen Verhoest et al.

about the other actor (Blomqvist 1997; Lewis and Weigert 1985; Oakes 1990). Before a 'trustor' decides to place trust in a potential 'trustee,' the trustor considers certain characteristics of that particular trustee. Trust will be placed only when the trustor perceives the trustee as being trustworthy. Good (1988) posited trust to be grounded in expectations of the behavior of another actor, based on that actor's current and previous implicit and explicit claims. In a similar vein, Mayer, David, and Schoorman (1995) suggested that certain traits of these actors act as determinants for the amount of trust given to them. The link between trustworthiness and certain traits of the trustee has been corroborated by others (Good 1988; Johnson-George and Swap 1982).

The trustworthiness of an organization encompasses different organization-specific sources of trust. *Competence-based trust* is based on previous behavior of the trustee as a predictor of future behavior. It refers to the competences and expertise of the trustee (Sako 1992). *Identity-based trust* is based on repeated interactions between actors that lead to the formation of emotional attachments (Lewicki and Bunker 1996). A trustor believes in the good intentions and the integrity of a trustee, who is believed to have internalized the trustor's norms and values.

In order to decide whether to place trust, a trustor will rely on signals that are produced by the trustee. The concept of 'active trust' has been used to argue that trustees can play an active role in initiating, shaping, sustaining, and changing trust (Möllering 2006, 79). Trustees may partially determine themselves which signals are being sent to the trustor (Giddens 1994). For instance, in order to increase identity-based trust, actors may appeal to the norms and values of the trustor by 'constructing' a shared identity (Phillips and Hardy 1997). Such mechanisms include gift giving and conforming to the opinion of the trustor (see Bottom et al. 2006; Lawler and Yoon 1996).

Organizational reputation is an important informative signal that functions as a mechanism for stakeholders to evaluate the risk of interacting with the organization (Aqueveque and Ravasi 2006; Davies and Chun 2003; Fombrun and van Riel 1998). As such, organizational reputation can be regarded as an important source of trust (see also Picci in this volume).

Trusting Behavior

Organizational trustworthiness may lead to trust and several types of trusting behavior. First, research on inter-organizational relations has pointed toward 'trust' as a key factor in explaining collaboration (Huxham 2003; Lane and Bachmann 1996; McEvily and Zaheer 2006; Nooteboom, Berger, and Noorderhaven 1997; Ring and van de Ven 1992). Partners that trust each other will engage in increased information sharing, especially the sharing of tacit information (Edelenbos and Klijn 2007). Partners will also engage in joint problem solving and joint action (Dyer and Chu 2003;

Organizational Reputation and Trust   125

Muthusamy and White 2005). A second effect of high trust is that the need for formal control is reduced (Ring and van de Ven 1992).

These effects can also be applied in the context of independent agencies. According to Grey and Garsten (2001), the concept of trust is relevant in post-bureaucratic environments, which are characterized by participative management styles and consensus building. Others have suggested that, when trust is high, agencies will report higher levels of autonomy and ministers will use formal controls less rigidly in practice (Lægreid, Roness, and Rubecksen 2005; Verhoest 2002, 2005).

Similarly, the literature on bureaucratic reputation has also argued that political reactions (in the form of granting or reducing agency autonomy) depend on organizational reputations. Carpenter (2001) found that elected institutions delegate autonomy to agencies that had built an organizational reputation (through capacities and networking) for solving policy problems. Carpenter and Lewis (2004) showed that failure by an agency, accompanied by negative media coverage (thus damaging organizational reputation), increases the likelihood of agency termination. A similar mechanism was described in the context of Australian public service providers (Macintosh 2007). MacDonald and Franko Jr. (2007) demonstrated a direct link between low agency performance and a subsequent loss of autonomy.

In this chapter, we will argue that mechanisms of trust building based on reputation are at work in the context of VREG. These mechanisms help to explain why the de facto autonomy of VREG is much more extended than formally stipulated. We focus on the effects on policy autonomy, which refers to the freedom to decide on content or results of the primary organizational process (see Verhoest et al. 2010). The extent to which an agency enjoys policy autonomy depends on the extent to which it is steered on processes, outputs, or effects. Policy autonomy may concern operational issues (e.g., discretion to make decisions in individual, specific cases, such as deciding to grant a license to a particular regulatee), or more strategic affairs such as the discretion to prioritize organizational objectives for the next year, or the extent to which the organization is involved in the policy-making process (i.e., discretion to evaluate current policy and/or prepare and draft new policy).

METHOD

The empirical material presented is based on a single case study. Case studies allow researchers to study a phenomenon (i.e., the autonomy of regulators and their interactions with the minister) within its real-life context (e.g., the specific routines and rules that have developed over time) (Yin 2009). Although case studies are not suitable for measuring causal effects, they can be used to identify a causal *mechanism:* "they allow one to peer into the box of causality to the intermediate causes lying between some cause

126 *Koen Verhoest et al.*

and its purported effect. Ideally, they allow one to see X and Y interact" (Gerring 2004, 348). Case studies should describe 'what' happens, but also 'how' and 'why' things unfold (Miles and Huberman 1994, 4). Therefore, the objective of the case study was to describe how an independent regulator interacts with other actors (e.g., via which mechanisms, on what topics) and to explain how these interactions affect the decision-making autonomy of the organization.

Interviews were performed according to an interview protocol that was sent to informants one week before the interview. The protocol contained questions on the perception of autonomy of VREG for three types of issues: (1) *Operational affairs* relate to daily decisions concerning individual firms (e.g., granting licenses to specific firms); (2) *tactical affairs* are more abstract, such as decisions concerning methodology (e.g., deciding how to perform market studies); and (3) *strategic affairs* refers to determining objectives and priorities for the next years, the evaluation of current policy, and the preparation of new policy.

The data was transcribed and coded in ATLAS.ti, which allows researchers to define associational relations between codes. ATLAS.ti allows the researcher to define the following links: '*is associated with*,' which is used when codes seem to covary but the researcher cannot determine whether the relation is positive or negative; '*hampers*,' which points to a negative relation between codes; '*increases*,' which points to a positive relation; and '*is cause of*,' which can be used when one finds a causal relation between two codes. Whereas these links are defined by the researcher, the 'co-occurrence explorer' is a tool to assess proximity or association among coded quotations in a more automated way. Two codes are labeled as 'co-occurring' when they code quotations that are in some way touching each other (i.e., the first code either 'overlaps,' 'is overlapped by,' 'follows,' 'precedes,' 'encloses,' or is enclosed by' the second code). A high extent of co-occurrence between two codes points to a certain association or covariance between codes. For instance, when interviewees systematically mention 'coordination on operational affairs' in combination with 'reduction in autonomy,' it is likely that these codes are associated (see Malina and Selto 2001). However, whereas the tool allows one to detect association and proximity, it does not allow one to unravel causality. Therefore, we focused mainly on the associational relations as defined by the researcher and used the co-occurrence explorer as an additional source to interpret the relations between codes.

FINDINGS

The structure of our findings is based on the theoretical framework presented in Figure 7.1. We will first demonstrate that VREG rationally pursued a unique organizational reputation of technical expertise, which was cultivated and maintained through several relational strategies. We will show

how this socially rooted reputation and related signals of trustworthiness were recognized by the political principal. However, VREG not only pursued an organizational technical reputation based on unique expertise. It also aimed to build a moral reputation toward its political principals related to traits such as reliability, openness, and sensitivity to their needs. After discussing how VREG bolstered its reputation on these aspects and managed to grow corresponding trust, we will highlight how this resulted in high levels of de facto policy making and deeper forms of collaboration with the political principal.

Before we enter into further details, let us first set out that VREG *rationally* pursues more policy autonomy and a higher involvement in the policy process. According to the agency head, being involved in policy is important:

> Our core task is to regulate the market, not to prepare policy. But you cannot separate these two very strictly. Exerting oversight and making rules are complementary: we can see where things are going wrong and where policy should be adapted. When we feel that the market needs a new legislative initiative, we signal that to the minister. Sometimes you really have to take the initiative yourself.
>
> (Interview 5, quote 10)

Technical Reputation and Competence-Based Trust by Developing Unique Expertise

Organizations actively develop a reputation for technical expertise in order to be perceived as having the unique technical capacity and skills required to do their jobs (regardless of the actual performance) (Carpenter and Krause 2012; see phase 1 in Figure 7.1). Because all regulatory competences are allocated to VREG, it is evident that the expertise for regulatory policy is available only at VREG. The capacity of the political principal is limited because the ministerial cabinet consists of only two personal advisors to the minister for energy.

VREG accumulated and further developed its technical expertise by extensive contacts with multiple actors. On the *supranational* level, VREG coordinated with other national regulators and the European Commission via European Regulatory Networks (Eberlein 2008). The European Regulators Group for Electricity and Gas (ERGEG) was established to "facilitate consultation, coordination and cooperation of national regulatory authorities, contributing to a consistent application, in all Member States of the energy Directives" (European Commission 2003). ERGEG provided a forum for energy regulators to participate in policy making at the EU level. ERGEG could "advise and assist the Commission in consolidating the internal energy market, in particular with respect to the preparation of implementing measures on any matters related to the internal energy market" (European Commission 2003). The Belgian regional

128 *Koen Verhoest et al.*

regulators have been members of the ERGEG working groups on consumer protection and on renewable energy, whereas the Belgian federal regulator represented the Belgian viewpoint in the other working groups (e.g., cross-border trade). In July 2011, the Agency for the Cooperation of Energy Regulators (ACER) replaced ERGEG, but some ERGEG working groups have continued to meet on a regular basis (Agency for the Cooperation of Energy Regulators 2011).

On a *national and regional level,* VREG had frequent contacts with the other regional energy regulators of Belgium (Wallonia, Brussels region) as they exchanged information, practices, and opinions. VREG also targeted regulatees and stakeholders. Via written consultation procedures, regulatees can comment on draft decisions or opinions of the regulators. In addition, there are monthly meetings between VREG and the CEOs of the two distribution network operators (*Eandis* and *Infrax*). A third way of consultation occurred through asking the opinion of market actors via surveys. Two important examples are the 'market model study' *(Studie Marktmodel)* and the 'stakeholder survey.' The former is a study undertaken jointly by the regulatees and VREG, with the aim to develop a common long-term vision on the governance of the energy market (VREG 2009, 1). The latter is a survey involving consumers, industry federations, and social partners.

The networking with international and national regulators, and with the regulated field, is a deliberate strategy of the agency head: "My personal task is to make sure that the relations are well-managed. It is important that we consult very closely with all involved actors" (Interview 27, quote 4). It allowed VREG to expand its expertise on regulatory policy and on wider energy policy issues:

> It is good to have an informal network to rely on, when we perform a certain market study. We can ask colleagues to pass on data, or ask their opinions regarding the methodology that we should apply.
>
> (Interview 23, quote 33)

In addition, it allows VREG to build consensus on regulatory objectives, together with the other Belgian regional energy regulators. Interviewees indicated that the energy regulators often shared the same opinions regarding regulatory objectives: "The other regional regulators live in the same situation and we know each other very well."

However, before a reputation can be used as a political asset, the recognition by the political authorities of a unique organizational and socially rooted expertise is of crucial importance (see phase 2 in Figure 7.1). The minister expressed a large amount of *competence-based trust* in VREG:

> The de facto role that the organization plays differs from the formal role. How can VREG strengthen its role? By writing valuable reports. Those reports are worthy to be read and they are widely read. You can

see that VREG has developed expertise, its CEO is frequently interviewed by the media, when it concerns rising energy prices. In a similar vein, when people have complaints about their energy supplier, they contact VREG, even when the topic is not a competence of VREG. So, they have become the single point of contact for many stakeholders and the spokesperson of the Flemish energy policy.

(Interview 25, quote 94)

Hence, being considered as a reputable actor by the stakeholders was an important factor for playing a larger role in the policy process. Reports and advices gained considerable credibility when VREG could demonstrate that they were supported by these influential and knowledgeable actors. For instance, interviewees mentioned that ERGEG membership has led to a higher reputational power of VREG. ERGEG documents gained a large weight because they represented the uniform viewpoint of the European regulators, and because they usually resulted in European Commission decisions. Interviewees indicate that it was much harder for a minister to ignore an advice of VREG when it reflected the same opinion of the ERGEG network, because "the minister would not risk to contradict what Europe wants."

Because it has built such extensive contacts with stakeholders, VREG succeeded in embedding its capacities in several networks so that the parent minister could no longer ignore its unique expertise regarding energy policy. As mentioned by a personal advisor of the minister, the cabinet had "really nobody else to turn to." In other words, because VREG had developed a unique expertise, supported by multiple audiences at the supranational, national, and regional levels of government, it would be politically costly for the political principal to deny the regulator a role in the policy process.

Moral Reputation and Identity-Based Trust by Signaling Reliability and Openness

VREG wants to be perceived by the minister as being honest, reliable, and open. Before VREG formally publishes a regulatory decision, a market monitoring report, or a policy opinion, it has usually discussed this informally with the ministerial cabinet first. Interviewees mentioned that VREG has frequent informal contacts with the ministerial cabinet via email and telephone as well, almost on a daily basis:

We have set up a communication system with the cabinet that runs very well. We see them a lot and we try to maintain those channels, so that they are not surprised of the things we are doing. That is a kind of informal trust between us.

(Interview 23, quote 9)

130   *Koen Verhoest et al.*

The interviewee from the ministerial cabinet confirms this informal way of working: "In practice the collaboration between us is very informal and goes very smoothly."

VREG and the minister seemed to adhere to the same values, as they both attached importance to maintaining an informal culture, where policy issues are discussed via personal contacts. Personal relations were emphasized repeatedly and were reportedly very good. VREG even signals that it is sensitive to the needs and objectives of its political principal. When the European Commission presented the Third Legislative Package on energy in 2009, the Flemish minister for energy asked VREG to prepare and draft the transposition of these directives into Flemish law. These directives were aimed at further developing the Single Market for energy. An important objective was to safeguard the autonomy of the national regulatory authorities vis-à-vis the parent minister. For instance, article 35 of Directive 2009/72 states that national regulators should not take direct instructions from any public entity, including government. When VREG was asked to draft the transposition of these directives into Flemish law, it had much discretion to interpret the directives and to decide to what extent its legal statutes would have to be modified in order to comply with the directives. The Third Legislative Package initially sparked a discussion within the regulatory agency regarding its structural autonomy. Some actors argued to place VREG under the authority of parliament instead of the executive branch. However, in its draft proposal of the Flemish energy law, VREG confirmed itself as a part of the executive branch and as partly being under the authority of the minister. The agency head stated that: "You cannot just detach yourself and be completely 100% autonomous." In fact, interviewees argued that a sole focus on safeguarding independence might produce a reverse effect:

> Organizations that strictly defend their independence often create the opposite effect: they get a very strenuous relation. Of course, it works in two ways: when ministers behave in a very threatening manner, then this will evoke very defensive behavior.
>
> (Interview 23, quote 66)

Instead, VREG asked to remove only some steering instruments, whereas others could be maintained. The main focus was on removing the possibility that *commissaires du gouvernement* would be appointed and on expanding the Board of Directors, to allow for the appointment of independent directors (VREG 2010, 44–52). However, VREG still needs to negotiate its multi-annual objectives with the minister via a performance contract. In addition, the minister still appoints the chairman of the Board of Directors. We could say that, even though the Third Package provided arguments to further reduce the influence of the minister, VREG has not pushed for this. Instead, VREG seemed to leave some space for steering by the minister and appears to differentiate between steering instruments that were found to be too intrusive and steering instruments that did not violate its independence.

Interviewees said that VREG does not want to insulate itself completely from the parent minister. Instead, it prefers an approach of close collaboration between regulator and minister, which would give the regulator a larger de facto role in policy making. These relational strategies resulted in identification-based trust by the political principal in VREG.

Apparently, closeness and informal contact may build up trust and give influence on the political leadership because of increased access. But it might be a risky strategy, as this might also lead to more influence on the agency and its leadership from the ministry.

Effects of Reputation and Trust: Autonomy and Collaboration as Trusting Behavior

There are some indications of the need for reciprocity in the relationship between VREG and the parent minister. We would argue that a certain extent of 'gift-giving behavior' can be observed. For instance, despite the alleged need for credible commitment and depoliticization, VREG seems to leave some space for political influence. In return, the minister has granted a large extent of de facto policy autonomy to VREG. Although VREG is formally only competent for giving nonbinding advice on legislative proposals, it plays a more important role in practice. For instance, the transposition of the Third Legislative Package into Flemish legislation was drafted entirely by VREG and was adopted by the Flemish government with only minor adjustments. The minister acknowledged the need for more autonomy under the Third Package (Van den Bossche 2010). In 2011, a new decree came into force, to transpose the directives into Flemish law (Vlaams Parlement 2009, art. 1.1.2). Under the new decree, the agency head and the members of the Board of Directors were appointed for a fixed term of five years, renewable once, making early dismissal by the minister much harder. In addition, the new decree abolishes the *commissaires du gouvernement*.

In fact, many proposals for which it produced a formal advice have actually been prepared (informally) by VREG:

> It sometimes leads to strange situations, where the minister asks us informally to prepare the proposal. After we have sent it to the cabinet, it returns to us as part of the legally prescribed procedure, so we then have to give a formal advice on our own proposal.
>
> (Interview 23, quote 4)

Interviewees from the ministerial cabinet considered this high extent of de facto policy autonomy as a gift to VREG: "I believe it is very motivating for them" (Interview 25, quote 53).

132 *Koen Verhoest et al.*

VREG has even collaborated with the minister in highly political processes. Until 2011, the authority to regulate distribution network operators in Belgium was fragmented across the regional and federal levels of government. Whereas the regional regulators were competent for technical regulation (e.g., monitoring the safety and capacity of distribution networks) and social regulation (e.g., imposing public service obligations), the federal level remained responsible for tariff setting. From 2008 onward, VREG requested the Flemish government to negotiate a new division of competences with the federal government:

> In order to be able to develop a coherent Flemish energy policy, the region must have the authority over distribution tariffs. Flanders should continuously argue for a transfer of this competence to the regions.
>
> (VREG 2008, 2)

The Flemish government has supported this request (Van den Bossche 2010). In December 2011, the newly elected federal government announced that tariff setting for distribution networks would be delegated to the regional level as part of a large-scale reform of the state (Federale Regering 2011). These examples of 'gift-giving behavior' demonstrate that both the minister and VREG seem committed to achieve each other's objectives, signaling a high level of identity-based trust.

DISCUSSION AND CONCLUSIONS

This chapter aimed to explain the high de facto policy autonomy of VREG. VREG presented an intriguing empirical puzzle given that both its de facto policy autonomy and collaboration efforts with its political principal, i.e., the Flemish Minister of Energy, were much larger than formally stipulated. We developed and used a framework based on bureaucratic reputation theory, integrated with insights from trust literature.

The concepts of organizational reputation and trustworthiness seem to be closely connected, as they have multiple corresponding elements (cf. Table 7.1). Both concepts refer to the perceptions/beliefs of one or more external audiences about one or more traits of the agency. Both reputation theory and trust theory point toward the ability of (regulatory) agencies to actively craft the signals that are being sent out to external audiences. Both make a distinction between different types of traits in which reputation/trust is grounded. Whereas reputation theory puts the emphasis on traits linked to the performative/technical/moral/procedural capabilities of the regulator, trust theory distinguishes between competence-based, identity-based, and routine-based types of the trustor-trustee relationship. Finally, both theories posit that a regulator, conscious about the traits/signals that are being sent out, can actively determine which relational strategies to adopt.

Table 7.1 Corresponding elements in reputation and trust theory

Reputation theory		Trust theory	
Concept	Definition	Concept	Definition
Organizational reputation	Refers to a set of symbolic beliefs about the unique or separable capacities, intentions, roles, obligations, history, and mission of an organization that are embedded in a network of multiple audiences	*Trustworthiness*	Refers to a general belief about how trustable the organization is, expressed in terms of trust intentions
Reputation consciousness	Agencies are no passive actors; on the contrary, they strategically craft and manage their organizational reputations	*Active trust*	Trustees are not merely passive actors but can play an active role in initiating, shaping, sustaining, and changing trust
Performative reputation	Refers to whether an agency can execute its tasks competently and efficiently	*Competence-based trust*	Refers to the competences and expertise of an organization
Technical reputation	Means an agency has the technical capacity and skill required to do its job (regardless of its actual performance)		
Moral reputation	Means that an agency is sensitive, flexible, honest, and protective of the interests of its clients	*Identity-based trust*	Refers to when partners know and share each other's interests, norms, and values
Relational strategies	Strategies to achieve social embeddedness in a network of multiple audiences	*Trust as a relational concept*	Refers to trustees determining themselves which signals are being sent to the trustor and how the relationship with the trustor is maintained

134 *Koen Verhoest et al.*

However, close inspection of both theories also highlights some important differences. First, reputation theory states that the abovementioned traits (performative/technical/etc.) that a regulator might choose to bring forward might be conflicting. Regulators must choose to which trait they give priority. Trust theory is less clear about this prioritization of strategies and seems to highlight the multidimensionality of the trust concept (as opposed to uniqueness). Second, whereas trust theory seems to focus on dyadic trustor-trustee relations, reputation theory also emphasizes that a unique reputation must be socially rooted in diverse networks. An agency encounters multiple audiences that need to be managed simultaneously. Third, reputation theory makes different underlying assumptions when looking at the behavior of actors. Although it clearly deviates from principal-agent theory in identifying unique organizational reputations as sources of bureaucratic power, bureaucratic reputation theory is still grounded in rational choice theory and its assumptions of cost-calculating behavior guided by self-interest. It is only when the political principals see it in their interest to grant de facto autonomy to an agency, or when denying this autonomy would come at a political cost, that we expect to see an increase in de facto autonomy. Trust theory, on the other hand, in particular when referring to nonrational identification-based trust, sees the behavior of political and administrative actors rather as intrinsically motivated, collectivistic, and confident of each other's motivations. Fourth, the organizational traits identified by reputation theory refer to features of the organization and its behavior, which are seen as intangible political assets used to generate political support. The different types of trust, however, refer to features of the trust relationship and can be seen as end results of different organizational and environmental factors rather than pure antecedents (although they might be antecedents as well). A fifth difference lies in the degree to which a regulator is in control of the crafting of its reputation/trustworthiness. Reputation theory stresses the ability of regulatory agencies to craft their own reputations (although Maor takes a different stance on this than, for instance, Carpenter, who has less faith in the ability of agencies to strategically manage their reputation in response to changing circumstances). Trust theory, while also suggesting strategies that agencies can pursue to actively improve their trustworthiness, places more emphasis on the reciprocal nature of the relationship between trustor and trustee.

Future research could focus more on how these theories complement each other. First, reputation can be considered as an antecedent of trust and as an intangible asset for public organizations because it underpins the trustworthiness of public organizations. Second, trust may act as a feedback mechanism, which might result in the use of other *complementary* relational strategies (in this context, strategies that promote moral reputation in addition to technical reputation). Third, trust complements reputation theory in explaining the mechanisms behind the recognition of a unique organizational reputation by the political principal. Next to this, relational-based

Organizational Reputation and Trust 135

trust points at the importance of moral reputations. At the moment, reputation literature is strongly focused on reputations for technical expertise or performance. Other types of reputation that refer more to moral and character-based traits like benevolence, openness, and sensitiveness should get more attention in literature in terms of how they are created, signaled, and sustained over time. Finally, an important element is that reputation and trust might reinforce each other. But future research might study what happens in situations where there is a crisis or conflict—will this reinforcement work then? Or will it become a situation where ministry and agency are trying to avoid blame? In that case, are closeness and informal contact more a problem than an advantage?

REFERENCES

Agency for the Cooperation of Energy Regulators. 2011. "2012 Work Programme of the Agency for the Cooperation of Energy Regulators." www.acer.europa. eu/Official_documents/Acts_of_the_Agency/Publication/ACER%20Work%20 Programme%202012.pdf.

Aqueveque, Claudio. 2005. "Signaling Corporate Values: Consumers' Suspicious Minds." *Corporate Governance: The International Journal of Business in Society* 5:70–81.

Aqueveque, Claudio, and Davide Ravasi. 2006. "Corporate Reputation, Affect, and Trustworthiness: An Explanation for the Reputation-Performance Relationship." Paper presented at 10th Annual Corporate Reputation Institute Conference, New York, NY.

Blomqvist, Kirsimarja. 1997. "The Many Faces of Trust." *Scandinavian Journal of Management* 13:271–286.

Bottom, William. P, James Holloway, Gary J. Miler, Alexandra Mislin, and Andrew Whitford. 2006. "Building a Pathway to Cooperation: Negotiation and Social Exchange between Principal and Agent." *Administrative Science Quarterly* 51:29–58.

Carpenter, Daniel. 2001. *The Forging of Bureaucratic Autonomy: Reputations, Networks, and Policy Innovation in Executive Agencies 1862–1928*. Princeton, NJ: Princeton University Press.

Carpenter, Daniel. 2002. "Groups, the Media, Agency Waiting Costs, and FDA Drug Approval." *American Journal of Political Science* 46:490–505.

Carpenter, Daniel. 2010. *Reputation and Power: Organizational Image and Pharmaceutical Regulation at the FDA*. Princeton, NJ: Princeton University Press.

Carpenter, Daniel, and George A. Krause. 2012. "Reputation and Public Administration." *Public Administration Review* 72:26–32.

Carpenter, Daniel, and David E. Lewis. 2004. "Political Learning from Rare Events: Poisson Inference, Fiscal Constraints, and the Lifetime of Bureaus." *Political Analysis* 12:201–232.

Christensen, Tom, and Per Lægreid. 2007. "Regulatory Agencies—The Challenges of Balancing Agency Autonomy and Political Control." *Governance* 20:499–520.

Davies, Gary, and Rosa Chun. 2003. "The Use of Metaphor in the Exploration of the Brand Concept." *Journal of Marketing Management* 19:45–71.

Dyer, Jeffrey H., and Wujin Chu. 2003. "The Role of Trustworthiness in Reducing Transaction Costs and Improving Performance: Empirical Evidence from the United States, Japan, and Korea." *Organization Science* 14:57–68.

136 Koen Verhoest et al.

Eberlein, Burkard. 2008. "Formal and Informal Governance in Single Market Regulation." In *The Organizational Dimension of Politics. Essays in Honour of Morten Egeberg,* edited by Ulf Sverdrup and Jarle Trondal, 304–330. Bergen: Fagbokforlaget.

Edelenbos, Jurian, and Erik-Hans Klijn. 2007. "Trust in Complex Decision-Making Networks: A Theoretical and Empirical Exploration." *Administration & Society* 39:25–50.

European Commission. 2003. *Commission Decision of 11 November 2003 on Establishing the European Regulators Group for Electricity and Gas. 2003/796/ EC.*

European Parliament and Council. 2009. *Directive 2009/72/EC of 13 July 2009 Concerning Common Rules for the Internal Market in Electricity and Repealing Directive 2003/54/EC.* Brussels: European Parliament and Council

Federale Regering. 2011. "Ontwerpakkoord voor het Algemeen Beleid." Brussels: Federale Regering. http://www.premier.be/files/20111206/Regeerakkoord_1_ december_2011.pdf.

Fombrun, Charles, and Cees van Riel. 1998. "The Reputational Landscape." *Corporate Reputation Review* 1:5–14.

Gambetta, Diego. 1988. "Can We Trust Trust?" In *Trust: Making and Breaking Co-operative Relations,* edited by Diego Gambetta, 213–237. Oxford: Blackwell.

Gerring, John. 2004. "What Is a Case Study and What Is It Good for?" *American Political Science Review* 98:341–354.

Giddens, Anthony. 1994. "Risk, Trust, Reflexivity." In *Reflexive Modernization,* edited by Ulrich Beck, Antony Giddens, and Scott Lash, 184–197. Cambridge: Polity Press.

Gilad, Sharon, Moshe Maor, and Pazit Ben-Nun Bloom. 2013. "Organizational Reputation, the Content of Public Allegations, and Regulatory Communication." *Journal of Public Administration Research and Theory.* doi: 10.1093/jopart/ mut041.

Good, David. 1988. "Individuals, Interpersonal Relations, and Trust." In *Trust,* edited by Diego Gambetta, 131–185. New York: Basil Blackwell.

Grey, Chris, and Christina Garsten. 2001. "Trust, Control and Post-Bureaucracy." *Organization Studies* 22:229–250.

Groenleer, Martin. 2009. *The Autonomy of European Union Agencies: A Comparative Study of Institutional Development.* Delft: Uitgeverij Eburon.

Huxham, Chris. 2003. "Theorizing Collaboration Practice." *Public Management Review* 5(3):401–423.

Jensen, Michael C., and William H. Meckling. 1976. "Theory of the Firm: Managerial Behavior, Agency Costs and Ownership Structure." *Journal of Financial Economics* 3:305–60.

Johnson-George, Cynthia, and Walter C. Swap. 1982. Measurement of Specific Interpersonal Trust: Construction and Validation of a Scale to Assess Trust in a Specific Other. *Journal of Personality and Social Psychology* 43:1306–1317.

Jordana, Jacint, and David Levi-Faur, eds. 2004. *The Politics of Regulation: Institutions and Regulatory Reforms for the Age of Governance.* Cheltenham: Edward Elgar.

Lægreid, Per, Paul G. Roness, and Kristin Rubecksen. 2005. "Regulating Regulatory Organizations: Controlling Norwegian Civil Service Organisations." Working Paper 5, Stein Rokkan Centre for Social Studies.

Lane, Christel, and Reinhard Bachmann. 1996. "The Social Constitution of Trust: Supplier Relations in Britain and Germany." *Organization Studies* 17:365–395.

Lawler, Edward J., and Jeongkoo Yoon. 1996. "Commitment in Exchange Relations: Test of a Theory of Relational Cohesion." *American Sociological Review* 61:89–108.

Organizational Reputation and Trust 137

Lewis, J. David, and Andrew Weigert. 1985. "Trust as a Social Reality." *Social Forces* 63:967–985.

Lewicki, Roy J., and Barbara B. Bunker. 1996. "Developing and Maintaining Trust in Work Relationships." In *Trust in Organizations: Frontiers of Theory and Research,* edited by Roderick Kramer and Tom Tyler, 114–39. Thousand Oaks: Sage.

Lyon, Fergus. 2006. "Managing Co-operation: Trust and Power in Ghanaian Associations." *Organization Studies* 27:31–52.

MacDonald, Jason A., and William W. Franko Jr. 2007. "Bureaucratic Capacity and Bureaucratic Discretion. Does Congress Tie Policy Authority to Performance?" *American Politics Research* 35:790–807.

Macintosh, Andrew. 2007. "Statutory Authorities." In *Silencing Dissent. How the Australian Government Is Controlling Public Opinion and Stifling Debate,* edited by Clive Hamilton and Sarah Maddison, 148–174. Crow's Nest, Australia: Allen & Unwin.

Maggetti, Martino. 2009. "The de Facto Independence of Regulatory Agencies and Its Consequences for Policy Making and Regulatory Outcomes." Unpublished PhD Thesis, Université de Lausanne, Switzerland.

Malina, Mary A., and Frank H. Selto. 2001. "Communicating and Controlling Strategy: An Empirical Study of the Effectiveness of the Balanced Scorecard." *Journal of Accounting Research* 13:47–90.

Maor, Moshe. 2007. "A Scientific Standard and an Agency's Legal Independence: Which of These Reputation Protection Mechanisms Is Less Susceptible to Political Moves?" *Public Administration* 85:961–978.

Maor, Moshe. 2011. "Organizational Reputations and the Observability of Public Warnings in 10 Pharmaceutical Markets." *Governance: An International Journal of Policy, Administration, and Institutions* 24:557–82.

Maor, Moshe, Sharon Gilad, and Pazit Ben-Nun Bloom. 2013. "Organizational Reputation, Regulatory Talk, and Strategic Silence." *Journal of Public Administration Research and Theory* 23:561–608.

Maor, Moshe, and Raanan Sulitzeanu-Kenan. 2013. "The Effect of Salient Reputational Threats on the Pace of FDA Enforcement." *Governance: An International Journal of Policy and Administration* 26:31–61.

Mayer, Roger C., James H. Davis, and F. David Schoorman. 1995. "An Integrative Model of Organizational Trust." *Academy of Management Review* 20:709–734.

McEvily, Bill, and Akbar Zaheer. 2006. "Does Trust Still Matter? Research on the Role of Trust in Inter-organizational Exchange." In *Handbook of Trust Research,* edited by Reinhard Bachmann and Akbar Zaheer, 280–300. Cheltenham: Edward Elgar.

Miles, Matthew B., and Michael A. Huberman. 1994. *Qualitative Data Analysis. An Expanded Sourcebook. Second Edition.* Thousand Oaks: Sage.

Moffitt, Susan. 2010. "Promoting Agency Reputation through Public Advice: Advisory Committee Use in the FDA." *The Journal of Politics* 72:880–893.

Möllering, Guido. 2006. *Trust: Reason, Routine, Reflexivity.* Amsterdam: Elsevier.

Muthusamy, Senthil K., and Margaret A. White. 2005. "Learning and Knowledge Transfer in Strategic Alliances: A Social Exchange View." *Organization Studies* 26:415–41.

Nooteboom, Bart, Hans Berger, and Niels G. Noorderhaven. 1997. "Effects of Trust and Governance on Relational Risk." *Academy of Management Journal* 40:308–338.

Oakes, Guy. 1990. "The Sales Process and the Paradoxes of Trust." *Journal of Business Ethics* 9:671–679.

Phillips, Nelson, and Cynthia Hardy. 1997. "Managing Multiple Identities: Discourse, Legitimacy and Resources in the UK Refugee System." *Organization* 4: 159–186.

Ring, Peter S., and Andrew van de Ven. 1992. "Structuring Cooperative Relationships between Organizations." *Strategic Management Journal* 13:483–493.

138 *Koen Verhoest et al.*

Sako, Mari. 1992. *Prices, Quality and Trust: Inter-Firm Relations in Britain and Japan.* Cambridge: Cambridge University Press.

Scott, Colin. 2004. "Regulation in the Age of Governance: The Rise of the Post-Regulatory State." In *The Politics of Regulation: Institutions and Regulatory Reforms for the Age of Governance,* edited by Jacint Jordana and David Levi-Faur, 145–174. Cheltenham: Edward Elgar.

Smaiziene, Ingrida, and Robertas Jucevicius. 2009. "Corporate Reputation: Multidisciplinary Richness and Search for a Relevant Definition." *Inzinerine Ekonomika-Engineering Economics* 2:91–100.

van Thiel, Sandra, and Kutsal Yesilkagit. 2011. "Good Neighbours or Distant Friends? Trust between Dutch Ministries and their Executive Agencies." *Public Management Review* 13:783–802.

Van den Bossche, Freya. 2010. "Beleidsbrief Energie 2010–2011. Brussel: Vlaamse Regering.

Verhoest, Koen. 2002. Resultaatgericht Verzelfstandigen. Een Analyse vanuit een Verruimd Principaal-Agent Perspectief." Unpublished PhD Thesis, K.U. Leuven, Belgium.

Verhoest, Koen. 2005. "Effects of Autonomy, Performance Contracting, and Competition on the Performance of a Public Agency: A Case Study." *The Policy Studies Journal* 33:235–258.

Verhoest, Koen, Sara Demuzere, and Jan Rommel. 2012. "Agencification in Latin Countries: Belgium and Its Regions." In *Government Agencies: Practices and Lessons from 30 Countries,* edited by Koen Verhoest, Sandra van Thiel, Geert Bouckaert, and Per Lægreid, 84–97. Basingstoke, Hampshire: Palgrave Macmillan.

Verhoest, Koen, Paul G. Roness, Bram Verschuere, Kristin Rubecksen, and Muiris MacCarthaigh. 2010. *Autonomy and Control of State Agencies. Comparing States and Agencies.* Basingstoke: Palgrave Macmillan.

Vlaams Parlement. 2009. "Decreet Houdende Algemene Bepalingen Betreffende het Energiebeleid." *Belgisch Staatsblad,* 07 July 2009.

VREG. 2008. *Advies van de Vlaamse Reguleringsinstantie voor de Elektriciteits- en Gasmarkt van 29 april 2008 met Betrekking tot het Voorstel tot Wijziging van de Bijzondere Wet tot Hervorming van de Instellingen op het Vlak van de Energiebevoegdheden. ADV-2008–4.* Brussel.

VREG. 2009. *Project Marktmodel. Visietekst Studie Marktmodel.* Brussel: VREG. http://www.vreg.be/sites/default/files/rapporten/rapp-2009–1.pdf.

VREG. 2010. *Advies van de Vlaamse Reguleringsinstantie voor de Elektriciteits-en Gasmarkt van 23 maart 2010 met Betrekking tot de Omzetting in Vlaamse regelgeving van de Richtlijn van de Europese Unie 2009/72/EG van 13 juli 2009 Betreffende Gemeenschappelijke Regels voor de Interne Markt voor Elektriciteit en tot Intrekking van Richtlijn 2003/54/EG en de Richtlijn van de Europese Unie 2009/73/EG van 13 juli 2009 Betreffende Gemeenschappelijke Regels voor de Interne Markt voor Aardgas en tot Intrekking van Richtlijn 2003/55/EG. ADV-2010–1.* Brussel: VREG.

Yin, Robert K. 2009. *Case Study Research. Design and Methods. Fourth Edition.* Thousand Oaks: Sage.

8 Organizational Reputation, Public Protest, and the Strategic Use of Regulatory Communication

Yael Schanin*

INTRODUCTION

This chapter proposes to examine how organizational reputation affects the way a bureaucratic organization reacts to public protest. To this end, I will gauge the differences between the effects of public protest on the communication policy of the bureaucratic organization and the effects of the protest on its regulatory policy, and whether and how these differences are connected to organizational reputation.

These questions will be examined by means of a case study investigating how the social protest of the summer of 2011 in Israel affected the communication policy and the regulatory policy of the Banking Supervision Department in Bank of Israel (hereafter: the BSD). The methodology will consist of content analysis and quantitative analysis of changes in the reactions of the BSD to the way it was perceived in the media and the change in BSD outputs toward the banks following the protest of summer 2011.

Unlike previous research, it is found that the bureaucratic organization reacts to criticism in the media not only in situations of media salience regarding the organization's activities but also in the reverse situation, when organizational media salience is low. These findings are important for deepening the evolving discussion in the literature dealing with theories of reputation and blame avoidance regarding strategies of organizational reputation management and the way a bureaucratic organization reacts to external signaling.

The findings also contribute to the understanding of how the different strategies of organizational reputation management—statements to the media and regulatory activity—correspond with each other. The research results appear to indicate a gap in the way a bureaucratic organization applies the various strategies to manage reputation. This gap is likely to point to the fact that every strategy serves a different type of reputational threat: media policy takes care of a short-term reputational threat, whereas regulatory policy takes care of a long-term reputational threat.

140   *Yael Schanin*

The chapter is organized as follows: First, we will survey the relevant literature, the theoretical framework, and the research hypotheses; then, we will present the case study; subsequently, we will describe the research and its results; and finally, we will conclude with discussion and conclusions.

STRATEGIES FOR REPUTATION MANAGEMENT

The theories of bureaucratic reputation maintain that organizational reputation is a valuable political asset that rational organizations will want to strengthen and protect (Carpenter 2001, 2002; Carpenter and Krause 2012; Maor 2011; Maor and Sulitzeanu-Kenan 2013). Organizational reputations, according to Carpenter, "can be used to generate public support, to achieve delegated autonomy and discretion from politicians, to protect the agency from political attack, and to recruit and retain valued employees" (Carpenter 2002, 491).

Considering the aspiration of a bureaucratic organization to receive positive reactions and public support, signs of public dissatisfaction with the organization's role will lead the organization to react in order to change public opinion (Jennings 2009; Moe 1985; Noll 1985; Olson 1995, 1996; Wood and Waterman 1991).

A public protest is an event that poses a threat to the reputation of a bureaucratic organization. It is a significant external signal indicating the dissatisfaction of the protesting public. This signaling, by nature, might reverberate with politicians and elected officials. These officials could try to influence the public dissatisfaction by curtailing the authority of the organization or by imposing priorities on it.

The literature focusing on reputation maintains that various external signals have different effects on the bureaucratic organization. The way these external signals affect the organization is a consequence of an agency's wish to protect its organizational reputation. This means that organizational reputation is a tool to manage external signaling and to control the way these signals create threats for the organization. Thus, bureaucratic organizations invest great resources in managing their reputations.

Bureaucratic organizations aspire to design their reputations as reflecting unique abilities and exclusive characteristics (Carpenter 2001; Carpenter and Krause 2012; Gilad and Yogev 2012; Maor 2011; Maor, Gilad, and Ben-Nun Bloom 2013). Carpenter (2001, 2002) defined "reputation uniqueness" as the ability of an organization to show that it can supply solutions and services that no other governmental agency can provide (Carpenter 2001, 2002; Carpenter and Krause 2012).

Gilad and Yogev have pointed to three regulatory reputation-management strategies: (1) managing reputation by defining the regulatory task boundaries so that tasks will be limited only to those that correlate

Reputation, Public Protest, and Communication 141

to the core of organizational identity and that do not create negative reputation; (2) managing reputation by regulatory communications that arouse consciousness, shape public perceptions, and enable a reaction to criticism; and (3) managing reputation by regulatory operation determining priorities among the regulatory tasks, tools, and accepted practice (Gilad and Yogev 2012). This chapter will focus and the latter two strategies.

Strategic Use of Regulatory Communication

A basic premise of the political science approach to reputation is that, as a rule, bureaucratic organizations are rational and are politically aware (Carpenter 2001; Krause and Douglas 2005; Maor 2011; Maor and Sulitzeanu-Kenan 2013; see also Wæraas and Maor in this volume). This premise provides the basis for explaining agencies' communication strategies, the content of their public statements, and their actual choice of whether to react to criticism or to remain silent. All of these are a consequence of organizational reputation-management strategies rather than incidental whim.

When a bureaucratic organization encounters media criticism, it may choose whether to react to the criticism or to avoid reaction. According to Maor, Gilad, and Ben-Nun Bloom (2013), absence of response and maintaining silence as a response are both reactions that may shape public opinion. Silence could stem from the wish to not cause damage in the short term, such as shock to financial markets (Blinder et al. 2008). Silence even transmits the message to the public that the bureaucratic organization is occupied with finding a solution to the problem rather than a solution to the public criticism about it (Maor, Gilad, and Ben-Nun Bloom. 2013). Maor and Sulitzeanu-Kenan (2013) point out that considerations of blame avoidance and reputation protection affect the content of response to criticism or its absence (Maor and Sulitzeanu-Kenan 2013; Sulitzeanu-Kenan 2010). However, beyond that, research has indicated that the choice between reaction and silence is intimately connected to organizational reputation.

According to Maor and colleagues (2013), an agency can afford to keep silent regarding opinions about core functional areas in which it enjoys a strong reputation. An agency can also afford to keep silent when facing challenges regarding domains that are secondary to its overall reputation. On the other hand, an agency with a weak or uncertain reputation might fight hard to protect its reputation. Therefore, it is more likely to respond to opinions about functional areas in which it generally has a weak or evolving reputation (Maor, Gilad, and Ben-Nun Bloom 2013).

Our analysis so far anticipates that the strength of a regulator's reputation and its reputation across functional areas shape its choice between silence and talk. Therefore, our first hypothesis is that (a) a bureaucratic

142   *Yael Schanin*

organization is more likely to respond to opinions expressed about it in the media after a public protest than it did before the protest; and (b) a bureaucratic organization is more likely to respond to opinions concerning issues regarding whether its reputation is negative or is still evolving after a public protest than it did before the protest and keep silent about issues on which it generally enjoys a strong reputation.

Strategic Use of Regulatory Policy

A second reputation-management strategy is regulatory operation to determine bureaucratic organizational priorities and the means to achieve these objectives (Gilad and Yogev 2012). Reputation risk management is embedded in the mode of decision making by the bureaucratic organization and by its deeds (Carpenter 2002; Gilad, Maor, and Ben-Nun Bloom 2013; Krause et al. 2005; Maor and Sulitzeanu-Kenan 2013). In accordance with theories dealing with reputation, prioritization among bureaucratic organizational objectives is a product of the calculation of danger to the public on the one hand, and reputational risk resulting from an error in the estimation of danger and coping with it on the other hand (Gilad 2012; Olson 1996).

The aspiration to protect a unique reputation and positive public opinion, under certain circumstances, results in behavior that contradicts public opinion and is likely to lead to negative criticism in the short term. In other words, not every external signal will bring about a change in the behavior of the regulator, which is weighing considerations of long-term reputation. In prioritizing tasks, regulators will act to protect the core reputation of the organization (Gilad 2012). In addition, sociopolitical theories maintain that prioritization among objectives, formulated in response to external signals, are a function of the organization's internal structure and its implication on the division of organizational attentiveness (Carpenter 1996; May, Workman, and Jones 2008; Workman, Jones, and Jochim 2009). In many cases, changes in policy take place following changes in public opinion. However, for the most part, there is a time gap that stems from the period necessary to implement the change in policy (Jennings 2009).

Changes in regulatory policy are therefore a consequence of the institutional structure of the bureaucratic organization (Olson 1996). Bureaucratic organizations are rigid and inflexible, and they are slow to internalize changes and to adopt a new policy adapted to these changes (Noll 1985). Following a significant external signal, top management's attention will be directed toward the criticism, and a slow organizational process will begin moving down the organizational hierarchy. This will stop when public attention turns to another significant direction (Gilad 2012).

Therefore, our second hypothesis is that (a) following public protest, the number of outputs of a bureaucratic organization will not increase in the short term; and (b) following public protest, there will be no change, in the short term, in the way a bureaucratic organization prioritizes between different policy tasks.

By *outputs* we mean regulatory actions that can be counted and measured as individual regulatory actions in one of the agency's functional areas.

CASE DESCRIPTION: THE EFFECT OF PUBLIC PROTEST ON THE COMMUNICATION POLICY AND REGULATORY POLICY OF THE BSD

The BSD in Israel, Its Distinct Reputation, and Its Communication Policy

The BSD in Israel is a statutory unit, located within the Bank of Israel, which is an independent central bank. Various documents that are issued by the Bank of Israel and the BSD indicate that the BSD views itself as responsible first and foremost for the stability of the banking system (Ben-Bassat 2007; Maor, Gilad, and Ben-Nun Bloom 2013; Gilad, Maor, and Ben-Nun Bloom 2013).

Another role of the BSD is to handle all aspects of bank-customer relations—fairness in relations between the banks and their customers, and protection of the rights of the banking consumer. This means that the BSD resolves issues with regard to protecting the consumer and maintaining competitiveness in the banking system. The BSD views consumer protection and competition as it secondary role (Ben-Bassat 2007).

The Bank of Israel has a positive reputation based on its success in safeguarding the stability of the banking system. The fact that the Israeli economy exited almost unharmed from the international financial crisis of 2007–2009 strengthened the reputation of the BSD in that context (Gilad, Maor, and Ben-Nun Bloom 2013). However, the reputation of the BSD for protecting the stability of the banks was achieved at the price of its reputation in implementing its other tasks. The Supervision Department has been subject to public criticism in its role of consumer protection (Gilad, Maor, and Ben-Nun Bloom 2013). In addition, through the years, proposals have been raised to transfer responsibility for protecting the consumer to a body outside the Bank Supervision Department—that is, to another unit of the Bank of Israel or to another designated regulator (Parliamentary Inquiry Committee on Bank Fees—Summary Report 2007, 12; Gilad, Maor, and Ben-Nun Bloom 2013). Consumer organizations, as well, have criticized the activity of the BSD in this realm.

The Bank Supervision Department has also received a negative reputation with regard to the promotion of competition in the realm of banking, which suffers from a high degree of concentration (Ben-Bassat 2007; Gilad, Maor, and Ben-Nun Bloom 2013), and it is viewed as preferring stability at the price of competition in the system.

144   *Yael Schanin*

In their research, Maor, Gilad, and Ben-Nun Bloom (2013) analyzed the choice of the BSD to either respond or not respond to media criticism, given the focus of the bureaucratic task that was criticized. The research found that the BSD tended not to respond to criticism toward its activities in the realm of stability, an area in which it enjoyed a positive reputation. Also, the BSD tended not to respond to criticism in the realm of competitiveness, as this was viewed as a secondary goal that was primarily under the jurisdiction of another regulator, the Israel Antitrust Authority. In contrast, the BSD tended to respond to criticism regarding its activities in the realm of consumer protection, in which its reputation was negative (Maor, Gilad, and Ben-Nun Bloom 2013).

The 2011 Social Protest in Israel

In the summer of 2011, a social protest erupted in Israel. The protest began in a spontaneous building of a tent city in many cities throughout Israel. The protest aroused hundreds of thousands of people to participate in giant demonstrations protesting the high cost of living and demanding social justice. The protest was widely covered in the media, including live broadcasts from the demonstrations on commercial television stations.

During the social protest, objections to the cost of living were raised again and again, referring to the high prices of products and services and, in particular, the price of apartments. In addition, the protest focused on the reasons for the high cost of living, including a low level of competition and the concentration of ownership in a small number of wealthy individuals. Although banking did not play a central role in the protest, the banks and their owners are perceived by the Israeli public as another striking example of a centralized domain controlled by a small elite that is influential in a variety of other sectors.

Consequent upon the protest and the huge demonstrations, the Israeli government announced a number of steps toward solving the housing problem and established the Committee on Socioeconomic Reform. On September 26, 2011, the committee published a list of recommendations. The committee recommended the establishment of another committee to deal with competition in the banking system. So even though public discourse had not explicitly expressed criticism or threat toward the banking system, the committee members assumed that the social protest implied the need for a change in banking as well.

Following this proposal, on December 7, 2011, the Minister of Finance and the Governor of the Bank of Israel appointed an inter-ministerial working team to examine how to increase competitiveness in the banking industry, headed by the BSD. The team presented interim findings on July 15, 2012, and its final report on March 19, 2013. The report included various recommendations with the aim of "increasing competitiveness in the market for banking services in Israel, improving the bargaining power of households and small businesses, [and] expanding the options available to the customer" (Bank of Israel 2012, 1).

THE EFFECT OF THE SOCIAL PROTEST ON THE COMMUNICATION POLICY OF THE BSD

Methodology and Data Collection

In order to investigate the effect of the social protest on the media policy of the BSD, a database of opinions was constructed. This included all articles that expressed an opinion toward the BSD between June 2009 and June (inclusive) 2013 and that existed in the database of the Globes newspaper.[1]

A total of 173 articles expressing an opinion were found during the stated period. Each opinion that was expressed about the BSD, whether by the writer of the article or by another person or body mentioned in the article, was coded separately. In cases in which the same person expressed a number of opinions on various issues, each opinion was coded separately. A total of 225 opinions were collected.

In order to validate the database, we used a database that had been coded by Dr. Sharon Gilad for another study (Gilad, Maor, and Ben-Nun Bloom 2013; Maor, Gilad, and Ben-Nun Bloom 2013), while using the same categories and referring to the same period. Krippendorff-alpha results for the relevant variables were higher than 7 (ranging from 0.7427 to 0.9097) for 151 positions out of the 225 positions that I had coded, indicating a high level of reliability for the database that was constructed.

Further to the article by Maor and colleagues (2013), multivariate logistic regression analysis (binary) was used to investigate the reactions of the BSD to opinions expressed about it in the media, both before and after the social protest. The regression examined the tendency of the BSD to respond or not respond to the criticism as depending on the number of explanatory variables and control variables.

The dependent variable is a binary explained variable that represents the media policy of the BSD. The variable is the response of the BSD to an opinion expressed with regard to its activity or lack of activity concerning the aforesaid opinion. A reaction brought up in an article about an opinion expressed in the article was coded as a response[2] (1) even if the response was not directly expressed as a reaction to the article but rather to the opinion expressed in the article (for example, a reaction to a position expressed in a parliamentary discussion that had received a response during the discussion). The absence of response in an article regarding an opinion expressed in the article was coded as an absence of response (0).[3]

The independent variables were the existence of a significant external signal about public opinion, and organizational reputation. The social protest that erupted in the summer of 2011 represents a significant external signal

146   *Yael Schanin*

expressing public opinion. The explanatory variable examines the situation before and after the social protest.

The social protest broke out on July 14 and reached its peak on September 3 at a giant demonstration that was termed the "march of the million" by the media. As the protest was spread over the period of a month and a half, the timing of the case study as 'before' and 'after' was determined by the high point of the social protest, ending on September 3, 2011. This was the last date for intensive media coverage, including direct broadcasts on the three leading television stations. After that demonstration, the protest organizers announced the dismantling of the tents, and media coverage waned.[4]

The amount of time investigated as before the social protest was two years and three months, and the period of time examined as after the social protest was a year and nine months. The number of opinions expressed regarding the BSD in the period preceding the social protest was 132, whereas 93 positions were expressed in the period following the protest.

In addition, in order to investigate the effect of bureaucratic organizational reputation on the organization's motivation to react or not to react to criticism, we created a categorical variable according to the areas of the BSD's responsibility, as representing organizational reputation: (1) banking stability—opinions regarding the BSD's conduct in maintaining banking system stability, capital requirements, limiting activity in certain areas, and more; (2) consumer protection—opinions regarding the BSD's protection of banking customers (and not consumers in general); (3) competition—opinions about the BSD's conduct in the creation or prevention of competition in the banking system; (4) corporate governance—opinions regarding supervision over shareholders and bank managers, and banking decision-making practices; and (5) others. Each opinion was categorized in accordance with the area of responsibility to which it referred.

In addition to the detailed variables, the effects of the following variables were also investigated: the nature of the opinion (positive or negative), the place where expressed, and media salience.

To evaluate expressions of the BSD's media salience, we examined the general scope of media coverage relating to it as expressed in the Globes newspaper. For each article, we counted the number of other articles published during that month that mentioned the BSD and whether they included an opinion about it or not. A total of 1,093 articles were found to mention the BSD, whereas the average number of articles per month was 28.13 and the median number was 28 articles per month.

This variable investigates the effect of public salience of the bureaucratic organization and not of the policy area. This is similar to Maor and colleagues (2013) and differs from Gormley's opinion (1986), according to which it is more correct to investigate the public salience of the policy area and not of the bureaucratic organization. The reason that the research investigates the extent of media coverage of the bureaucratic organization

Reputation, Public Protest, and Communication 147

is, in fact, the estimation that the public salience of the bureaucratic organization has an independent effect on the organization, independent of the public salience of the area of policy. In other words, a bureaucratic organization will be affected by its public salience in its reactions to the media even if the policy area about which the position is expressed is not media salient.

Results

As demonstrated in Table 8.1, the BSD responded to 44 out of 225 opinions (20 percent). In other words, the BSD commonly chose not to respond. In research by Maor and colleagues (2013) that examined an earlier period (1998 to mid-2009), the findings were similar.[5]

In the period preceding the social protest, the rate of response by the BSD was 11 percent of the total opinions expressed in that period. In the period after the social protest, the BSD responded to 31 percent of the total opinions expressed in that period. This means that the rate of response by the BSD tripled after the social protest.

After the social protest, the BSD responded more often to criticism that was directed toward its roles of protecting the consumer and corporate governance. In contrast, the BSD reacted less to criticism directed toward its role in regulating competition after the social protest. Similarly, there was

Table 8.1 Descriptive statistics

	Overall	Before Protest	After Protest
	225	132	93
Response			
Response	20% (44)	11% (15)	31% (29)
Non-Response	80% (181)	89% (117)	69% (64)
Opinion content			
Negative	48% (109)	19.5% (44)	29% (65)
Positive	33% (74)	21% (47)	12% (27)
Mix	19% (42)	11% (25)	7.5% (17)
Regulatory tasks			
Competition	7% (15)	4 (Response = 25%)	11 (Response = 18%)
Consumer Protection	26% (58)	22 (Response = 27%)	36 (Response = 33%)
Prudential	23% (52)	26 (Response = 8%)	26 (Response = 8%)
Internal Control	16% (37)	18 (Response = 17%)	19 (Response = 53%)
Other	28% (63)		
Venue	29% (65)		
Interview	4% (10)		
Knesset	2% (4)		
Correspondence	65% (146)		
Other			

148 *Yael Schanin*

no change in the rate of response to opinions relating to banking system stability after the social protest.

A qualitative investigation of responses made by the BSD indicates that before the social protest, few of these were direct responses to an article, and most responses had been quoted from responses made by the BSD or the Bank of Israel in other places. After the social protest, the number of direct responses to opinions in the media quadrupled (from three responses before the protest to 13 after it).

A quantitative analysis also shows the change in media response policy by the BSD. Table 8.2 demonstrates the results of the multivariate logistic regression analysis examining the BSD's tendency to react to criticism when

Table 8.2 The tendency of the BSD to respond to opinions in the media

	Model I	Model II
Log Odds (S.E.)		
Protest (ref = Before protest)	0.851 (0.411)**	−0.551 (0.603)
Opinion content (ref = Negative)		
Positive	0.023 (0.436)	−0.048 (0.456)
Mix	−1.043 (0.623)*	−1.281 (0.647)**
Regulatory tasks (ref = Other)		
Competition	0.323 (0.826)	0.172 (0.848)
Consumer Protection	0.946 (0.568)*	1.224 (0.604)**
Prudential	−0.281 (0.700)	−0.230 (0.718)
Internal Control	1.577 (0.598)***	1.622 (0.617)***
Venue (ref = Other)		
Interview	2.172 (0.830)***	2.483 (0.858)***
Knesset	1.554 (1.250)	1.019 (1.295)
Correspondence	−0.228 (0.442)	−0.298 (0.456)
Media Salience		−0.082 (0.27)***
Constant	−2.395 (0.574)***	0.454 (1.041)
N	225	225
Model Chi Square	$X^2(10) = 40.427$, $p < 0.01$***	$X^2(11) = 50.643$, $p < 0.01$***
Percentage Correct	83.1	84.9
−2 Log Likelihood	181.954	171.7373
Pseudo R Squares		
Cox & Snell R Square	0.164	0.202
Nagelkerke R Square	0.262	0.321

*$p < 0.1$ **$p < 0.05$ ***$p < 0.01$

expressed toward it (in comparison with the tendency to not react) as dependence on the number of explanatory variables and control variables.

Two models of regression were created in order to understand the effect of each variable when neutralizing the effects of other independent variables: Model I included only the first two control variables—site of opinion expressed and type of opinion. Model II also included the control variable of media salience—that is, the overall extent of media coverage referring to the BSD, in addition to all of the variables appearing in Model I.

Model 1 predicting the BSD's response to media-expressed opinions was found to be statistically significant. According to the model, following the social protest, the log odds that the BSD would respond to an opinion directed toward it in the media grew by 0.851 compared with non-response ($p < 0.05$). With regard to organizational reputation, results were statistically significant concerning criticism directed toward the BSD in its role of consumer protection and corporate governance with an increase of 0.946 and 1.577, respectively, in its tendency to respond to the criticism ($p < 0.01$ and $p < 0.01$, respectively).

Regarding critical variables, it was found that only when an opinion was expressed in an interview or at a press conference was there a significant effect on the BSD's tendency to respond to criticism ($p < 0.01$). In contrast to previous research (Maor, Gilad, and Ben-Nun Bloom 2013), the type of criticism (positive or negative) did not significantly affect the BSD's tendency to respond (except for the tendency to not respond to complex opinions that included both positive and negative aspects).

Model II was also found to be statistically significant. As in Model 1, organizational reputation with respect to consumer protection and corporate governance had a significant effect on the tendency of the BSD to respond to criticism by 1.224 units ($p < 0.1$). Criticism directed toward the BSD dealing with corporate governance raises the log odds by 1.622 units per reaction in comparison to non-response ($p < 0.1$). Regarding control variables, a result similar to Model 1 was indicated.

The –2 Log Likelihood test is lower in Model 2 than in Model I, which may indicate that Model 1 is more suitable. On the other hand, the percentage of anticipated cases in Model II is higher. The Residuals Diagnostics analysis in Model II is identified as one extreme observation in the opinion dataset. Coding of the opinion was retested, and it was found that it had been correctly coded. In addition, the Analog of Cook's Influence Statistics and Leverage Value tests yielded low value results, indicating no real effect on the findings.

As described above, Model II is distinguished from Model I by the control variable, extent of media coverage. According to Model II, the extent of media coverage of the BSD had a significant effect on the tendency of the BSD to respond to the criticism, so that a *rise* in the amount of media coverage actually *lowered* the log odds of response to criticism in comparison with no response by 0.082 units ($p < 0.01$). In other words, the association between salience and the tendency to respond is negative and bidirectional, so that a decrease in salience also leads to a rise in the tendency to respond to criticism. In addition, it was found that, following the addition of the variable of extent of media coverage, the variable of social protest lost its significant effect on the tendency of the BSD to respond to media criticism directed to it, in contrast to the findings of Model I.

This finding is surprising, and it contradicts previous studies, which found that a rise in salience apparently leads to a rise in responsiveness (Maor, Gilad, and Ben-Nun Bloom 2013; Maor and Sulitzeanu-Kenan 2013). Considering this finding, we carried out an analysis of the mediating association, examining the effect of the independent variable—the social protest—on the tendency of the BSD to respond to criticism, when it was mediated by the salience of BSD in the media (the extent of media coverage).

A graphic representation of the examined relationship is detailed in Figure 8.1.

The results of the mediation model show that the association between the social protest and the extent of media coverage is negative (as, on average, in the period after the social protest, the number of articles covering bank supervision was lower by about 19 articles), and this effect was statistically significant ($p < 0.01$). Furthermore, as described in Table 8.2 (above), the association between salience and responsiveness is negative and significant ($p < 0.05$), so that a reduction in media coverage results in a rise in responsiveness, and the opposite is also true.

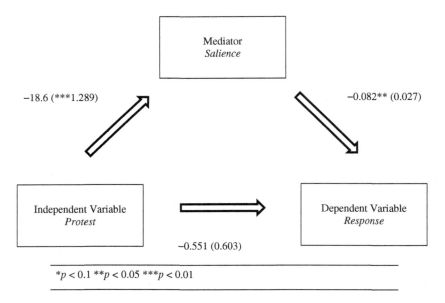

*$p < 0.1$ **$p < 0.05$ ***$p < 0.01$

Figure 8.1 The association between social protest, extent of media coverage, and response of the BSD

As seen in Figure 8.1, the social protest led to a reduction in the extent of media coverage of bank supervision and to an indirect *rise* in reactions linked directly (and negatively) to the reduction in coverage. Moreover, the diagram indicates that when controlling for the indirect effect by means of extent of media coverage, there was no direct effect of social protest on the BSD's responsiveness.[6]

In addition, it was found that the social protest had an indirect effect on the response of the BSD.[7] Log odds for indirect effect of social protest were 1.53.[8] This was an increase of 4.6 times the odds ratio for response in contrast to non-response.

THE EFFECT OF THE SOCIAL PROTEST ON REGULATORY POLICY OF THE BSD

Methodology and Data Collection

In order to examine the effect of the social protest on regulatory activity by the BSD, a dataset of outputs was constructed. To that end, all letters and circulars published by the BSD between June 2009 and June 2013 (inclusive) were assembled.

Letters and circulars constitute official directives by the BSD to banking corporations supervised by it, and they express its official positions in its realm of activity. The circulars express the BSD's directions to the banks: Proper Conduct of Banking Business Regulations, directives for reporting to the public and for reporting to the BSD, whereas the letters include directives to the supervised bodies. Due to problems of access to unofficial directions and instructions given by the BSD to the banks (in individual letters and directives, telephone conversations, informal meetings, and the like), these were not included in the research.[9]

Similar to the coding of the newspaper articles, and using identical operationalization, the circulars and letters from the supervision department were coded according to the type of activity discussed (that is, banking stability, consumer protection, competition, corporate governance, and others). In coding the documents, as in the article coding, each document was coded separately. If the document referred to more than one subject, each subject was coded separately. A total of 90 letters and 157 circulars were assembled that together included 247 outputs.

As with the effects of the social protest on media policy, September 3, 2011, was determined as the date distinguishing between before and after the social protest. Two years and three months were determined as the period before the social protest, and a year and nine months determined the after period.

Considering the 247 outputs, 134 had been issued before the social protest (27 months) at an average rate of 4.9 outputs per month. In contrast,

152   *Yael Schanin*

113 outputs were issued in the period following the social protest (22 months) at an average rate of 5.1 outputs per month. In addition, before the social protest, 46 percent of the total outputs referred to banking stability, whereas 48 percent of the total outputs dealt with stability after the protest. The rate of outputs concerning competition also rose, but the nominal number of outputs remained unchanged (1 output). Consumer protection was discussed in 20 percent of the total outputs in the period before the protest, but it decreased to 15 percent after the protest. The rate of outputs dealing with corporate governance remained unchanged for both periods, whereas outputs for other subjects went up from 18 percent before the protest to 27 percent after it.

Results

There was no significant change in the number of outputs after the protest. This was also true for the subjects of output policies. Additionally, a qualitative investigation of the subjects of the letters and circulars leads to similar conclusions. Regarding stability, the social protest did not change regulatory activity of the BSD. In the period preceding the social protest and after the social protest, the supervision department was greatly occupied with implementing the directives of the Basel II and III Accords, dealing, *inter alia,* with capital requirements to maintain bank stability in various risk scenarios.[10]

Another topic that greatly involved the BSD both before and after the social protest was the issue of bank loans for housing. This issue was also of great interest to the media. The regulations for housing loans affect both the stability of the banking system and the costs of purchasing an apartment. In terms of banking system stability, housing loans arouse fear of a real estate 'bubble' that might lead to banking instability as a result of a transverse crisis in the ability of customers to repay the loans. Therefore, both before and after the protest, the BSD worked actively to lower the risks in loans issued to customers and to buying networks.

Actions taken by the BSD with regard to stability also affect the ability of customers to receive housing loans, as these actions raised the costs of loans. However, although the social protest was concerned with the high cost of living in general and the high cost of housing in particular, the BSD did not change its policies in the realm of housing loans as a result of the protest.

In addition, with regard to activity in the realm of consumer protection, the BSD also did not change policy in the wake of the social protest.

These findings are in line with the research hypothesis that the BSD's regulatory activity did not change as a result of the social protest. These findings also conform to the fact that, during the investigated period after the social protest, the head of the BSD was chairing the team to investigate ways to increase competition in the system, which submitted its final report only on March 19, 2013, at the end of the period examined here. The report included recommendations for consumer protection and competitiveness in the banking system. This raised the conjecture that regulatory activity affected by the protest would be expressed only after the team had submitted its report.

Therefore, it was decided to examine the drafts for discussion issued by the BSD up to June 2013. These were drafts of letters and circulars that were issued for public comment before being published as binding official documents. In other words, this was regulatory activity in the pipeline that would also indicate changes in bureaucratic organizational policy change.[11]

By June 2013, 12 drafts for discussion had been issued, all appearing after the social protest. An analysis of the draft policy issues revealed that three drafts dealt with consumer protection, five concerned stability, three pertained to corporate governance, and one related to competition.

After adding the drafts to the discussion of output data, it was found that from 259 outputs, 134 were issued during the period preceding the social protest (27 months) at an average rate of 4.9 outputs per month, and 125 were issued following the protest (22 months) at an average rate of 5.6 outputs per month. In other words, there was an increase in outputs per month after the social protest. However, this increase was not found to be significant.

In addition, it was found that the rate of outputs pertaining to stability out of the total outputs rose to 47 percent after the social protest (in contrast to 48 percent, not including the drafts for discussion). The rate of outputs dealing with consumer protection out of the total number of outputs in the same period fell to 16 percent after the social protest (in contrast to 15 percent without the drafts for discussion). The rate of outputs referring to competition rose to 1.6 percent of the total outputs after the protest. The rate of outputs regarding corporate governance rose to 14 percent of the total outputs following the protest, whereas the rate of outputs concerning other issues rose to a rate of 24 percent (in contrast to 27 percent without drafts for discussion).

A qualitative examination of issues raised in the drafts for discussion indicated that, with regard to consumer protection, a possible change in regulatory behavior of the BSD may be discerned after the social protest. These findings are in line with the research hypothesis that following a public protest, regulatory activity of a bureaucratic organization will not change in the short term. On the other hand, in the long term, a public protest may have an effect on regulatory activity. It appears that in the time range of two years after the social protest, there are seeds of change in regulatory action. Notwithstanding, more research is needed to evaluate a longer period of time after the social protest to determine whether change has occurred.

154 *Yael Schanin*

DISCUSSION AND CONCLUSIONS

It was found that the BSD responded to criticism directed toward it to a greater extent after the social protest of summer 2011 than it did before the protest. These results are similar to results of earlier studies in this field (Maor, Gilad, and Ben-Nun Bloom 2013). Nevertheless, the results of the study also indicate that the effects of the social protest of summer 2011 on the tendency of the BSD to respond to criticism possibly result indirectly from the decrease in public salience of the BSD and not directly from the protest itself. It appears that, following the protest, public attention was shifted to other issues. Media visibility of the BSD, which was 37.33 on average (median: 37) before the protest, fell to 18.33 on average (median: 21) after it. Surprisingly, the decrease in public visibility in fact led to a rise in the tendency of the BSD to respond to protest (from 11 percent of the cases before the protest to 31 percent of the cases after the protest). This is in contradiction to previous research that found that a decrease in media visibility by a bureaucratic organization lessened its tendency to respond to criticism (Maor, Gilad, and Ben-Nun Bloom 2013; Maor and Sulitzeanu-Kenan 2013).

In seeking explanations for these findings, we may follow Carpenter's advice: "When trying to account for a regulator's behavior, look at the audience and look at the threats" (Carpenter 2010, 382). There may be a number of possible explanations for these findings:

First, after the social protest, although the public salience of the BSD decreased, the media discourse regarding it became more negative than before the protest. In comparison to the period preceding the protest, after the protest, the number of negative opinions about the BSD increased (from 38 percent of the total opinions expressed before the protest to 60 percent of the total opinions expressed after the protest).

It is possible that, although the BSD's media salience decreased, the fact that the criticism against it became more negative encouraged the BSD to respond more to it, in order to try to change public attitudes. This raises the possibility that the quality and the content of the opinions expressed about the BSD had a greater effect than the quantity of opinions expressed about it. This explanation is in line with previous studies (Gilad, Maor, and Ben-Nun Bloom 2013; Hood 2011; Maor, Gilad, and Ben-Nun Bloom 2013; Kahneman and Tversky 1979) that found that negative criticism increased the probability of reaction from a bureaucratic organization.

Second, it is possible that the findings indicate that a bureaucratic organization listens not only to 'noise' but also to 'silence.' In other words, the extent of media coverage affects the bureaucratic organization both when there is an especially great amount of coverage and also when the amount of media coverage is particularly low. Perhaps, in contrast to the way previous writers have viewed this, it is not only public salience but also its absence that constitute external signaling. A decline in media salience does not necessarily signal to a bureaucratic organization that there is no threat to it, but that a different type of threat exists.

In the context of the social protest of summer 2011, it is possible that the BSD viewed the fall in media salience as a signal that the public did not see it as part of the solution to its consumer distress. As an organization concerned that its reputation as a consumer protector is poor, it is possible that low media salience signaled to the BSD that its status was in danger. In that case, the BSD chose to respond more to criticism in the media in order to strengthen its reputation and prevent future loss of status.

In this context, one may view a public protest as it is perceived by the organization not only as a risk but also as an opportunity: a potential for broadening the powers of the bureaucratic organization and for receiving additional resources. Following a public protest, a change in government priorities is possible, as budgets and attention are directed from one realm of responsibility to another. One example is the case of the Israel Antitrust Authority. After the public protest, a new division was created in the Economics Department of the Antitrust Authority, which received additional budgets and authorities. In this situation, no bureaucratic organization wants to stay out of the discourse.

The BSD might have also been interested in receiving additional staff positions and an increase in its powers and, on the other hand, not losing the authority and resources that it already had. There is also the danger that those wishing to remove the Bank-Customer Division, responsible for protecting bank customers, from the Bank Supervision Department will get their wish. Thus, the BSD must be perceived in the public as a body working to solve problems raised in the social protest and, in order to find a solution, it needs the powers that it now has and the staff and resources it presently has at its disposal.

Beyond these findings, similar to previous studies (Maor, Gilad, and Ben-Nun Bloom 2013), the results of this research strengthen the argument that, following a public protest, a bureaucratic organization will respond more to criticism in the media about areas in which it has a weak reputation. The BSD responded more to opinions relating to consumer protection and to its supervision of corporate governance of banks after the social protest, topics for which it had a negative reputation. In contrast, it responded less to opinions about competition that was not perceived as a policy topic under its authority. Moreover, the BSD did not change its responses to the issue of stability, about which it had a strong and positive reputation.

The results of the research also reinforce the second hypothesis, according to which the number of outputs of a bureaucratic organization will not increase in the short term following the social protest. It was found that, in less than two years after the summer 2011 protest, the number of BSD's outputs did not increase significantly.

156   *Yael Schanin*

This finding is consistent with the literature preceding this study that indicated that a change in regulatory activity as a result of external signaling requires a process of internalization and application in a bureaucratic organization (Jennings 2009). Thus, in the short–medium term, after a public protest, no change will occur in the amount of regulatory activity.

Regarding division of resources between the various policy issues, the results of the research strengthen the second hypothesis, according to which, in the short and medium term, there will be no change in the policy issues of regulatory activity after the public protest. Nevertheless, a qualitative investigation of the outputs demonstrates a possible change in the inclination of regulatory activity in the realm of consumer protection. To complete the picture, the research should be expanded to the medium–long term following the social protest. This will enable an investigation into whether, after a period of processing and assimilation, there is a change in regulatory activity and will deepen understanding of bureaucratic organizational regulatory activity as a means of managing reputational risk.

Considering this, it appears that the findings of the research indicate that "talking is one thing, doing is another." A bureaucratic organization quickly responds to public voices in the media but is in no rush to alter its regulatory behavior, nor does it make more than minimal changes in reaction to these voices.

Moreover, it seems that, in the short term, regulatory behavior of the BSD is disconnected not only from its media policy but also from reputational threat. In the long term, the risk to the BSD's reputation resulting from a bank failure vastly exceeds the reputational risk stemming from exaggerated service charges from the public. There are even those who believe that the more the BSD encourages the existence of competition in the banking system and limits its incomes, the greater the danger of bank failure. Thus, in the framework of regulatory policy, the BSD persists in avoiding a risk to stability that is its core reputation. The BSD chooses its media policy in order to deal with the reputational risk resulting from the absence of competition and the harm to the consumer.

In other words, in the short term, the bureaucratic organization may cope with reputational threat by a change in its media policy. However, when considering its priorities in its regulatory policy, the bureaucratic organization considers long-term reputation with the objective of protecting the core reputation of the organization.

NOTES

*   This chapter is based on a master's thesis submitted in fulfillment of the requirements for the degree of Master of Arts in Public Policy, under the supervision of Dr. Sharon Gilad. I would like to express my deep gratitude to Dr. Gilad for her guidance, wisdom, and patience. This work could not have been accomplished without her.

1 The Globes database was selected because it is the only free Internet database of a newspaper that specializes in economic-business matters. This database includes all of the articles that were published in the printed and Internet newspaper from 1996 on.
2 In the articles examined, no statements like "no comment" were expressed by the BSD, although those would have actually been considered as a response.
3 This means that a late response of the BSD to criticism expressed about it in an article was not coded in that same article but would appear as a separate line. It seems that this should not distort the research findings considering the sensitivity test performed by Maor and colleagues (2012), which indicated that a late response by the BSD is uncommon.
4 It should be noted that the research investigates changes in policy in a bureaucratic organization (media policy and then regulatory activity). These are not quick changes that are carried out within a few days. Therefore, it is doubtful whether deviation in the number of days from the exact dates chosen to represent the social protest is significant.
5 In a study by Maor and colleagues (2012), the BSD responded to 19 percent of the cases examined between 1998 and the first half of 2009.
6 The application of a Sobel test (Sobel 1982) yielded a significant result supporting the existence of a mediation association ($2.971, p < 0.01$). The analysis was conducted by means of Preacher and Leonardelli (2001). In addition, an analysis was conducted that does not assume normal distribution by bootstrapping. The analysis was conducted using PROCESS for SPSS (Hayes 2013).
7 The indirect effect of the social protest on the BSD's response changed from 0 to 1.5317 (S.E.$0.5204, p < 0.01$), with a margin of error between 0.2922 and 2.8680 and Sobel Test Z: 2.94 (5000 replacements) (Preacher and Hayes 2004, 2008).
8 18.6 (average reduction in the extent of coverage) times -0.082 (log odds for effect of salience on BSD's responsiveness)
9 It may be assumed that unofficial instructions did not represent change in policy but were rather individual ad hoc guidance. Thus, it does not appear that these would diminish the validity of the research.
10 The Basel measures are international standards that are published by the Basel Committee on Banking Supervision, which meets at the Bank for International Settlements (BIS). The standards are available at http://www.bis.org/bcbs/basel3.htm.
11 Indeed, it was possible that public comment or other considerations would eventually mean that these drafts would not become binding documents, but they still pointed to bureaucratic organizational intentions and to a possible change in regulatory activity.

REFERENCES

Bank of Israel. 2012. "Interim Report of the Team to Examine How to Increase Competitiveness in the Banking System—Summary, 2012." http://knesset.gov.il/committees/heb/material/data/kalkala2012–07–17–04.pdf.
Ben-Bassat, Avi. 2007. "The Authorities of Agencies Regulating Capital Markets in Israel and Its Independence." In *Regulation of the Capital Market,* edited by Avi Ben-Bassat, 21–74. Jerusalem: Israel Democracy Institute.

158   *Yael Schanin*

Blinder, Alan S., Michael Ehrmann, Marcel Fratzscher, Jakob De Haan, and David Jan Jansen. 2008. "Central Bank Communication and Monetary Policy: A Survey of Theory and Evidence." CEPS Working Paper No. 161. www.princeton.edu/~blinder/papers/08ceps161.pdf.

Carpenter, Daniel P. 1996. "Adaptive Signal Processing, Hierarchy, and Budgetary Control in Federal Regulation." *The American Political Science Review* 90:283–302.

Carpenter, Daniel P. 2001. *The Forging of Bureaucratic Autonomy: Reputations, Networks, and Policy Innovation in Executive Agencies, 1862–1928*. Princeton: Princeton University Press.

Carpenter, Daniel P. 2002. "Groups, the Media, Agency Waiting Costs, and FDA Drug Approval." *American Journal of Political Science* 46:490–505.

Carpenter, Daniel P. 2010. "Institutional Strangulation: Bureaucratic Politics and Financial Reform in the Obama Administration." *Perspectives on Politics* 8:825–846.

Carpenter, Daniel P., and George A. Krause. 2012. "Reputation and Public Administration." *Public Administration Review* 72:26–32.

Gilad, Sharon. 2012. "Attention and Reputation: Linking Regulators' Internal and External Worlds." In *Executive Government in Crisis*, edited by Martin Lodge and Kai Wegrich, 157–178. Basingstoke: Palgrave.

Gilad, Sharon, Moshe Maor, and Pazit Ben-Nun Bloom. 2013. "Organizational Reputation, the Content of Public Allegations and Regulatory Communication." *Journal of Public Administration Research and Theory*. doi: 10.1093/jopart/mut041.

Gilad, Sharon, and Tamar Yogev. 2012. "How Reputation Regulates Regulators: Illustrations from the Regulation of Retail Finance." In *The Oxford Handbook of Corporate Reputation*, edited by Michael Barnett and Tim Pollock, 320–340. Oxford: University Press.

Gormley, William T. 1986. "Regulatory Issue Networks in a Federal System." *Polity* 18:595–620.

Hood, Christopher. 2011. *The Blame Game: Spin, Bureaucracy, and Self-Preservation in Government*. Princeton: Princeton University Press.

Jennings, Will. 2009. "The Public Thermostat, Political Responsiveness and Error-Correction: Border Control and Asylum in Britain, 1994–2007." *British Journal of Political Science* 39:847–870.

Kahneman, Daniel, and Amos Tversky. 1979. "Prospect Theory: An Analysis of Decision under Risk." *Econometrica* 47:263–291.

Krause, George A., and James W. Douglas. 2005. "Institutional Design versus Reputational Effects on Bureaucratic Performance: Evidence from U.S. Government Macroeconomic and Fiscal Projections." *Journal of Public Administration Research and Theory* 15:281–306.

Maor, Moshe. 2011. "Organizational Reputation and the Observability of Public Warnings in 10 Pharmaceutical Markets." *Governance* 24:557–582.

Maor, Moshe, Sharon Gilad, and Pazit Ben-Nun Bloom. 2013. "Organizational Reputation, Regulatory Talk and Strategic Silence." *Journal of Public Administration Research and Theory* 23:581–608. doi: 10.1093/jopart/mus047.

Maor, Moshe, and Raanan Sulitzeanu-Kenan. 2013. "The Effect of Salient Reputational Threats on the Pace of FDA Enforcement." *Governance* 26:31–61.

May, Peter J., Samuel Workman, and Bryan D. Jones. 2008. "Organizing Attention: Responses of the Bureaucracy to Agenda Disruption." *Journal of Public Administration Research and Theory* 18:517–541.

Moe, Terry M. 1985. "Control and Feedback in Economic-Regulation—the Case of the NLRB." *American Political Science Review* 79:1094–1116.

Noll, Roger G.1985. "Government Regulatory Behavior—A Multidisciplinary Survey and Synthesis." In *Regulatory Policy and the Social Sciences,* edited by Roger G. Noll, 9–63. Berkeley: University of California Press.

Olson, Mary. 1995. "Regulatory Agency Discretion among Competing Industries—Inside the FDA." *Journal of Law, Economics, and Organization* 11:379–405.

Olson, Mary. 1996. "Substitution in Regulatory Agencies: FDA Enforcement Alternatives." *Journal of Law, Economics, and Organization* 12(2):376–407.

Parliamentary Inquiry Committee on Bank Fees—Summary Report, 2007. http://www.knesset.gov.il/committees/heb/docs/bank_inq.pdf.

Preacher, Kristopher J., and Andrew F. Hayes. 2004. "SPSS and SAS Procedures for Estimating Indirect Effects in Simple Mediation Models." *Behavior Research Methods* 36:717–731.

Preacher, Kristopher J., and Andrew F. Hayes. 2008. "Asymptotic and Resampling Strategies for Assessing and Comparing Indirect Effects in Multiple Mediator Models." *Behavior Research Methods* 40:879–891.

Preacher, Kristopher J., and Geoffrey J. Leonardelli. 2001. "An Interactive Calculation Tool for Mediation Tests." http://quantpsy.org/sobel/sobel.htm.

Sobel, Michael E. 1982. "Asymptotic Confidence Intervals for Indirect Effects in Structural Equation Models." *Sociological Methodology* 13:290–312.

Sulitzeanu-Kenan, Raanan. 2010. "Reflection in the Shadow of Blame: When Do Politicians Appoint Commissions of Inquiry?" *British Journal of Political Science* 40:613–634.

Wood, B. D., and Richard W. Waterman. 1991. "The Dynamics of Political Control of the Bureaucracy." *American Political Science Review* 85:801–828.

Workman, Samuel, Bryan D. Jones, and Ashley E. Jochim 2009. "Information Processing and Policy Dynamics." *Policy Studies Journal* 37:75–92.

Part III

Reputation Management in Local Government

9 Struggles behind the Scenes
Reputation Management in Swedish Hospitals

Maria Blomgren, Tina Hedmo, and Caroline Waks

INTRODUCTION

This chapter departs from the notion that organizational reputation has become a current management trend in public sector organizations. Contemporary research reveals how social entities such as universities (Engwall 2008) and hospitals (Byrkjeflot and Angell 2007; Wæraas 2008) are seeking to manage their reputation by adopting managerial concepts and models for image making, branding, and strategic communication. Public organizations, which previously were portrayed as anonymous bureaucracies, are now expected to externally 'be known for something' and communicate their uniqueness in a more coherent and managed way. This is bound to be difficult as they, by tradition, internally encompass contradictory and even inconsistent values, identities, and technologies. In addition, they are embedded in complex institutional contexts covering multiple stakeholders such as consumers and citizens, politicians, the media, etc., having different expectations concerning what constitutes a favorable reputation. Hospitals, which are highlighted in this chapter, are no exceptions.

The multi-construct of reputation (c.f. Maor, Gilad, and Ben-Nun Bloom 2012) is particularly interesting to empirically study in relation to hospitals because their formal structures are known as being very robust and uniform. Ruef and Scott (1998, 879) describe hospitals as "a taken-for-granted arrangement for providing healthcare services, which rarely depart from the conventional format." The authoritative state and the medical professions have been pointed out as particularly influential in forcing hospitals toward incorporating certain attributes into their formal structures, making them more similar and, hence, legitimate (c.f. DiMaggio and Powell 1983; Greenwood, Suddaby, and Hinings 2002; Hwang and Powell 2009). These traditional conditions of hospital contexts, together with contemporary structural and ideological changes, force them into adopting a more market- and corporate-like behavior (see, e.g., Brock, Powell, and Hinings 1999; Brunsson and Sahlin-Andersson 2000). Consequently, they find themselves at the crossroad between more conventional pressures for how to behave

164 *Maria Blomgren et al.*

in order to gain legitimacy, and expectations that force them toward acting more strategically, opportunistically, and 'uniquely'—a situation challenging the professional norms and standards in health care (Blomgren et al. 2013). Now their legitimacy is expected to a greater extent to depend on how they manage their reputation vis-à-vis their internal and external stakeholders (Byrkjeflot and Angell 2007), as they simultaneously have to consider an increasing number of expectations when doing this.

Whereas ideas and managerial practices for organizational reputation are spreading in the public sector, there is still a lack of empirical studies investigating this phenomenon (Luoma-aho 2007; Carpenter and Krause 2012; see also Wæraas and Maor in this volume). The existing body of literature has mainly focused on the drivers and effects of organizational reputation (c.f. Rindova et al. 2005) and how the forming of reputation is contingent with the expectations of multiple target audiences operating in the surrounding context (Maor in this volume). There is an obvious need for an increased understanding of how organizational reputation manifests itself in public sector organizations, how it comes about, and how it is expressed (see Wæraas and Maor in this volume). Organizational reputation in the public sector is expected to deviate from prevailing, albeit vague and multifarious definitions of 'corporate reputation,' as such organizations are embedded in specific organizational contexts being characterized by other ideals and expectations. Accordingly, this chapter takes an intra-organizational perspective on reputation management in public sector organizations. It draws attention to the internal complexity and inconsistency of such social entities, conditioning reputation management. Such a view is assumed to be necessary for increasing our knowledge of how reputation comes about and is managed in public sector organizations, and previous research has not paid explicit attention to the organizing dimension in reputation management. This chapter aims to fill this gap. It seeks to contribute to a deeper understanding of organizational reputation in public sector organizations by studying what is going on behind the scenes in the shaping and management of reputation. More concretely, it investigates how the internal complexities, interactions, and dynamics are being managed; what the management of these types of processes are conditioned by; and what implications it might have for organizational self-presentations.

Empirically, this study focuses on specific and complex organizations in the public sector, Swedish hospitals. In similarity with health care sectors elsewhere (Kjær and Svejgaard Pors 2010; Wæraas and Byrkjeflot 2012), a new form of expertise has entered into Swedish hospitals and, consequently, new procedures for how to communicate properly and to express organizational uniqueness to multiple target audiences. For instance, the number of communication workers and communication managers has expanded significantly during the last years, and their functions and positions have also shifted from being dominated by administrative, routinized day-to-day practices to becoming increasingly strategic and professional. In line with previous research (Wæraas 2008; Maor, Gilad, and Ben-Nun Bloom 2012), it is argued that these communication features are strategic tools or mechanisms for reputation management. Hence, the strategic use of communication is expected to be central for the shaping, expressing, and managing of organizational reputation. The communication work and how it is organized within these constellations of actors are empirically described and analyzed in order to capture the reputation management at Swedish hospitals.

THEORIZING ORGANIZATIONAL REPUTATION IN PUBLIC SECTOR ORGANIZATIONS

Hospitals as Complex Public Sector Organizations

Historically, there has been a basic categorical distinction between private and public organizations in social scientific research (see, e.g., Christensen et al. 2007). Public sector organizations have been treated as a 'unitary' form of organization, and they are mostly portrayed as rigid, inefficient, bureaucratic, old-fashioned, and in need of drastic change (Wæraas 2008). In reality, however, the concept hides a variety of entities with various functions and roles (Luoma-aho 2007). Moreover, there is empirical evidence revealing that the distinction between what is private and what is public is increasingly blurred (c.f. Lindberg and Blomgren 2009), making the conceptualization of these organizations even more complicated.

Hospitals refer to a distinct form of public sector organization (see, e.g., Ruef and Scott 1998; Scott et al. 2000). In classical organizational literature, hospitals are conceptualized as professional bureaucracies (Mintzberg 1983), professional arenas (Brunsson and Sahlin-Andersson 2000), or hybrid organizations (Scott 2004) that rest on two parallel organizational structures—the professional and the bureaucratic/administrative. Their semi-bureaucratic and decentralized structure is mainly controlled by medical experts who are socialized by different cognitive and normative maps (Greenwood et al. 2011). By tradition, the professionals have been acknowledged as having particular occupational positions and status in the organization, and they operate rather autonomously with considerable power to make decisions and to control their own operating practices inside the organization. In addition, professionals often engage in open negotiation and bargaining activities, on the basis of professional worth and values (see, e.g., Bucher and Stelling 1969).

Consequently, hospitals form specific, dynamic, and multiprofessional public sector organizations that are, first, dominated by large collections of autonomous professionals and, second, also include an administrative structure, which plays an important and supporting role (c.f. Mintzberg 1983). The internal complexity of hospitals then opens up for inconsistent

166 *Maria Blomgren et al.*

values and multiple identities (Wæraas 2008). Their parallel and incompatible structures open up for disagreements, competition, and tensions, making it problematic to make decisions, to coordinate, and to formulate a coherent organization-wide identity and strategy (Brock, Powell, and Hinings 1999).

Besides the internal complexity of hospitals, they also operate in pluralistic and dynamic institutional contexts covering multiple expectations from target audiences (e.g., Schneiberg and Clemens 2006; Reay and Hinings 2009; Dunn and Jones 2010). As such, hospitals are assumed to be confronted by varying and in many cases incompatible pressures for how to behave from stakeholders operating both within and outside the organization. Even though hospitals are expected to be difficult to control and coordinate, they are under pressure to change due to the spread of new administrative means for management and control. Several studies have investigated empirically how public organizations, including health care organizations, respond to the spread of new ideals and principles for how to manage their operations more properly and efficiently. A common theme in much of the empirical work having roots in institutional theory (Bentsen et al. 1999; Scott et al. 2000; Lindberg and Blomgren 2009; Wæraas and Byrkjeflot 2012) is the implications of the New Public Management (NPM) reforms in the public sector on a global scale and how these reforms have opened up for the incorporation of more business-oriented ideas, practices, and organizational elements in public administration and management.

A managerial idea that is expanding in the public sector is the value of reputation and how to properly manage and express it (Wæraas and Byrkjeflot 2012).

Organizational Reputation in the Public Sector

Interest in the contested concept of organizational reputation has increased considerably in the social sciences during the last decades, and as an outcome we find a rich variation of definitions and conceptualizations (see, e.g., Barnett, Jermier, and Lafferty 2006; Lange, Lee, and Daio 2011). Previously, the concept has mainly been investigated in the fields of marketing, management, economics, and public relations (Deephouse 1997; Fombrun and van Riel 1997; Gray and Balmer 1998; Bromley 2002; Rindova et al. 2005), It has often been synonymous with corporate reputation, even outside the private sector. A common definition of the concept in organizational studies is "the extent to which an organization is widely recognized among stakeholders in its organizational field, and the extent to which it stands out relative to competitors" (Rindova et al. 2005, 1035). Yet the phenomenon of reputation has been rather unnoticed in research in the public sector (Hutton et al. 2001; Carpenter 2002; Luoma-aho 2007; Wæraas and Byrkjeflot 2012; Maor in this volume). Recently, however, there is a growing body of

Struggles Behind the Scenes 167

research acknowledging the importance of reputational considerations also in the public sector, as well as attempts to identify what characterizes organizational reputation in public sector organizations such as local governments (Nielsen and Houlberg Salomonsen 2012), public agencies (Carpenter and Krause 2012; Maor in this volume), and health care organizations (Byrkjeflot and Angell 2007; Wæraas 2008; Wæraas and Byrkjeflot 2012).

But what is organizational reputation in the public sector? In research there is a lack of a clear conceptualization. Carpenter and Krause (2012, 26) define organizational reputation as being exogenously prescribed, and contingent on "a set of beliefs about an organization's unique or separable capacities, intentions, history and mission that are embedded in a network of multiple audiences." In similarity with findings in other fields of reputation (see, e.g., Fombrun and van Riel 1997), this definition directs attention to the uniqueness of organizations, meaning the organization's capability to "be known for something" (Lange, Lee, and Daio 2011)— that is, a particular attribute or characteristic of interest or value for the receiver that distinguishes the organization from its equals (cf. Carpenter 2001). To be known for something can then be used to generate financial and moral support, autonomy, and discretion; for protection; and to attract the 'appropriate' workforce (see Fombrun and van Riel 1997). As such, reputation uniqueness forms a valuable and powerful intangible asset for the individual organization (Deephouse 2000), but it may also be associated with considerable risk and a loss of legitimacy (Carpenter 2001; Power et al. 2009).

In organizational literature, it is highlighted that reputation assumes consistency in terms of internal values, identities, and self-representations (cf. Fombrun and van Riel 1997). Previous studies of public sector organizations reveal that such social entities by nature are multifunctional and multiprofessional, covering inconsistent values and multiple identities (Luoma-aho 2007; Wæraas 2008). Besides being exposed to shifting external expectations from various target audiences, they also suffer from shared internal values and a strong sense of identity. These specificities may lead to multiple perceptions on the question 'who are we as an organization?' Consequently, public organizations need to balance and handle these inconsistencies in an appropriate way. To unite these into a shared and desired identity expression and reputation construct might be an organizational dilemma. What might appear is a variation of choices for how to shape and manage reputation (Wæraas and Byrkjeflot 2012) and an obvious risk that "satisfying some audience subset often means upsetting others or projecting ambiguity" (Carpenter and Krause 2012, 29). This means that the complexity and pluralism surrounding public sector organizations brings considerable uncertainty and ambiguity into the process of constructing and managing reputation.

One central means facilitating the shaping, managing, and protection of reputation is the use of *strategic communication* (Wæraas 2008; Maor,

168   *Maria Blomgren et al.*

Gilad, and Ben-Nun Bloom 2012). Strategic communication is understood as a social activity that, among other things, aims at expressing the uniqueness of an organization, thereby closing the gap between its desired and actual image (Wæraas and Byrkjeflot 2012). For public organizations, it also means the intriguing issue of transforming a broad collection of identities or expectations into a single and unitary one. Strategic communication thus assumes an idealized vision of self, meaning in essence a shared set of core values and a joint vision of the organization (van Riel and Fombrun 2007). To choose a proper strategy and to speak freely with a coherent voice in public sector communication is then expected to be highly problematic due to the internal and external inconsistencies in stakeholder expectations.

To summarize, this chapter ties in with the organizational institutional research tradition (see Wæraas and Maor in this volume), treating reputation as a 'man-made' or socially constructed product that is shaped on the basis of a dynamic social activity between the reputation-seeking organization and its target audiences (c.f. Rao 1994; Power et al. 2009). The intra-organizational perspective being employed in the chapter informs us that the critical organization-specific dilemmas of public sector organizations in general, and hospitals in particular, may expose them to considerable dynamics, uncertainty, and ambiguity regarding how to properly construct and manage their reputation uniqueness. Reputation presumes consensus and the forming of a shared identity, and this may be critical in complex organizations that encompass multiple values and identities. In addition, the inherently political nature of public sector organizations such as hospitals is expected to constrain their conditions to manage reputation.

Next follows a presentation of how Swedish health care is organized, continuing with a short note of the methodological considerations shaping the study.

THE ORGANIZATION OF SWEDISH HOSPITAL CARE

The health care system in Sweden is decentralized and mainly governed at the local level by 21 relatively autonomous bodies—county councils and regions. The 17 county councils and four regional bodies are responsible for the funding and provision of health care services to the inhabitants in Sweden (Anell, Glenngård, and Merkur 2012). Health and medical care is organized into three levels: regional medical care, county medical care, and primary care.

Since the 1990s, there has been a tendency toward regional concentration through mergers of hospitals and county councils (Anell, Glenngård, and Merkur 2012). The majority of the Swedish hospitals are located in the southern and middle parts of the country and in or around the more populated and urban geographical regions such as Stockholm, Gothenburg, and Skåne. In 2012, there were 77 operating hospitals in Sweden. Most of these had public principals (71), whereas the rest (6) were privately owned. The population covers a variety of hospitals providing specialized somatic care in Sweden. We find university hospitals, county hospitals, rural hospitals, etc. The hospitals differ largely in terms of size.

The focus of this study has been the communication work at seven Swedish hospitals. In a previous study (Blomgren et al. 2013), these hospitals were identified as using the largest amount of expressive tools in their website communication. The results showed that the hospitals communicating more intensively on their websites did this in a similar and rather 'ordinary' way—the external communication was grounded in established institutions of professionalism and bureaucracy. In order to find out more about the conditions behind the communication work, seven of the expressive hospitals' communication departments were selected for more in-depth analysis. To allow for sample variety, the hospitals varied in terms of size (four large hospitals and three smaller ones), ownership (four public and three privately run hospitals), and research intensity (two university/emergency hospitals, three emergency hospitals, and two hospitals for planned care). In-depth interviews were conducted with 13 persons (one or two at each hospital), including directors of communication and communications managers, professional communicators, web managers/web strategists, and one health care director. The professional background of the communication professionals varied. Many of them, but not all, were trained communicators and/or journalists, and some had a professional background as communication consultant, as art director, or in marketing. All but one had previously been employed in the private sector, and three had previous experience working in other parts of the public sector. The interviews lasted for approximately 1–1.5 hours and concerned the role and work of communicators in the communication department. Prior to the interviews, different types of written materials produced by the organizations—such as communication policies, annual reports, internal documents, and website texts—were consulted. The interviews then used this information as a source when discussing the practice and aim of the departments' communication work. Questions asked concerned the work being performed (both activities that involved branding, including work with core values, vision statements, etc., and other types of work and how this had changed over time); the construction of web pages (which groups and how different groups were involved, trade-offs that needed to be made, the reasons for that, etc.); the relationship between internal and external communication; and the role of the communication department vis-à-vis other departments and professional groups, etc.

170 *Maria Blomgren et al.*

COMMUNICATION WORK AT SWEDISH HOSPITALS

Reputation management and strategic communication as ideas have grown stronger at the managerial level of hospitals over the past years, with the effect of a changed perception of the communication department's role and tasks. If the communication function previously had been about responding to external inquiries, it is now perceived as more future-oriented and strategic. One of the communication workers argued that this change was linked to the introduction of marketization reforms in the Swedish public sector. The reforms partly meant that public hospitals could be transformed into partial corporations owned by the county council. The interviewee described how this transformation laid the foundation for a strategic approach toward communication in the hospital. When preparing for the corporatization reform, the hospital's first business plan was formulated, including both an internal and external communication plan. This work also implied a focus on branding and a careful consideration of the hospital's image, core values, and mission statement. An intranet was developed, and the need for qualified communicators who could work more strategically and formulate texts according to the management's assignments increased. One important part of the hospital's positioning in relation to other hospitals was to be seen as 'the expert' in Swedish health care. Professionalism and openness in relation to the media was therefore essential.

In a similar vein, a communication director at another hospital described how they wanted to appear as "an emergency hospital with a focus on the broad national diseases" and that their strategic concern was to figure out how to work in order to establish such an image:

> Everything we do and say relates to our brand. Everything we post in social media, press releases . . . everything is branding. Our ads are also branding. We have to make them look good in order to appear as a serious hospital.
>
> (Director of Communications, private large hospital)

The ambition to externally communicate an organizational image was evident at other hospitals as well. At one of the large university hospitals, the work of presenting the hospital's highly specialized care on the website was in progress. The role model was Karolinska University hospital, a large, well-recognized university hospital in Stockholm.

> We have gathered all information, but it has not yet been published [on the website] . . . so it is on its way. We will arrange all the highly specialized care we provide according to . . . well Karolinska is doing this already . . . the medical specialties are arranged according to diseases and functional areas and then it becomes possible to see "these are the diseases that we are treating, this is what we are good at."
>
> (Web manager, public university hospital)

Struggles Behind the Scenes   171

Compared to how the situation was in the late 1990s, when communication plans, image making, and the formulation of core values and coherent mission statements were considered novelties in health care management, most of the respondents experienced that much had changed. Hospitals had expanded their communication departments in size and scope, also making it more strategic. Communication policies had been formulated, and the number of external communication channels had increased. Although the resources for communication had not increased in all hospitals, there was a pervading perception that the demand for communication services was steadily growing. There is "a whole new media landscape now," one communication director said and argued that the new social media channels provided many opportunities to brand the hospital but that the systems needed maintenance that required competence and resources. Five of the interviewed communication directors were members of their hospitals' management teams, whereas two were not. This reflects a more general situation for professional communicators in Sweden.

Negotiating Hospital Communication

When it comes to communicating the activities of hospitals, it is impossible to disregard the specific knowledge technology this type of organization is built on and the interpretative prerogative of the medical profession:

> Of course, in this knowledge intensive organization, and we being such a small specialty, you need to show what you can offer all the time. Make it simple and clear to the management and the co-workers at the wards and clinics otherwise you are not trustworthy. . . . It is very difficult to compete with heart-lung machines, but you have to.
> (Former Director of Communications, public university hospital)

The communication officials also saw a need to position themselves within the hospital because their role (even in projects that concerned communication) wasn't always self-evident. This meant finding ways to convince the medical professionals about the advantages of presenting things in a simpler and more patient-friendly way. A recurrent task for the communicators was to edit complex medical terminology and present it in a less academic manner on the websites. In many cases this meant that the number of authorized website editors had been reduced and that courses on 'how to write on the web' had been provided. The communication officials also needed to convince the health care professionals (especially doctors) about the advantage of a more comprehensive and clear language and that the information was targeted toward patients and not toward other medical professionals:

> The big challenge is probably not to present it in a way that makes people comprehend but rather to make the clinics accept that we don't

172 *Maria Blomgren et al.*

use a medical terminology. . . . One has to point out the advantages of our formulations and to a great extent I think we have to take on the role as being in charge. This is how it should be. This is the strategy for the website. It's aimed at the patient. It's not aimed at your colleagues!

(Web strategist, private hospital)

However, editing also required that there actually were texts to edit. Feedback from different medical subspecialties on texts that were aimed for publication on the website was not always easy to receive. One communicator described that although many health care professionals had criticized the website's design and content, they had been very reluctant to actually contribute with new texts, although it concerned their own area of responsibility. This was a problem because it was the health care professionals who 'owned' the information, and the communicators needed their input.

However, one working area within the communication officers' domain, which did not seem as contested although it did involve a lot of hard work, was the form, structure, and orientation of the website. A 'good' website should, according to the communication officers, be adapted to the needs of its primary target groups. The websites' primary target group was the patients/relatives, followed by journalists, job seekers, and other health care providers in need of making referrals to the particular hospital. One of the main objectives was to restructure the website so it was designed in accordance with the information that the patients and their relatives needed and could easily comprehend. The communicators talked about the struggle to abandon the 'internal perspective' and to 'remember who they were talking to':

No one understands what 'colposcopy' is. What you want to know is: 'my stomach hurts and I want a medical assessment, where should I go?'

(Professional communicator, private hospital)

This was a challenge because hospital communication had traditionally been designed on the basis of the science of medicine and how different clinical specialties were organized, rather than in accordance with how the patients experienced their problems. At one of the hospitals they had actually tried to construct a website that was structured according to a more patient-friendly logic, but due to the complexity of medicine it had been impossible to implement:

We tried to have a search . . . you clicked on a small figure and if you clicked at the stomach, then ten different health problems to ten different specialties emerged. You cannot present it in such a way, so you need to go back to how healthcare is organized.

(Director of Communications, private hospital)

Struggles Behind the Scenes   173

From the descriptions above we can conclude that the position and the work of the communicators as a group at the hospitals were under negotiation and also that how to best present health care services was complicated and framed by tradition. Because external communication was directed toward different stakeholders—in this case the patient and other caregivers—it wasn't obvious how to present health care on the webpage.

Another example of how the external communication of the hospitals was under negotiation could be found in the efforts to construct core values and brand names. In order to convincingly communicate what the hospital could offer and what it stood for, it was important that the organizational members shared the same view. There had been many activities going on in the hospitals in order to manifest, construct new, or modify already-existing core values, brand names, and logotypes, as well as choosing and constructing organizational stories. A majority of the hospitals had been occupied with different types of bottom-up work where discussions concerning the organization's core values were held and anchored in larger groups of employees. These meant time-consuming discussions, hosted in arenas where a wide range of subspecialties and health care professionals were represented—sometimes together with a professor specialized in ethics. The workshops concerned questions such as "who are we and for what purpose are we here?" but they also served as an arena for discussions about what the hospitals aspired to become. One of the hospitals was, by its external caregiver, perceived as the 'sophisticated' teaching hospital, superior to the smaller and less research-intensive hospitals in the periphery. This was perceived as a problem, and it was decided that one of the hospital's new core values should include being humble:

> We want to be perceived as humble, skilled and forward-looking. Humble was a word we choose because we weren't always perceived as such. . . . We were perceived as being a bit superior and arrogant so that's why we work on being humble and more receptive.
> (Director of Communications, public university hospital)

Another university hospital described how they chose not to communicate externally those core values that health care professionals already perceived as firmly anchored among the members of the organization, but rather to communicate values that expressed the desired identity of the hospital:

> It is of great importance to have core values that describe how we want to be perceived by the external environment. Two years ago we started to work on our core values. . . . We asked our co-workers to estimate which core values that prevailed today and which ones they thought should prevail in the future. . . . It was very interesting that the prevailing ones were classical and traditional ones such as professionalism, competence and excellence. Well, then we don't need to communi-

174   *Maria Blomgren et al.*

cate these! Instead we should use the ones that the co-workers want to emphasize. We should use the ones that would also push us in the right direction in a change process. So then the core values became much 'softer.' Considering that we are a teaching hospital of this caliber, it is very brave to use such a soft core value as 'compassion' but that was something that were perceived as missing today.

(Former Director of Communications, public university hospital)

However, it seemed important for the hospitals not to deviate too much from the taken-for-granted perception of what a hospital was and stood for. It was standard procedure to use established categories such as 'university hospital' and 'emergency hospital' and add minor specifications to that. At one university hospital, one wanted to be seen as 'one of the four largest university hospitals' and another one wanted to be positioned as 'an emergency hospital focusing on the broad national diseases.' Even in one of the hospitals, which actually marked a difference in relation to the others in the sense that it presented itself as a hospital resting on Christian values, it was important to emphasize that this was still a 'professional' hospital that dealt with cure and care just like 'any other hospital.'

So, from what has been described so far, we can conclude that the work with core values, brand names, etc., could be used to stimulate and gain approval for change. Even though it involved work aimed at presenting the organization externally, it also involved work aimed at presenting what one as an organization wanted to become. We have also seen how the hospitals did not want to deviate too much from the taken-for-granted perception of what a hospital is. This meant, among other things, that they used standard categories such as 'emergency hospital' and 'university hospital,' with only minor specifications when they presented themselves. In order to explain this phenomenon further, we elaborate below on the fact that the negotiations described above are also conditioned by the institutional environment of the hospital.

HOSPITAL CONTEXT CONDITIONING EXTERNAL COMMUNICATION

The conditions for a hospital's external communication are determined by the specific context in which health care services are being embedded. Part of that context includes laws and regulations that control hospitals' external communication. In the Marketing Practices Act there are general regulations about branding that concern all types of organizations and companies. There are also regulations that are aimed at different professional groups. The Swedish Medical Association has for instance developed regulations for how to market the exercise of physicians. The different county councils also constitute ethical guidelines for marketing health care in their specific

Struggles Behind the Scenes   175

regions. In the guidelines of one of the counties investigated here, it is specified that the marketing should be "genuine, objective and correct" and that it should not "misuse the public's trust in healthcare or feed from lack of knowledge." One communication manager expressed that:

> One has to be a bit humble and careful. You are not allowed to say: "come to us. You will be healthier with us than with anyone else."
> (Director of Communications, public university hospital)

Communication professionals also had to relate to, on the one hand, the law of confidentiality and on the other hand (something that is unique for the Swedish context) the principle of public access to official records. It was the task of the communication department to educate managers at different levels in matters that concerned these regulations, and over the years the idea of public transparency eventually had become more accepted in the health care context.

> The culture of healthcare has been to be rather secretive. You have patient confidentiality at the same time as you have the principle of public access to official records that makes the organization much more transparent. That's partly different traditions. I think there has been a development over the years because when I arrived to the organization for the first time in 2000 the principle of public access was perceived as not being a concern for healthcare services. One wasn't used to it. But now we deal in parallel with confidentiality and public access.
> (Director of Communications, public university hospital)

Apart from the fact that health care services are publicly financed and of great public interest, their core services (treatments and care) differ from the attributes of products in, for instance, the manufacturing industry. This uniqueness influenced the way hospitals choose or were able to brand themselves. To use a business language was not common among the hospitals. Only one hospital used the term 'customer,' but the rest rather referred to them as 'patients.' One communication director explained how they tried to avoid a 'business' language:

> We actually try to avoid using a business language when it's up to me. We are indeed operating in a 'market' one can say but we are there for a very particular reason. We want large volumes in order to be able to perform research and keep high quality because large volumes and high quality are interrelated. The more interventions you perform, the better you get at it.
> (Director of Communications, public university hospital)

A communicator in one of the private hospitals contrasted his work in communication to a similar position in the manufacturing industry. In

176 *Maria Blomgren et al.*

contrast to this, the focus in the hospital was not on traditional branding activities. Much of the external communication on the hospitals' web pages was of course directed toward patients—but not as a means to 'sell' health care services but rather as a source of information. Apart from practical information on where and how to find departments and descriptions of different procedures prior to a hospital visit, other types of information, determined by yearly circles of flu epidemics, weather conditions, holiday periods, etc., was communicated. The communication officers at the different hospitals in the county also met regularly for the purpose of finding ways to cooperate around these similar challenges.

Something that also shaped the external communication was the fact that health care services, by the public, were perceived as legitimate in its own right. High medical quality was more or less taken for granted. In surveys that some of the investigated hospitals conducted themselves, it could be concluded that the persons visiting the hospitals didn't complain about medical treatments or care. Instead, they were more concerned about waiting times, phone availability, lack of parking lots, etc. This is also established in an attitude survey from 2012 on the citizens' trust in community institutions conducted by the SOM Institute (an impartial organization at the University of Gothenburg that recurrently investigates public trust in public institutions). Health care was the community institution that the Swedish population trusted the most. The public trust in output quality thus seemed to affect what the hospitals communicated externally. Not so much effort was put into highlighting medical quality. Stories illustrating good examples of different health care interventions were indeed used as a way to inform patients on the work that was being performed at the hospitals, but this was not so much for the purpose of branding top medical quality but rather for the purpose of informing future patients and to make them feel comfortable. However, the quality of medical services would sometimes be communicated externally as a way for the organization to show their commitment to quality work. One large teaching hospital had as a routine to publish the reports that they were obliged to hand in to the Health and Care Inspectorate in cases of miss treatments (the so-called Lex Maria reports) on their web:

> It is part of our quality work. The more you report, the more you file, the more you learn from your mistake, the better it is.
> (Former Director of Communications, public university hospital)

To sum up, the idea to externally communicate health care services has grown stronger, and efforts invested in strategic communication have increased. However, the content and the form of this communication are subject for negotiations. The communication officials needed to convince the medical profession about the importance of communicating health care in a simple, accurate, and coherent way and that the main aim for this communication was targeted toward the patients. The medical profession, on the other hand, saw their peers as the main target group for communication. The construction of new and modification of old core values and brand names were also subjects for negotiations. This was an arena for establishing what one as a hospital stood for, but also what one aspired to become. The negotiations, on the other hand, were conditioned by the specific context of health care services. This knowledge-intensive context—consisting of specific rules and regulations, professional groups, and traditional hierarchies but also of institutional norms establishing health care services as part of the welfare state and as such highly trustworthy—influenced the conditions for external communication.

REPUTATION MANAGEMENT IN A HOSPITAL CONTEXT—DISCUSSION

In this chapter, the management of reputation in public sector organizations, with a focus on hospitals, has been described and analyzed. The aim of the study has been to contribute to a conceptual approach that can increase our understanding for the making, organizing, and consequences of reputation management in complex and dynamic organizational settings such as public organizations more generally and hospitals in particular. Hospitals are located at the crossroad between radical institutional transformation and intra-organizational dynamics and dilemmas. In addition, they are confronted by multiple and fragmented audiences and expectations from both inside and outside, stimulating inconsistencies, and multiple identities, complicating the management of reputation. This chapter has empirically investigated how strategic communication, with a focus on organizational web sites as an expression of a strategic organizational practice for managing reputation, is shaped and organized in a sample of Swedish hospitals. Below follows a selection of findings upon which we will further elaborate.

The Complex and Dynamic Context Conditioning Hospitals' Communication

Health care in general, and in the Swedish context in particular, is a sector that is at the heart of social welfare, providing a 'public good' attracting multiple stakes and public attention. It is also a sector that has been exposed to a trend spreading managerial ideals and ideologies for how to behave properly for being a 'good,' 'competent,' and 'qualitative' health care provider during the last decades (Bentsen et al. 1999; Dent 2003; Lindberg and Blomgren 2009). The values, beliefs, and management models entering into these complex professional bureaucracies have triggered expectations for strategic action, among other things, for how communication practices around the notion of reputation should be managed. However, the findings

178   *Maria Blomgren et al.*

of the study tell us that the hospital contexts are largely regulated and institutionalized. A nest of hard and soft rules in terms of laws, policies, and professional norms specify how hospitals should frame and express themselves toward their target audiences, what they should communicate, and where they should communicate it. As such, reputation management is a multidimensional and inherently dynamic process that responds to multiple expectations. For the communicator, strategic communication is about balancing these conditions and finding a proper solution to solve internal and external inconsistencies.

The empirical findings reveal how the 'double structure' of hospitals demand an organizing of communication work that is ideally a bottom-up process—a condition that is familiar in professional organizations where organizational authority is mainly located at the lowest organizational level (Mintzberg 1983; Scott 2004). Even though the external communication is largely a managerial or administrative practice, it strongly presumes the support of the health care professionals. The medical profession is to a high extent represented in the hospital boards, constituting the executive role in hospital management, and, as such, the professionals positioned at the strategic level of the hospital organizations promote the making of communication. At the clinical level, however, it seems like professionals are rather moderately interested in communication practices. Even though communication work opens up an arena for influence and power, it appears that those processes are rather slow and exhaustive due to intra-organizational dynamics having roots in the professionals' protection of values and beliefs, the inherent difficulties in describing and structuring medical data in an accurate and user-/patient-friendly way, and the strong links between communication and information technology. This is made explicit in the 'repackaging' and translation of complex medical information and terminology into a simpler and more user-/patient-friendly vocabulary—a process in which the medical profession has an interpretive prerogative. However, the findings also support the beginning of a new direction in the external communication of hospitals. The introduction of a media logic in communication—aimed at simplicity, accuracy, and coherence of communication—challenges the traditional logic of professionalism. Below we elaborate on how external communication could be understood both as institutionally embedded and constructed through active bargaining.

Reputation-Management Work—A Result of Institutional Embeddedness and Active Bargaining

The negotiations between communication and health care professionals could be understood as a result of how public organizations, even though constrained by institutional norms and values, act adaptively, strategically, and/or opportunistically in relation to external reputation-management demands (see Oliver 1991; Carpenter 2001; Maor in this volume).

By interpreting external communication as socially constructed in everyday interactions and through an intra-organizational approach, it becomes clear that reputation management is not exclusively about rational top-down managerial control. It is also a response to institutional pressures of the environment and a product of negotiations between actors within the organization. The hospital is a professional organization, and it is hard to ignore the very core of health care activities and the complexities of trying to communicate these activities to a lay audience. Through an intra-organizational approach—when investigating what is going on behind the scenes—strategic communication seems to a great extent to be driven by stakeholder interests. It is also subject to negotiations and dialogue between members of the organization. This fuels the discussion concerning whether organizational reputation could be managed at all (Wæraas 2008; Carpenter and Krause 2012; Maor in this volume). Our results indicate that there certainly are attempts to do so. Through strategic storytelling, good practices were being highlighted to the members of the organization as tools for organizational learning at the same time as the work with core values and brand names became foundations for activities aimed at stimulating internal legitimacy and gaining approval for change. This was particularly evident in the description of how one of the hospitals chooses not to communicate externally 'traditional' core values (i.e., professionalism, competence, and excellence) because those were perceived as already internalized among the employees. Instead, new and 'softer' core values (such as compassion) that described what the organization wanted to achieve and become were worked out. We expand on this below.

Being Special in an Ordinary Way—The Construction of the 'Humble' and 'Compassionate' Hospital

Our investigation shows that the management of reputation leans against values that are familiar for the traditional category(ies) of 'hospitals,' such as professionalism, quality, competence, etc. It is not considered as important to deviate and to be visualized as unique and special even though the 'core service' itself is assumed to be unique and different. It is also obvious that the communication does not necessarily revolve around the 'core services' of hospitals—namely, the quality of medical treatments and care—but rather around the services provided in relation to these services, such as accessibility and the way patients are encountered. Rather than being seen as unique, it was vital to dress the hospital in organizational attributes relating to 'ordinary pictures' of what is believed as constituting a 'hospital.' Consequently, we found few traces of core values being associated with a more business- and management-oriented vocabulary prescribing efficiency, competition, and distinctiveness. However, our findings revealed how core values such as 'humbleness' and 'compassion' were entering into the vocabulary of the hospitals, expressing and reflecting a mixture of old and new ideals. Professional

180 *Maria Blomgren et al.*

values related to professional skills, competence, and knowledge had not disappeared but been accompanied by relational values such as compassion, empathy, and humbleness. This supports an earlier study (see Wæraas 2010) of 25 regulatory agencies who in their core value statements simultaneously emphasized so called 'people-related' and professional values in order to distance themselves from a more authoritative and bureaucratic identity. But it also gives a hint on the future orientation of hospitals. It could be defined as a type of 'aspirational talk' (Christensen, Morsing, and Thyssen 2013)—a performative activity that has the potential to change the reality of hospitals and of how professionals perform their work. This is an area of research that demands further empirical investigations.

CONCLUSION

In correspondence with public sector organizations more generally, hospitals are currently expected to externally express and communicate their distinctiveness in a more coherent and managed way than before. Earlier studies tell us that this might be complicated because these types of organizations internally encompass contradictory and even inconsistent values, identities, and technologies. The aim of this study has been to go behind the scenes and investigate how this complexity is being managed, how the management of these types of processes are being conditioned, and what implications it might have for organizational self-presentations. Through an analysis of the communication work in seven Swedish hospitals, it could be concluded that the external communication of the hospitals has multiple roles—to provide information to target audiences such as patients, relatives, and principals; to attract coworkers; to communicate with other referral health care providers; etc. If previous research has been concerned with managerial responses to external stakeholder pressures, our findings reveal that reputation management in hospitals also refers to a complex and dynamic bottom-up process involving, and being conditioned by, negotiations within the focal organization. These negotiations are vital because they concern both what should be considered good health care quality and how this quality should be communicated externally, as well as the self-representation of the hospital. Reputation management and, ultimately, what is to be defined as good health care quality are conditioned by the institutional embeddedness of health care—i.e., rules, regulations, and professional norms on how health care is to be communicated. The parallel governing structure of health care, including the complexity of medical care and the prerogative of the medical profession, also condition reputation management. On top of that, the communication professionals play a central role in shaping the organizations' external communication. They have emerged as a group of experts on information technology and are fostered in a communication logic that includes 'filtering' complex medical data into something more 'user friendly.' The role of the communication department is dichotomized. It has both a more traditional supporting role in the professional bureaucracy that concerns information exchange and a more strategic role that concerns impression management and normative control in order to create consistent internal values and self-representations. In the interactions between different groups, both on the level of the shop floor and on the management level, the external communication of hospitals is being framed and seemingly coherent representations of the hospitals are being presented on the hospitals' web pages. We opened this chapter by saying that previous literature has underestimated the ability of public organizations to act adaptively and strategically in developing good reputations. This holds true for our investigation. In the backyard of communication work, the skills, knowledge, and interests of different groups are being played out and result in a representation of hospitals where traditional categories of hospitals such as 'knowledge intensive' and 'professional' coexist with new representations of hospitals as being 'humble' and 'compassionate.' In light of previous research on reputation management, departing from an 'economics perspective,' where organizations are viewed as being manageable and rational, our findings point to the complexity of managerial control and to outcome uncertainty.

Hospitals are often referred to as a distinct category of public sector organization—that is, a professional bureaucracy. However, professionals are not typical for only the health care sector; they can also be found in other forms of public sector bureaucracies. This suggests that the findings of organizational reputation and its management in this study could also apply to other public sector organizations. However, in order to draw such conclusions, there is a need for further empirical studies.

REFERENCES

Anell, Anders, Anna H. Glenngård, and Sherry M. Merkur. 2012. "Sweden: Health System Review." *Health Systems in Transition* 14:1–159.
Barnett, Michael, L. John Jermier M., and Barbara A. Lafferty. 2006. "Corporate Reputation: The Definitional Landscape." *Corporate Reputation Review* 9:26–39.
Bentsen, Eva, Finn Borum, Gudbjörg Erlingsdottir, and Kerstin Sahlin-Andersson. 1999. *Når styrningsambitioner møder praksis—den svære omstillning af sygehus- og sundhedsvæsenet i Danmark og Sverige.* København: Handelshøjskolens Forlag.
Blomgren, Maria, Tina Hedmo, Caroline Waks, and Peter Lundqvist. 2013. "Being Special in an Ordinary Way—Swedish Hospitals' Strategic Web-Communication." Paper presented at XVII IRSPM Conference, Prague, April 10–12.
Brock, David M., Michael J. Powell, and Christopher R. Hinings. 1999. *Restructuring the Professional Organization. Accounting, Health Care and Law.* London: Routledge.

182 *Maria Blomgren et al.*

Bromley, Dennis. 2002. "Comparing Corporate Reputations: League Tables, Quotients, Benchmarks, or Case Studies?" *Corporate Reputation Review* 5:35–50.

Brunsson, Nils, and Kerstin Sahlin-Andersson. 2000. "Constructing Organizations: The Example of Public Sector Reform." *Organization Studies* 21:721–746.

Bucher, Rue, and Joan Stelling. 1969. "Characteristics of Professional Organizations." *Journal of Health and Social Behavior* 10:3–15.

Byrkjeflot, Haldor, and Svein I. Angell. 2007. "Dressing up Hospitals as Enterprises? The Expansion and Managerialization of Communication in Norwegian Hospitals." In *Mediating Business. The Expansion of Business Journalism,* edited by Peter Kjær and Tore Slaatta, 235–263. Copenhagen: Copenhagen Business Press.

Carpenter, Daniel P. 2001. *The Forging of Bureaucratic Autonomy: Reputations, Networks and Policy Innovation in Executive Agencies, 1862–1928.* Princeton: Princeton University Press.

Carpenter, Daniel P. 2002. "Groups, the Media, Agency Waiting Costs, and FDA Drug Approval." *American Journal of Political Science* 46:490–505.

Carpenter, Daniel P., and George A. Krause. 2012. "Reputation and Public Administration." *Public Administration Review* 72:26–32.

Christensen, Lars T., Mette Morsing, and Ole Thyssen. 2013. "CSR as Aspirational Talk." *Organization* 20:372–393.

Christensen, Tom, Per Lægreid, Paul G. Roness, and Kjell A. Røvik. 2007. *Organization Theory and the Public Sector. Instrument, Culture and Myth.* New York: Routledge.

Deephouse, David L. 1997. "Part IV: How Do Reputations Affect Corporate Performance? The Effect of Financial and Media Reputations on Performance." *Corporate Reputation Review* 1:68–72.

Deephouse, David L. 2000. "Media Reputation as a Strategic Resource: An Integration of Mass Communication and Resource-Based Theories." *Journal of Management* 26:1091–1112.

Dent, Mike. 2003. *Remodelling Hospitals and Health Professionals in Europe: Medicine, Nursing and the State.* London: Palgrave.

DiMaggio, Paul J., and Walter W. Powell. 1983. "The Iron Cage Revisited: Institutional Isomorphism and Collective Rationality in Organizational Fields." *American Sociological Review* 48:147–160.

Dunn, Mary B., and Candace Jones. 2010. "Institutional Logics and Institutional Pluralism: The Contestation of Care and Science Logics in Medical Education." *Administrative Science Quarterly* 55:114–149.

Engwall, Lars. 2008. "The University: A Multinational Corporation." In *The University in the Market,* edited by Lars Engwall and Denis Weaire, 9–50. London: Portland Press.

Fombrun, Charles J., and Cees B. M. van Riel. 1997. "The Reputational Landscape." *Corporate Reputation Review* 1:5–13.

Gray, Edmund R., and John M. T. Balmer. 1998. "Managing Corporate Image and Corporate Reputation." *International Journal of Strategic Management* 31:695–702.

Greenwood, Royston, Roy Suddaby, and Christopher R. Hinings. 2002. "Theorizing Change: The Role of Professional Associations in the Transformation of Institutionalized Fields." *Academy of Management Journal* 45:58–80.

Greenwood, Royston, Mia Raynard, Farah Kodeih, Evelyn R. Micelotta, and Michael Lounsbury. 2011. "Institutional Complexity and Organization Responses." *The Academy of Management Annals* 5:317–371.

Hutton, James G., Michael B. Goodman, Jill B. Alexander, and Christina M. Genest. 2001. "Reputation Management: The New Face of Corporate Public Relations?" *Public Relations Review* 27:247–61.

Hwang, Hokyu, and Walter W. Powell. 2009. "The Rationalization of Charity: The Influences of Professionalism in the Nonprofit Sector." *Administrative Science Quarterly* 54:268–298.

Kjær, Peter, and Anja Svejgaard Pors. 2010. "Patient og styrning i det kommunikationsliggjorte hospitalvaesen." In *Ledelse gennem patienten. Nye styrningsreformer i sundhedsvæsenet,* edited by Peter Kjær and A Reff, 46–74. Copenhagen: Handelshøjskolens forlag.

Lange, Donald, Peggy M. Lee, and Ye Daio. 2011. "Organizational Reputation: A Review." *Journal of Management* 37:153–164.

Lindberg, Kajsa, and Maria Blomgren. 2009. *Mellan offentligt och privat: om styrning, praktik och intressen i hälso- och sjukvården.* Stockholm: Santérus Academic Press.

Luoma-aho, Vilma. 2007. "Neutral Reputation and Public Sector Organizations." *Corporate Reputation Review* 10:124–143.

Maor, Moshe, Sharon Gilad, and Pazit Ben-Nun Bloom. 2012. "Organizational Reputation, Regulatory Talk and Strategic Silence." *Journal of Public Administration Research and Theory* 23:581–608.

Mintzberg, Henry. 1983. *Structures in Five: Designing Effective Organizations.* Englewood Cliffs, NJ: Prentice Hall.

Nielsen, Jeppe Agger, and Heidi Houlberg Salomonsen. 2012. "Why All This Communication? Explaining Strategic Communication in Danish Local Governments from an Institutional Perspective." *Scandinavian Journal of Public Administration* 16:69–89.

Oliver, Christine. 1991. "Strategic Responses to Institutional Processes." *The Academy of Management Review* 16:145–179.

Power, Michael, Tobias Scheytt, Kim Soin, and Kerstin Sahlin. 2009. "Reputational Risk as a Logic of Organizing in Late Modernity." *Organization Studies* 30:301–324.

Rao, Hayagreeva. 1994. "The Social Construction of Reputation Certification Contests, Legitimation, and the Survival of Organizations in the American Automobile Industry: 1985–1912. *Strategic Management Journal* 15:29–44.

Reay, Trich, and C.R. Hinings. 2009. "Managing the Rivalry of Competing Institutional Logics." *Organization Studies* 30:629–652.

Rindova, Violina P., Ian O. Williamson, Antoaneta P. Petkova, and Joy Marie Sever. 2005. "Being Good or Being Known: An Empirical Examination of the Dimensions, Antecedents and Consequences of Organizational Reputation." *Academy of Management Journal* 48:1033–1049.

Ruef, Martin, and W. Richard Scott. 1998. "A Multidimensional Model of Organizational Legitimacy: Hospital Survival in Changing Institutional Environments." *Administrative Science Quarterly* 43:877–904.

Scott, W. Richard. 2004. "Competing Logics in Healthcare: Professional, State and Managerial." In *The Sociology of the Economy,* edited by Frank Dobbin, 267–287. New York: Russell Sage Foundation.

Scott, W. Richard, Martin Ruef, Peter J. Mendel, and Carol A. Caronna. 2000. *Institutional Change and Healthcare Organizations: From Professional Dominance to Managed Care.* Chicago: The University of Chicago Press.

Schneiberg, M., and Elisabeth S. Clemens. 2006. "The Typical Tools for the Job: Research Strategies in Institutional Analysis." *Sociological Theory* 24:195–227.

184 Maria Blomgren et al.

van Riel, Cees B.M., and Charles J. Fombrun. 2007. *Essentials of Corporate Communication: Implementing Practices for Effective Reputation Management.* New York: Routledge.

Wæraas, Arild. 2008. "Can Public Sector Organizations Be Coherent Corporate Brands?" *Marketing Theory* 8:205–221.

Wæraas, Arild. 2010. "Communicating Identity: The Use of Core Value Statements in Regulative Institutions." *Administration & Society* 42:526–549.

Wæraas, Arild, and Haldor Byrkjeflot. 2012. "Public Sector Organizations and Reputation Management: Five Problems." *International Public Management Journal* 15:186–206.

10 Dealing with Stakeholders in Local Government
Three Norwegian Cases of Municipal Reputation Management

Hilde Bjørnå

INTRODUCTION

Increasingly in Norway, local councils and municipal executives are taking action to improve their image and promote their reputation among relevant stakeholders. Building on a political science perspective in its analysis of municipal reputation management strategies, this chapter is about what municipalities do, how they deal with stakeholders, and the success of their reputational strategies. Local councils are perceived in this sense as actors that compete with each other in relevant arenas to attract and retain residents, businesses, and skilled workers. Success in these competitive 'games' is likely to reward political leaders with further electoral support. Two basic assumptions are made: Local councils largely want to be in control of the reputational signals they put out; they signal their 'true' attributes through actions, and they form reputations with "specific stakeholders regarding specific characteristics" (Maor in this volume; Noe 2012; Wæraas and Maor in this volume).

In most of the reputation management literature, reputation is treated as an asset in a for-profit context. Little is said, however, about reputation as an asset in the political arena and what public and political institutions do to manage and improve their reputations (Mahon and McGowan 1999; Mahon and Wartick 2003). Reputation is obviously an asset in these arenas as well (Carpenter 2010). A favorable reputation among private enterprises, tourists, and potential settlers can lead to economic advantages for municipalities (Kotler, Haider, and Rein 1993; Papadopoulos 2004). A reputation for being a good service-providing organization can lead to increased autonomy (Carpenter 2010) and increased access to qualified labor (Balmer 2001). In the political and public arenas, however, the 'product,' the 'customers,' and the 'moral standards of performance' are different and perhaps less clear than in the for-profit sector. The challenges facing local authorities are different from what we find in the for-profit sector. The questions posed in this chapter, therefore, are the following: What are the key elements of municipal reputational strategies and whom do these strategies target? What sort of expectations do council leaders have regarding stakeholder demands?

186 *Hilde Bjørnå*

How are these expectations likely to affect the design of the reputational strategies, or indeed the wider reputation of the municipality itself? We will address these questions by analyzing data obtained by studies of reputation building in three Norwegian municipalities.

Our basic contention is that stakeholders' requirements and expectations differ according to whether the operative sector is public or private. We further hypothesize that stakeholders' expectations and requirements in the public and political domains pose an additional challenge to the officials in charge of designing and implementing reputation-building strategies. Council leaders consider demands, expectations, and options and adjust their reputational framing to this context accordingly.

Municipalities have two crucial groups of stakeholders: those inside the municipality and the external stakeholders. Reputations as competitive assets require that external stakeholders, such as tourists and businesses, need to be interested in what this particular council can offer in comparison with all the others. At the same time, the council leadership needs the support of its internal stakeholders—that is, its constituency. Councils have to do well on service delivery; prove they are dynamic, innovative, and caring; and set high moral standards—even beyond what is required legally—to uphold trust and get politicians reelected. Municipalities that target only a narrow selection of external stakeholders will fail to generate broad enough support for the local council's leadership. This is unlike major companies like Volvo and Nike, which can afford to target a small niche of the global market.

In the next section I discuss the competitive importance of a favorable reputation to municipalities. I briefly outline the main elements of a traditional market-oriented reputational strategy, which I then discuss in relation to the political and public context and the demands that stakeholders have in this realm. I then present the reputational strategies of three local councils and their anticipations about stakeholder demands and requirements. I discuss challenges pertaining to stakeholder reactions and how these are likely to affect the municipality's reputation. I conclude by asking why political organizations ('democracies') face additional challenges in their attempts at reputation building compared to for-profit organizations.

THE COMPETITIVE IMPORTANCE OF REPUTATION TO MUNICIPALITIES

Reputation building is a concerted effort to highlight comparative advantages. It involves finding a way to convey to stakeholders an impression of uniqueness. It is reflected in Carpenter's definition of organizational reputation: It is a set of symbolic beliefs about the unique or separable capacities, intentions, roles, obligations, history, and mission of an organization that are embedded in a network of multiple audiences (Carpenter 2010, 33, 45).

Reputation management builds on a notion that every organization has a reputation that should and can be managed (Doorley and Garcia 2011), and if properly managed will improve the organization's competitive ability (Fombrun 1996; Fombrun and van Riel 2004). Competitive assets can be derived from several sources, by providing information about attributes not so easily observed and the ability to produce quality. Depending on the actions under consideration, different attributes of the same organization can have different reputations among different stakeholder groups. The competitive value of reputation will depend on how a targeted stakeholder group evaluates the organization on a specific measure compared to others. Stakeholders that are crucial for the organization's prosperity and survival will receive the most attention inasmuch as other organizations most likely will be attempting to influence them in a competitive game (Campbell and Alexander 1997). This corresponds to an economic view of reputation building (Rindova and Martins 2012, 20) according to which specific attributes of organizations have reputations with particular stakeholder groups: There are several firms, stakeholder groups and strategies, interdependent decisions, and sets of choices that generate specific sets of rewards (see also Wæraas and Maor in this volume). The reward of each player in the game further depends on the choices made by others, not only their own. Thus each firm and stakeholder group has to make its decision on the basis of what it anticipates other(s) will do (Elster 1989, 28–29).

An organization's reputation reflects how it is perceived across the broad spectrum of stakeholders, and this again is dependent on how it acts. At the same time, we find that "symbolic beliefs about an organization" implies that this is not completely under anyone's control and thus difficult to manipulate (Fombrun 1996, 59). How a municipality acts will affect its reputation, and what it does must align with the tasks and expectations others have of it.

Reputational Strategy Elements and Stakeholder Claims

Formulating new reputational strategies involves strategic thinking and is, first of all, an expression of the senior management's goals and what the organization aspires to be in the future (Collins and Porras 1994). It cannot, however, be based on utopian wishes and aims. Aspirations must be realistic, include some pragmatic concerns, and 'connect' with the organization's history and identity. As Collins and Porras have demonstrated, strategic visions must align with the organization's core values to be successful. An organization will therefore, it is believed, gain high esteem among its different stakeholders when it is *authentic,* behaves *consistently,* and emphasizes *transparency* (Fombrun and van Riel 2004). Fombrun and van Riel also cite *differentiation* as an element of building a strong reputation by means of distinctive slogans, trademarks, and logos, as well as corporate stories. For private sector organizations it is important to stand out from competitors

188 *Hilde Bjørnå*

and emphasize unique qualities and exceptional resources in the reputation-building processes (Deephouse 1999; Kotler and Armstrong 2004; Porter 1980). The basic argument is that organizations pursuing a differentiation strategy benefit because they face less competition. Organizations can be quite similar but not have the same strategy, and their success lies in finding and defending unexploited niches. This argument should also hold in a municipal context.

However, it is vital in reputation management to reflect not only on how to deal with authentic representation, transparency, consistency, and differentiation but also on reputation *of what and according to whom*. There are different aspects to the reputation of an organization such as a local council. Mahon and Wartick (2003) and Wigelt and Camerer (1988) distinguish between the *company* reputation, the *product* reputation, and the reputation associated with *culture*. We will be using these categories rather broadly when we look at municipal reputation strategies. Company reputation can be measured, like financial soundness and notions about corporate social responsibility. For a municipality, this notion corresponds to how it is ranked compared to others, measured on various performance indicators, and how its policies on issues like integration, public participation, and innovation stack up, along with its record as a spokesman for the business environment, i.e., perceptions of *municipality ideas*. Favorable reputations on dimensions like these will likely strengthen the council's appeal to stakeholder groups outside and inside the municipality; they may make businesses and people want to settle in the municipality and those there already to continue living there. Product reputation is associated with the *quality* of local services pertaining to welfare, education, and technical 'support.' Whereas this approach is perceived as a fairly narrow reputation strategy, it still has the potential to attract stakeholder groups from inside the municipality and elsewhere. Cultural reputation deals with the *work environment* and how it is evaluated both internally and externally. For the municipality it is a question of how the organization is perceived as an employer and the attractiveness of working in the municipal organization; a favorable reputation on this dimension is likely to attract a competent labor force. All these reputational aspects add up to the municipality's wider reputation.

A key attribute of an organization's reputation is, however, that it is embedded in a network of multiple audiences and stakeholders—that is, groups whose attitudes, beliefs, and expectations are likely to differ (Bromley 1993; Freeman 1984). Each stakeholder targets specific dimensions of reputation. In the same vein, each organization chooses which dimensions will receive priority and which will not (Carpenter and Krause 2012). For example, as opportunistic organizations, municipalities are likely to target stakeholder groups that bring benefit to the municipality, but choosing a reputational strategy and targeting a stakeholder group could also undermine its reputation among other stakeholder groups. Municipalities must define which stakeholder groups they want to attract. When that is done, they will likely set about considering their qualities and practices, needs, and challenges.

Scandinavian municipalities are likely to run into difficulties defining key stakeholders because they are expected to perform across a wide range of areas of importance to different stakeholders. Reputation building in a competitive perspective involves strategies that make a municipality stand out from other municipalities, and efforts must somehow be directed at *external* stakeholders—with the aim of attracting new inhabitants and businesses as well as skilled workers. But as political and public organizations, municipalities are likely to be continuously aware of the needs of *internal* municipal stakeholders. The local constituency will have legitimate expectations of and demand a certain standard of service delivery, municipal ideas, and local norms of social responsibility, services, and working environment. Stakeholders have a variety of demands; some may want council executives to improve services; some may want to boost the social life of the community; some may want to attract private businesses and tourism to the area; and others would like to see a more caring and socially responsible municipal organization.

In addition, local councils are constrained by stricter morals and higher performance standards than the market-oriented sector. Norwegian law requires, for instance, very high standards of transparency and openness (Offentleglova 2006). Documents, minutes, and meetings are usually open to the public. These local democracies also adhere to strong principles of inclusion and citizen participation in decision making (NOU-2006).

Finally, the moral behavior of council and political leaders will also affect reputation and political careers; untoward behavior in fiscal matters and personal scandals can cost reputations and electoral support. The room for maneuver in the municipal reputational space is thus both large and constrained.

Norwegian Municipalities and Reputation Building

Municipalities in Norway are quite small; the average population is only 10,400. There were 428 municipalities in Norway in 2013. Larger and smaller municipalities have the same powers and duties on behalf of the state. They are responsible for providing and running schools, nurseries/child care, care for the elderly and disabled, social services, and urban and local planning; they attend to environmental issues, road building and maintenance, waste disposal, water supplies, and sewers. Vested with these responsibilities, municipalities command substantial organizational and economic resources, most of which are from individual taxes and central government grants. The system encourages in-migration, which leads to an increase in the number of taxpayers. The municipalities employ about a fifth of the nation's workforce, and aggregate running costs of all municipalities is 18 percent of mainland Norway's GDP (Statistisk sentralbyrå 2013).

190   Hilde Bjørnå

They have considerable autonomy—at least in principle—as they are authorized to undertake any activity that is not prohibited by law or falls under the exclusive jurisdiction of other public authorities (Page and Goldsmith 1987). Local authorities are set up to tailor their services to local challenges.

The growth in reputation- building activity among local governments has not come out of the blue. There is a national policy on municipal reputation management. The Ministry of Municipal and Regional Development (MRD) seeks to institutionalize awareness of the value of reputation among local councils. The Ministry has set up a specialized agency, the Centre for Competence on Rural Development, which runs a 'Reputation School' for senior local politicians and council officers (http://distriktssenteret.no/omdommes-kolen/). Seventy-seven municipalities, mostly small (<5,000 inhabitants), have availed themselves of the program since its inception in 2008. The Ministry also set up a program in the fall of 2011 that is more attuned to the municipality as an employer. Twenty-two municipalities have participated in this program. The Norwegian Association of Local and Regional Authorities, regional councils, and the State Housing Bank also encourage councils to boost their public images.

There is considerable interest in reputation building among Norwegian municipalities (Wæraas, Bjørnå, and Moldenæs 2014). Their reputation-building strategies have many different aims, including improving services, facilitating economic growth and business development, attracting qualified workers, and nurturing a sense of belonging and contentedness among the population. Service integration and citizens' trust are two further targets. Councils describe their communities and needs differently. Most (70 percent) point to business partners and civil society as important stakeholders and key target groups. For the municipal leadership it is important to maintain a good reputation—not least among citizens and council or city employees (almost 100 percent), local businesses, users of municipal services, and potential employees (95 percent), and tourists (about 60 percent). It is also very important for them to be seen as successful local democracies with competent politicians (about 75 percent) (Wæraas, Bjørnå, and Moldenæs 2014). Norwegian municipalities generally involve a broad range of citizens in the reputation-building procedures, and the projects involve community meetings, surveys, and consultations with a broad range of stakeholders.

METHODS

My three cases are a fairly random sample of Norwegian municipalities, chosen from a larger pool of examined municipal reputation-building processes (in total 13). They are not necessarily representative examples of the total pool of municipal reputation building, and they differ when it comes to size, the challenges they face, and how far they have come in the process

Dealing with Stakeholders 191

of reputation building. They were chosen because each of them illustrates certain strategies and dilemmas common to the larger pool. They also illustrate the thinking and contexts of the larger pool, by and large. Because we wanted to obtain a broader picture than what a single case study could provide, we chose to study and analyze three municipalities. Three cases give breadth to our understanding of reputation building in Norwegian municipalities, although there is less room for individual presentations.

The empirical groundwork was largely done before deciding on a theoretical framework and was followed up with additional interviews, some by telephone, following a more precise definition of the research problem. The interviews were supported by information obtained from municipal documents, media reports, and statistics. I studied the reputational strategies (two municipalities) and the formal municipal plan processes dealing with reputation management (one municipality). I also looked into statements about visions and established reputational procedures on their web pages and analyzed relevant minutes from council meetings, especially in the municipality that is in the making of a formal strategy (five relevant minutes). Furthermore, I searched for service provision debates in local newspapers (one municipality) and reports about special projects and planned projects (one municipality). I also Googled local newspaper articles on reputation management as a popular trend. From Statistics Norway I obtained data pertaining to population numbers and migration, service provisions, and finances—that is, I aimed for methodological triangulation and verification of information given in interviews. I am keeping the case municipalities anonymous, as agreed to with the interviewees. Indeed, the promise of anonymity persuaded them to tell me more about the difficulties and conflicts they face in this area. Between two and four senior council officers/politicians in each municipality were interviewed for about an hour, with additional shorter interviews later. I asked about strategies, how the program evolved, the program's objectives, and which stakeholder groups they wanted to approach. I also asked them about the challenges and difficulties associated with the process. The empirical data are, however, from reputation-conscious municipalities. Such municipalities can be assumed to have a special interest in making a good impression. This may have influenced the statements the informants gave in interviews.

THREE CASES ILLUSTRATING REPUTATIONAL STRATEGIES

I begin with an examination of what municipal politicians and officials think of stakeholder demands and which difficulties they experience in handling and meeting these demands. Data on these issues will help clarify how the councils' anticipations of stakeholder demands in this particular setting shape their strategies.

Kappa Municipality

The municipal council of Kappa is close to formally adopting its reputational strategy. The population is numerically stable, but aging. They need new residents who can use municipal services; they want more taxpayers and business development. Kappa is a fairly remote community. It does have exceptional things to offer—it is a tourist hotspot thanks to excellent skiing facilities, famous festivals, and historic grounds. Another special feature is that the number of cabin or second-home owners almost equals the number of permanent residents.

They have struggled to find the right slogan. Initially it was "Kappa—a plus municipality." During the reputation design process they changed it to (in a literal translation) "Kappa—pure nature joy," which is in use today. Municipal leaders are still discussing the wording of the reputational vision (municipal documents, September 2013) but have agreed on the general direction. At the outset, the leadership strategy was to build Kappa's reputation as an attractive place for people outside the municipality, especially cabin owners:[1] It would attract new residents and boost economic growth. In an earlier interview, the mayor said, "If we manage to become the most visited municipality we will be able to get people to come and live here." According to the chief administrative officer, they were a little worried about these aims:

> The leadership has made its priorities clear, but we don't know whether all the involved groups will approve. If something is prioritized, something else will be downgraded. The important stakeholders here are the cabin owners and permanent inhabitants, and there are some differences in the interests of the two.

They started their reputational work in December 2012. Council leaders followed the Reputation School 'recipe' and started out with a survey of the citizens. The survey indicated that the municipality had a much better standing among cabin owners than the locals. They then set up a special group of municipal and business leaders. Public meetings were organized in four villages where people could say what they thought about the "most visited municipality" idea and what *they* wanted the council to include in the reputation strategy. Few of these meetings were well attended, but some ideas surfaced. They had also consulted several public institutions, including the county council and county governor, along with civil society groups. All were generally positive. "There was a lot of harmless talk," said one municipal officer, and it was the "usual people" who responded. The strategy leaders encouraged other groups of stakeholders to come forward with their wishes and expectations, and they did.

In August 2013, the mayor wrote on the web, "By knowing Kappa's positive sides, our possibilities and qualities, we now see what future development we want and what to put efforts into. . . . Business, cabin owners and the young are the groups we want to reach." Additional groups were included in fall 2013. The council needed young local people to stay as residents, as well as general business development. They found it "hard to prioritize" among the many stakeholder groups (municipal chief officer).

Council members also found it hard to find measures of success and something that made the reputation-building idea stand out as more than just a collection of loose ideas and wooly visions. They are therefore currently, at the Reputational School's bidding, making the reputational aims part of their general municipal plan. This has brought forth even more goals and objectives, as well as additional groups of stakeholders they want to target. Living conditions, regional cooperation, and skilled workers are also to be targeted. Some of these objectives are measurable, like the number of visitors. Others are not, like the ability to encourage regional cooperation. This irritates the municipal chief administrative officer, as he wants to tick off how they are progressing on the performance rankings.

Kappa now targets both external and internal stakeholders and addresses a variety of reputational matters in its strategy. They have attended to authenticity and transparency, but the strategy hardly stands out as a consistent plan. The reputation-building process proceeds by identifying and articulating the interests of the community, but the participatory approach makes it harder to formulate a clear strategy given the need to prioritize and make decisions. It is likely to be difficult to give all stakeholder groups equal attention in a reputational strategy that is differentiated and appeals to an external audience. Its competitive value may therefore be tenuous.

Beta Municipality

Beta has more experience in the business of reputation building. The vision of the city of Beta is "People in Beta should have access to information on all aspects of their municipality." This is "our way of building our reputation and saying how the municipality is run: this is the way we are doing it here," says the information director. Their vision encapsulates their reputational strategy. The council's employees are encouraged to be open about all aspects of their job; all employees also know what the vision is. The information department gives staff advice on handling the media.

Reputation building is very important and on the daily agenda, we were told. "Expectations to the municipality are formed in meetings between suppliers and users. This is about how we do our work" (information director). The strategy is based on an awareness of the generally negative opinion of the municipality a whole, combined with a positive attitude to the work of the different municipal units. "But it is in meetings between

194   Hilde Bjørnå

citizens and units that we actually build our reputation. It is no more difficult than doing a good job," says the information director. They want users to have realistic expectations of what the municipality can deliver. A member of the city council seconded this understanding of the thinking behind the strategy.

It is a clear vision; it targets staff in the various municipal departments and the public. They have had it since 2007, and it is explained to all new employees. And transparency is practiced in the municipality, we were told (by all three interviewees): "All employees have to make information available and be open to the public, they should be able to tell what is right and wrong in the organization," preferably by informing their superiors before telling the media. "Having the vision integrated into the daily life of the municipality boosts credibility," the council members tell us. The vision is handled by administrative officers, a politician told us, but is supported by the politicians, who are happy to promote it. It is "normative for what we do and the city council leader repeats it all the time" (politician).

Beta municipality has its own coat of arms, as all Norwegian municipalities do. It is cherished and used carefully. Rather than employing pollsters, marketing, or PR agencies, they publish a municipal magazine, distributed to all citizens four times per year. Here they respond to criticism in the media, and say what they do and what is happening around in the municipality: They want to promote the good stories and show that they are doing a good job. It conveys the 'corporate story' to all the citizens. But as the information director and the administrative director told us, they are criticized for boasting and accentuating achievements, while shying away from the problems in the municipality.

Their reputation strategy clearly emphasizes the value of transparency, and as they have practiced it in their work, it comes across as a fairly consistent scheme. As it is so embedded among council workers and within the organization, it must be understood as authentic and distinct. Although other municipalities have transparency as a key reputational element, only in Beta it is the main issue. It is about informing about things as they really are, as they think that this will contribute to credibility. At the same time it is quite scary: What might the employees not reveal about the council? Things might surface in the service sector that potentially could undermine the council's reputation. The vision is "obscure" and "incredibly difficult to live up to" (information director). As one official put it, "It is difficult to get a focus on the good stories in Beta because the media has a different agenda." The media want headlines, not rosy descriptions. They are well aware of the council's commitment to transparency and use it to get all manner of information that is likely to harm the municipality.

This focus on transparency is clearly intended to influence the public's experience of service availability and proximity to the municipal organization. It is an integrated policy that informs service delivery and the work environment, not so much the 'municipal ideas'—that is, it is not a recipe telling the municipal leadership what they can do in other areas to move the municipality forward. The reputational strategy is thus only partly consistent.

Whether the strategy works as intended—i.e., it facilitates the release of information about all aspects of municipal services, good or bad, and promotes the municipality's reputation—is doubtful. This is because the stakeholders do not seem to think quite like municipal leaders expect them to.

Gamma Municipality

Gamma is a medium-sized municipality, located near a large city. Its population is growing fast, and providing sufficient housing and public services is a challenge. Visitors are 'greeted' by the town's logo and municipal coat of arms. The logo stands atop the city hall entrance and can be seen on municipal vehicles and information sheets. Accompanying the logo is the vision "Gamma—a community with the power to grow and renew"—"Gamma inspires" for short. The council's reputation-building policy is both very thorough and well thought through: The strategies are detailed, expressed in very practical terms, and summarized in a small 'business card'-like folder. Here the corporate story is outlined in a figure and in a few but consistent ideas and words.

The mayor is the main figure and inventor of this strategy, and he works closely and trustfully with the chief officer. He has been in office for more than a decade and survived personal scandals. His support has, however, declined since the turn of the century. The council has worked on the strategy since 2005. "We started before anyone else," says the mayor. The vision expresses the ideals Gamma wants to be known for: "We want to create results, we listen with respect, we are enthusiastic and will support anyone who accomplishes anything, and we do what we say." It has an innovative element. "This is what we live by," say both the mayor and chief officer. "We ask every applicant for a council job whether they can adhere to these values."

The senior citizens' center, the vacation tours, and the organizing of a major building project are examples of how this vision is translated into practical politics, according to the municipal chief officer and the mayor. The senior citizens' center is a 50/50 'public/private venture' with private actors running half of it, the municipality the other half. This is an alternative to either privatizing the whole unit or keeping it public. The two units are frequently evaluated and compared to find out which performs best. The difference between them is miniscule, and they seem to learn from each other and copy each other: When the privately run part started giving the elderly waffles on Saturdays and organizing Sunday outings, the publicly

196 Hilde Bjørnå

run part did as well. The model has received much publicity and stands as an example for other municipalities, many of which have come to study it. Several municipalities have copied the idea of public/private collaboration. Another example is the vacation tours for the elderly to the Mediterranean organized by the council, whereby pensioners pay their own fare and are accompanied by a small number of municipal employees. It is very popular and includes groups of disabled people. It has also been copied by other municipalities. Gamma municipality has established "a sort of culture whereby those who criticize innovation have to prove their case" (mayor). It has made many think differently. The principle is perhaps especially apparent in the development and planning sector, where decision making proceeds at a speed unheard of in most other municipalities. Ideally, the political and administrative units in such projects should be separate, but this municipality has project groups involving both. This, we are told, shows politicians how the units are managed and spurs respect for their managerial skills. The strategy, along with many new approaches to service provision, ensures an excellent working environment, according to the chief administrative officer. The mayor says:

> I use this vision, and people in surrounding municipalities know about Gamma and what we are like; they come to me with their ideas and ask me to help them put them into practice.

Furthermore, "people know they can trust us when we say something," says the municipal chief administrative officer.

Gamma has a creative approach to what it does. Theirs is an authentic vision that stands apart from the rest, a vision that is integrated and informs political decisions, service provision, and the working environment. It is consistent. As the mayor and the coalition he leads have enjoyed a substantial majority for over a decade, this is a strategy with broad appeal. It targets external and internal stakeholders. Some have criticized the council for overspending and taking risks, criticism that may undermine the credibility of its reputation over time (opposing politician).

Summing up, we find that all these municipalities wanted to concretize the reputational idea in their reputational strategies. They did, however, have different answers to "what it is important to do" to gain a good reputation. They target different stakeholder groups. Kappa wants to include both internal and external stakeholders in a broadly oriented approach. Beta addresses internal stakeholders, whereas Gamma engages both internal and external stakeholders in a consistent strategy. We found some possible challenges with these reputational strategies. Table 10.1 sums up the key elements of the reputational strategies: the targeted stakeholder groups, the philosophy informing the reputational design, and (possible) challenges for these three municipalities.

Table 10.1 Reputational strategies and challenges in three municipalities

	Key elements	Targeted stakeholders	Thinking behind municipal leaders' approach to reputation building	Challenges with internal stakeholder thinking	Risk to municipal reputation
Kappa	Leisure activities Service	Cabin holders Business Young people	"Tourists and cabin holders are positive to our services and provide income to the municipality; we address their needs." "We also want businesses, we want young people to stay and we want skilled workers."	Might lose support among the local population if only cabin holders needs are prioritized	Likely to end up as a vague strategy that loses impact because of multiple targeted stakeholders
Beta	Transparency	Employers Citizens	"Transparency in what we do in different service sectors will give a good overall reputation."	Might be just as much evaluating on the basis of negative things surfacing	Strategy is not much externally directed— could be too narrow in a competitive game
Gamma	Innovation	Citizens Potential citizens	"A consistent innovative approach gives us a distinct and good overall reputation." "The mayor will see to this."	Few, but could be losing support because of risk taking and declining economy	Few at the moment, but very leader-dependent

198   *Hilde Bjørnå*

DISCUSSION

A good reputation is based on values that encompass future needs and current core values. It highlights the uniqueness of the organization but has to align with perceptions among core groups of stakeholders and with the reputational idea that the council wants to project. Strategies have to line up with what the municipality is and does.

As the case studies show, municipalities try to do many of the things that are done in the for-profit sector. They provide information about aspects of the municipality not so easily observed, especially in Beta. Consistent with the economics perspective on reputation (Noe 2012; Rindova and Martins 2012) as well as the political science approach to reputation (Maor in this volume; Wæraas and Maor in this volume), the municipalities all seek to control their reputational signals in a specific way, and they choose the dimension on the basis of which to build a favorable reputation (cf. Carpenter and Krause 2012). In Kappa, reputation building is about being a tourist municipality that provides good living conditions for the local population. They address cabin dwellers' and tourists' needs, and by reaching out to the population in an inclusive process, they prove that they take them and their needs seriously. In Beta, reputation building is about transparency, signaled by integrating this value in municipal staff and by providing information about municipal services, high-quality as well as lower-quality ones. Thus, Beta is concerned about its moral reputation (Carpenter and Krause 2012). Being transparent and open could be seen as a way to safeguard the interests of inhabitants as well as signaling 'honesty' as a main 'municipal idea.' Conversely, in Gamma, reputation building is about doing things differently, signaled through innovative approaches throughout the entire span of municipal activities; it has to do with a differentiated 'municipal idea' and an appearance as a competent and efficient organization (Carpenter and Krause 2012). The municipalities highlight different reputational characteristics—services, working environment, tourism, and 'ideas'—and do it in a way that reflects the regular work of the organization. They also target different 'customers,' i.e., stakeholder groups, groups essential to the municipality's ability to meet different challenges or stakeholder demands. In this process they apply the same standards as those often used in the for-profit sector (authenticity, transparency, consistency, and differentiation)—sometimes rather successfully. The exception here is Kappa. Kappa's reputational strategy is neither consistent nor distinctive.

The findings also illustrate how municipalities rationally adapt their reputation-building strategies to the demands of the stakeholders in an attempt to reap reputational rewards, although on this point the three cases choose different paths. As in the for-profit sector, the competitive value of a municipal reputation will depend on how the targeted stakeholder group evaluates municipal performance on different reputational dimensions,

Dealing with Stakeholders 199

compared to others. There are different stakeholder groups and reputational strategies, and there are interdependent decisions and sets of choices that generate specific sets of rewards. The reputational reward to each municipality depends on the choice of stakeholder groups. Council leaders know this and attempt to anticipate how key stakeholders are likely to react. Indeed, councils frequently adjust their strategies to accommodate stakeholder reactions. In our cases, some of the council's expectations were 'wrong,' and in another, steps were taken to realign the strategy.

Kappa is at the beginning of its reputation-building process and experienced that they had different reputations on different attributes among different stakeholder groups (local survey). Tourists and cabin owners were the first two groups of stakeholders the council wanted to target with its reputational strategy because they provide the income that keeps the municipality viable. By catering to their needs, Kappa could highlight the exceptional resources and assets of the municipality. The leadership subsequently found it difficult to relegate the locals down its priority list. There were conflicts of interest between locals and cabin owners, and the permanent residents wanted to be involved in the reputation-building process and shape the strategy. The support of the local population is crucial to councilors, and their demands were duly incorporated into the reputational strategy.

Beta, on the other hand, targets employers and the public, based on the belief that transparency in all service sectors will add up to a good reputation. This strategy does, however, also lead some to focus on the negative aspects of "what Beta is," and the media have been extraordinarily adept at pursuing negative stories. The receiver end of the reputational strategy is both service users and newsreaders, and the audience is likely to be influenced by positive as well as negative information. This strategy does not lead straight to a good reputation, and the strategy is perhaps too internally oriented to make the municipality stand out in the competition for skilled workers.

The findings also illustrate some crucial challenges that are likely to be shared by any reputation-seeking public sector organization concerning how the relationship between public organizations and their stakeholders shapes reputational strategies. The findings complement prior studies (e.g., Luoma-aho 2007; Wæraas and Byrkjeflot 2012) concerning the difficulties of public sector organizations of maintaining high standards of transparency and participation. For example, the principle of broad public participation poses an extra challenge in the Kappa example. It is a slow-moving process that encourages different stakeholder groups to add something to the strategy as it progresses to a final design. It can be hard for councils not to make room for suggestions because they have asked for input from an increasing number of stakeholder groups and interests targeted by the strategy. This poses a problem because the strategy is likely to end up as neither consistent nor differentiated.

200 *Hilde Bjørnå*

Furthermore, as we have seen in the Beta case, the strategy of highlighting transparency might not improve perceptions of Beta's trustworthiness and might not even represent a competitive advantage, although it is important to the moral standard of behavior expected of public organizations. The findings suggest that transparency could actually threaten reputation, which makes it even harder for this municipality to get ahead in the rivalry for skilled workers and satisfied citizens. It would also be extraordinarily difficult to modify this reputational strategy, because if they demoted transparency, they would probably reap more public suspicion and distrust.

Together, these three cases illustrate some of the intricacies of building reputation in a public sector context. Local democracies are reputation-oriented and stakeholder-sensitive when developing their reputational strategies, and tailor the content of their strategies to what they perceive as the needs and requirements of key stakeholder groups (Campbell and Alexander 1997). However, the success—and pitfalls—of their reputational campaigns depend on the relationship between the council and the stakeholders. By implication, all public organizations need to consider their special position and relationship to key stakeholder groups when they set out to build a reputation. Public sector organizations can be assumed to freely choose which reputational dimensions they want to promote; however, freely choosing to attract an exclusive stakeholder group's attention and goodwill can be detrimental.

CONCLUSION

We have seen that municipal reputational strategies differ and target different key stakeholders. The councils seek to control their reputational signals by firm actions, and they tailor the content of their strategies to what they perceive as the needs and requirements of key stakeholder groups. They do many of the things that are done in the for-profit sector. What these examples can teach us is that a consistent and authentic strategy embracing all aspects of the council's activities seems most successful, but it is difficult to accommodate the demands and expectations of targeted stakeholders. We have also seen how their choice of strategies and targets affects their competitive standing. They are not always entirely successful.

Compared to private firms, municipalities face additional challenges in the reputational process. Here we have seen that council leaders know that whereas transparency is important, too much of it in a media-saturated world society that wants juicy news is perhaps not good for a council's overall reputation. We have seen that councils know they are expected to be inclusive and encourage participation. This can, however, result in multiple and sometimes conflicting input from strong stakeholder affiliations, thrusting a wider variety of concerns into the reputation-building strategy than originally envisaged. And it is a slow-moving process. Another challenge is the potential of the chosen strategy to adversely affect other moral standards, like financial probity, or dependency on key persons; political leaders may easily change. Many of these challenges are likely to be shared by any reputation-seeking public organization and concern the special relationship between public organizations and their stakeholders.

The main challenges for these reputation-building entities derive from their being political and democratic organizations. In a democracy, leaders are obligated to address internal stakeholder needs and expectations. Reputation building in the for-profit sector is more about becoming widely known for something and achieving standing with a chosen stakeholder group outside the firm. Municipal leaders want the same for their organization: They want to compete externally, but also need local support to survive as leaders. They know they have to conform to democratic standards such as consulting with the public and promoting transparency and accountability, and also know it will affect both the content and outcome of their reputational strategies. Public consultation can make strategies too fragmented, whereas focusing overmuch on internal stakeholders can make them too narrow. This does not help them when they try to stand out from the other municipalities taking part in a competitive game.

NOTE

1 In Norway, owning a mountain cabin in another municipality is very common. It is used for recreational purposes.

REFERENCES

Balmer, John M.T. 2001. "Corporate Identity, Corporate Branding and Corporate Marketing: Seeing through the Fog." *European Journal of Marketing* 35:248–291.

Bromley, Dennis B. 1993. *Reputation, Image and Impression Management.* Chichester: John Wiley.

Campbell, Andrew, and Marcus Alexander. 1997. "What's Wrong with Strategy?" *Harvard Business Review* 75:42–51.

Carpenter, Daniel P. 2010. *Reputation and Power. Organizational Image and Pharmaceutical Regulation at the FDA.* Princeton: Princeton University Press.

Carpenter, Daniel P., and George A. Krause. 2012. "Reputation and Public Administration." *Public Administration Review* 72:26–32.

Collins, James C., and J. Porras. 1994. *Built to Last.* New York: Harper Business.

Deephouse, David L. 1999. "To Be Different, or To Be the Same? It's a Question (and Theory) of Strategic Balance." *Strategic Management Journal* 20:147–166.

Doorley, John, and Helio Fred Garcia. 2011. *Reputation Management: The Key to Successful Public Relations and Corporate Communication.* New York: Routledge.

Elster, Jon. 1989. *Nuts and Bolts for the Social Sciences.* Cambridge: Cambridge University Press.

202 Hilde Bjørnå

Fombrun, Charles. 1996. *Reputation: Realizing Value from the Corporate Image.* Boston: Harvard Business School Press.

Fombrun, Charles J., and Cees B.M. van Riel. 2004. *Fame & Fortune: How Successful Companies Build Winning Reputations.* Upper Saddle River, NJ: Prentice Hall.

Freeman, R. Edward. 1984. *Strategic Management: A Stakeholder Approach.* Boston: Pitman.

Kotler, Philip, and Gary Armstrong. 2004. *Principles of Marketing,* 10th ed. Upper Saddle River, NJ: Pearson/Prentice Hall.

Kotler, Philip., D.H. Haider, and I. Rein. 1993. *Marketing Places: Attracting Investment, Industry, and Tourism to Cities, States and Nations.* New York: Cambridge University Press.

Luoma-aho, Vilma. 2007. "Neutral Reputation and Public Sector Organizations." *Corporate Reputation Review* 10:124–143.

Mahon, John F., and Richard A. McGowan. 1999. "Corporate Reputation, Crises, and Stakeholder Management." *Global Focus* 11:37–52.

Mahon, John F., and Steven L. Wartick. 2003. "Dealing with Stakeholders: How Reputation, Credibility and Framing Influence the Game." *Corporate Reputation Review* 6:19–35.

Noe, Thomas. 2012. "A Survey of the Economic Theory of Reputation: Its Logics and Limits." In *The Oxford Handbook of Corporate Reputation,* edited by Mike Barnett and Tim Pollock, 114–139. Oxford: Oxford University Press.

NOU-2006:7. *Det lokale folkestyret i endring?* Oslo: KRD.

Offentleglova. 2006. LOV 2006–05–19 nr 16: Lov om rett til innsyn i dokument i offentleg verksemd (offentleglova).

Page, Edward, and Michael Goldsmith, eds. 1987. *Central and Local Government Relations: A Comparative Analysis of West European Unitary States.* London and Beverly Hills: Sage.

Papadopoulos, Nicolas. 2004. "Place Branding: Evolution, Meaning and Implications." *Place Branding* 1:36–49.

Porter, Michael E. 1980. *Competitive Strategy. Techniques for Analyzing Industries and Competitors.* New York: Free Press.

Rindova, Violina P., and Luis L. Martins. 2012. "Show Me the Money: A Multidimensional Perspective on Reputation as an Intangible Asset." In *The Oxford Handbook of Corporate Reputation,* edited by Mike Barnett and Tim Pollock. Oxford: Oxford University Press.

Statistisk sentralbyrå. 2013. "Statistics Norway." http://ssb.no/.

Wæraas, Arild, and Haldor Byrkjeflot. 2012. "Public Sector Organizations and Reputation Management: Five Problems." *International Public Management Journal* 15:186–206.

Wæraas, Arild, Hilde Bjørnå, and Turid Moldenæs. 2014. "Place, Organization, Democracy: Three Strategies for Municipal Branding." *Public Management Review.* doi: 10.1080/14719037.2014.906965.

Weigelt, Keith, and Colin Camerer. 1988. "Reputation and Corporate Strategy: A Review of Recent Theory and Applications." *Strategic Management Journal* 9:443–454.

11 Investigating the Politics of Reputation Management in Local Government

The Case of Denmark

Heidi Houlberg Salomonsen and Jeppe Agger Nielsen

INTRODUCTION

Reputation management represents a recent example *par excellence* of a management strategy traveling from the private to the public sector (Røvik 2007). Whereas public administration research has discussed how such a generic strategy poses challenges that are unique to public sector organizations (Luoma-aho 2007; Carpenter and Krause 2012; Wæraas and Byrkjeflot 2012), more research is needed in order to understand how these challenges present themselves in practice. Such knowledge is needed in order to bring forward the growing theoretical interest in the distinctiveness of public sector reputation and its management. Additionally, it may inform the practical performance of this type of strategy for public managers. This chapter addresses this research gap by investigating the politics of reputation management in local governments by asking: *What are the interests, roles of, and relationships between the politicians and the administration in the development of reputation strategies and performing reputation management in practice?*

The chapter combines organizational and political science perspectives on reputation (see Wæraas and Maor in this volume). In keeping with an organizational perspective, the research focus is directed at how public entities, in this case local governments, "cope with the challenges of reputation and how they develop strategies for influencing various aspects of reputation formation" (Wæraas and Maor in this volume). However, the challenges of reputation investigated here stem from one of the basic premises of political science in general: that all public organizations are ultimately led by a political authority (e.g., Moe 1990; Rainey 2009). Once established, however, bureaucracies become "players in politics" (Moe 1990, 131) and therefore "generally rational and politically conscious organizations" (Wæraas and Maor in this volume). Accordingly, the management of public organizations always involves some element of balancing politics with administrative concerns and interests. It therefore remains an empirical question as to how the relationship between the politicians and administration is organized, institutionalized, negotiated, and bargained (Hood and Lodge 2006) regarding the

204   *Heidi Salomonsen and Jeppe Nielsen*

management of public sector organizations in general and the management of local governments' reputations in particular.

An organization's reputation may be defined as "a set of beliefs about an organization's capacities, intentions, history and mission that are embedded in a network of multiple audiences" (Carpenter 2012, 34; Carpenter and Krause 2012, 26). That reputations are based on perceptions has at least five implications: First, reputations can be both positive and negative; second, the reputation of an organization does not necessarily reflect the organizational reality (Walker 2010, 369); third, reputations are always comparative in the sense that they are formed based on comparisons of the organization either with other organizations or against the organization's past performance, reputation, and so forth (Deephouse and Carter 2005, 331; Walker 2010, 370); fourth, organizations can have multifaceted reputations, as the organizational reputation may vary according to its different functions and identities as well as across different internal and external stakeholders (Walker 2010, 369); and fifth, reputations tend to have a relatively stable, enduring character (Fombrun 2012, 100). Taking this approach, we recognize that reputation management is about affecting external as well as internal stakeholders' perceptions and beliefs about an organization. Further, it is suggested that an organization's reputation develops from the

> personal experience that stakeholders have with an organization, the corporate initiatives and communications that managers make to strategically influence stakeholder perceptions, and the specialized coverage the organization receives from influential intermediaries such as analysts, journalists, and other central gatekeepers linked through social networks.
>
> (Fombrun 2012, 103)

Hence, reputation management may involve a number of different types of activities and strategies for improving stakeholders' perceptions, ranging from strategies aimed at improving the quality of the core activity to strategic communication. This chapter focuses on reputation management as a communication practice to affect perceptions and beliefs about an organization, which also has proven to be crucial for reputation management in the public sector (Maor, Gilad, and Ben-Nun Bloom 2013, 22; Gilad, Maor, and Ben-Nun Bloom 2013).

Local governments can benefit from a positive reputation in several ways. In fact, reputation management may be an integrated part of positioning them strategically and differently from their peers (Porter 1996). The literature on local governments describes how they are engaged in strategic thinking and planning (e.g., Worrall, Collinge, and Bill 1998; Parry 1999; Twewdr-Jones, Morphet, and Allmendinger 2006), but most studies have paid scant attention to local government efforts toward integrating reputation work in their strategic positioning. Although local governments should

The Politics of Reputation Management   205

not be associated with regular market dynamics (Rainey 2009), they generally benefit from increasing their population (more citizens paying taxes), recruiting the best employees, and attracting business investors. A positive reputation also makes it easier for public organizations to handle potential crises in the media and public in general (Watson 2007) and may contribute to ensuring more autonomy in the organization's relation to the political principal (Carpenter and Krause 2012, 30; Nielsen and Salomonsen 2012).

However, there are several obstacles that can hinder the realization of the promise of public sector reputation management. One key challenge for public organizations is the fact that they are led by a political authority. This poses an array of politics problems distinct to public sector organizations performing reputation management, as accounted for by Wæraas and Byrkjeflot (2012, 193–194). First, because any public organization's *raison d'être* is politically decided (Wæraas and Byrkjeflot 2012, 194), there is limited discretionary power for public managers when deciding how to develop the reputation and reputational platform (van Riel and Fombrun 2007, 136–144). Second—and strongly related to the first—public organizations cannot decide for themselves what the core activity or production is. This poses limitations not only regarding the type of identity public managers wish to attain; not necessarily in terms of changing the identity of the organization understood as " 'who we are' and/or 'what we stand for' as an organization" (Hatch and Schultz 2000, 15), but in terms of changing the identity related to what the organization actually produces, e.g., being an educational, regulative, or military organization. Moreover, the fact that the core activity is decided politically poses challenges to the organization if the service produced *per se* suffers from a bad reputation (Wæraas and Byrkjeflot 2012, 1994). Whereas the first two elements of the politics problem refer to the political nature of public organizations, the third element of the problem refers to the relation between the political authority vis-à-vis the administration and the basic premise that politics and administration in practice are less distinct from one another than prescribed in Weber's bureaucracy ideal type (1971). However, as politicians expectedly won't relinquish their control over the local government, as far as reputation management is concerned, this means that politicians may criticize public organizations if doing so serves their own individual or partisan interests (Wæraas and Byrkjeflot 2012, 194), reflecting opposing (party) political interest. Hence, just as is the case for opposing political players, politicians and their administrations do not always share the same interests or worldviews, nor do they always act in complementary relationships (Svara 2001, 2006a).

This third element of the politics problem possibly poses a serious challenge to the basic premise of reputation management: the premise of performing a consistent self-presentation and behaving loyally in relation to the same corporate identity (Fombrun and van Riel 2004). A central competence in the administrative realm is not only to serve the political principals, the government of the day, and the immediate and short-term

206 *Heidi Salomonsen and Jeppe Nielsen*

interests of such principals, but also to have "an eye to the long-term interests" (Aberbach and Rockman 1994, 461), "a vested interest in continuity," (Heclo 1975, 82), and a broader viewpoint than the politicians. Conversely, politicians may have a shorter time perspective influencing their political decisions in order to safeguard their ultimate interest: being re-elected (Moe 1990, 130). In summary, then, problems related to politics not only include the formal, institutional constraints imposed on public managers by the political nature of the context, they are also related to the political authority *per se* and the fact that (1) politicians may act in a manner to serve their own or their partisan interests, which may be against the interests of opposing political players as well as the public organizations, and (2) the relation between politicians and the administration may reflect conflicting interests and worldviews.

By identifying the interests, roles of, and relationships between the politicians and the administration in the development of reputation strategies and performing reputation management in practice, this chapter investigates this third element of the politics problem of reputation management. Accordingly, we aim at identifying the roles and relationships between politicians and their administrations in local governments.

The research question is examined in the context of Danish local government, as bodies of local government have been profoundly engaged in professionalizing their strategic communication for at least the last 5–10 years (Salomonsen 2008; Frandsen and Johansen 2009; Nielsen and Salomonsen 2012). The politics problems should also be salient in local governments, where the political level is often present in the daily management of the central parts of the local government. However, our study in Danish local governments does not lend support to expectations that the politics problem may pose a serious challenge to the basic premise of reputation management. Instead, we demonstrate how politicians and administrators appear to share the same interests and worldviews on reputation issues, and the politics of reputation management may not be characterized as a process of conflicting interests and rivalry—neither between the politicians and top civil servants nor between the political parties. We have studied the politics of reputation management relying on the opinions of our respondents as they are reflected in a survey sent to top managers in all 98 Danish local governments. Additional data sources (e.g., qualitative interviews with administrators and politicians and observations of actual reputation-management processes) might have revealed a more politicized and conflicting process.

Next, we elaborate on the concept of politics and formulate four expectations related to the politics of reputation management. Our research design and method are then accounted for, and the formal system of Danish local governments is briefly described, followed by an empirical investigation of the four expectations. The conclusion discusses the findings and limitations of the empirical study.

THEORETICAL BACKGROUND AND EXPECTATIONS: THE POLITICS OF REPUTATION MANAGEMENT

The concept of politics refers to bargaining and negotiating activities and the behavior of members of governments aimed at influencing policies, political initiatives, and strategies (Allison 1971, 163). Politics therefore refers to the negotiation of the different and potentially conflicting interests and perceptions of different political issues and strategies that the respective players bring to the decision-making process (Allison 1971, 166). Politics (or political behavior) consists of intentional acts of influence and power undertaken by groups or individuals to enhance or protect their interests when conflicting courses of action are possible. Although the concept of politics originally refers to the political actors in politico-administrative systems, public servants and managers also develop both individual and institutional interests, which may be promoted as behavior reflecting bureaucratic politics (Peters 2001). Hence, 'the politics of reputation management' is not merely about the relations (and potential political struggles) between politicians; it is just as importantly about the relations and differences between politicians and key stakeholders from the administrative realm.

Based on the premise that the separation of politics and administration is *de facto* challenged across different levels of government as well as types of democracy, a number of classical ideal types reflecting different types of pure or hybrid roles of the bureaucracy have been put forward. In particular, Aberbach, Putnam, and Rockman's (1981, 1–21) four role images, ranging from total separation (Image I) to the 'pure hybrid' form of Image IV, have been prominent in the literature on these relationships. A somewhat similar four-role model has been formulated by Svara (2001, 2006a), which is often applied in the local government context (e.g., Svara 2006a; Mouritzen and Svara 2002). Based upon differences among the dimensions of the level of control political principals have over the administration and the degree of distance and differentiation between those parties, Svara (2006a) suggests role models labeled "separated," "autonomous," "responsive," and "overlapping." In the first model, separation is the dominant norm, and the public managers identify themselves as clearly subordinated to the politicians to whom they primarily offer neutral, expertise-based counsel (Mouritzen and Svara 2002, 34), although some contribution to policy making is recognized (Svara 2006a, 957). In the autonomous administrator model, we find in its extreme form a bureaucracy not "simply beyond but in control" (Svara 2006a, 965); bureaucratic politics prevail in this model. In the responsive model, the political principal is in control, the administration providing not only neutral but also responsive counsel to the politicians and performing supportive behavior that meets "the expectations and preferences" of the politicians. In the final model ("overlapping"), we find two parties sharing "influence and functions" in an "extensive interaction" (Svara 2006a, 962).

208 Heidi Salomonsen and Jeppe Nielsen

Based upon these four ideal models, Svara forwards an argument for complementarity based upon the idea that "elected officials and administrators interact extensively but in a way that preserves the unique contributions of each set of actors" (Svara 2006a, 966). The model is primarily based on the overlapping model but reflects elements from the others, including (1) an idea of distinctness and the fact that there are limits to the degree of functional politicization of the public manager's portfolio, (2) an element of responsiveness to the political principals beyond the provision of expertise but within the limits of partisan behavior (Mouritzen and Svara 2002, 277), and (3) an element of autonomy for the administration to exert some influence on policies and strategies as well as balancing the responsiveness with responsible advice, which may go against the politicians' immediate preferences (Mulgan 2008, 347).

Might we expect complementary or possibly even conflicting relationships and interests regarding reputational strategies in the context of local government political-administrative actors? The following section formulates the expectations investigating both the relations between politicians and the politician-administration relations.

The first expectation relates to the question of whether reputation management is a process involving negotiating political players or rather an administrative exercise. It then becomes crucial to ask whether the politicians are engaged in the development of reputation-management strategies and whether they are involved in performing reputation management in practice. Thus far, investigations have demonstrated that strategic communication in local governments represents a rather depoliticized activity primarily involving the administrative realm of the local government, where the politicians are only marginally involved (Salomonsen 2011). Therefore, we expect:

> E1: Reputation management is a depoliticized activity, where the politicians' involvement in (a) developing strategies and (b) performing reputation management in practice is low compared to the involvement of the administration.

The next expectation relates to the political-administrative relationship. A more or less implicit assumption in reputation management is the idea that formulating a reputation strategy involves a process of integration and collaboration whereby different stakeholders within an organization come together in a common and shared vision of the corporate identity and story. Whether the interests and worldviews of politicians and administrators complement each other or not regarding this task remains an open question. However, we may expect some differences regarding the preferences for the identity base when choosing from among the different identities present in the local government organization (Salomonsen 2011). We may expect politicians to prefer reputation-oriented initiatives aimed at a local democratic identity, whereas public managers may primarily be preoccupied with the identity of the local government as an efficient policy-implementing body. Such differences possibly also result in differences regarding the purpose of performing reputation management. Further reputation management represents a strategy, which, as is often the case to "accomplish objectives in local governments," requires awareness for "the long-term" interests and efforts (Mouritzen and Svara 2002, 11), as it involves substantial resources not only to change a negative reputation but also to preserve and sustain a positive reputation (Byrkjeflot, Salomonsen, and Wæraas 2013). This may cause conflicts among the two types of actors when deciding upon the strategy and time frame for implementing the initiatives aimed at improving the reputation, reflecting the difference in interests for protecting "the long-term" interest compared to the politicians' "short-term" interest with respect to re-election. This may be reflected in disagreements regarding what types of initiatives are not only attractive but also necessary. Based on these reflections, we expect:

E2: The politicians and administration disagree on the (a) identities of the local governments upon which they base their reputation strategy, (b) strategies for performing reputation management per se, and (c) purposes for performing reputation management.

Due to their concerns for the "institutional health" (Aberbach and Rockman 1994, 461) of the local government beyond the interests of the local government of the day (Peters 2001), public managers may prefer that, once politically decided, the reputation strategies should be isolated from both political disagreements as well as political critique from the politicians. This may be the case when politicians are confronted with potential crises when policy areas suddenly become the object of media and central government interest, such as cases of misconduct in elderly care. In such cases, politicians may prefer a strategy of publicly criticizing the public organization, distancing themselves from the administration, but also potentially damaging the reputation even further. Here, the crucial question becomes whether reputation management therefore becomes subject to bureaucratic politics, where the administration tries to 'keep politics out.' 'Keeping politics out' may include not only strategies for reducing the role of the politician in reputation management but also strategies for ensuring the political loyalty to the reputation platform, even in times where partisan differences and disagreement could be vented in public. We therefore expect:

E3: The administration tries to 'keep politics out' of the reputation management.

Also, the politicians may have different interests *per se* and, as argued by Wæraas and Byrkjeflot (2012, 194), might decide to pursue their own or

210　*Heidi Salomonsen and Jeppe Nielsen*

partisan interests, possibly to the detriment of the reputation of the public organization. We therefore investigate whether reputation management is subject to party-oriented disagreements and politicization. Such behavior is not only expected but also perfectly legitimate in democratic institutions such as local governments (Salomonsen 2011, 213), for which reason we expect:

> E4: The politicians are loyal to the reputation and strategy only as long as it is not against their partisan interests.

The section below presents the research design and data used to empirically investigate the expectations.

RESEARCH CONTEXT, DESIGN, AND METHODS

The research is contextualized in Danish local governments, which can formally be described as a 'committee-leader form' where one person is identifiable as 'the political leader,' being in Denmark the mayor (Mouritzen and Svara 2002, 56). The political bodies consist of the city council, the executive committee, and a number of standing committees, which share the executive powers (Mouritzen and Svara 2002, 60). Although being the daily and most important political leader of the administration, the mayor's formal power is restricted, as he or she can neither interfere with nor block decisions taken by the committees (Mouritzen and Svara 2002, 60). In spite of this relatively restricted formal role, in practice the mayors constitute by far the most powerful politicians throughout the Danish local governments (Berg and Kjær 2007, 14).

The research design represents a cross-sectional design based upon quantitative data collected at a single point in time (Bryman 2004, 41). The data used to investigate the politics of reputation management include a survey sent to all *mayors* of the 98 Danish local governments, all *chief administrative officers* (the CAO of the local government being the highest appointed administrator), as well as the *persons responsible for strategic communication*. The questionnaire was submitted electronically with the help of the Rambøll Management product SurveyXact®. All of the target respondents received an email in which they were informed about the research project together with a link to an online survey.

Respondents were asked to answer questions related to each of the four expectations. Complete details of the survey questions are accessible upon request to one of the authors. We used a 5-point Likert scale to reflect the respondent's level of agreement/disagreement on most of the questions. However, we may admit that if a respondent disagrees (or agrees) completely, none of the alternatives are capable of fully reflecting this response, because the most extreme alternatives were "to a very high degree" and "to a very low degree."

To promote the efficiency and ensure the construct validity of the questions (de Vaus 2002, 96), communication managers from two local governments tested the questionnaire and provided feedback regarding both the content of the questions and the structure of the questionnaire.

The data was collected in May–June 2013. To increase the response rate, we emailed a number of reminders and made telephone calls to the respondents. In the 98 local governments, 25 percent (24) of the mayors, 56 percent (55) of the CAOs, and 59 percent (56) of the persons responsible for strategic communication have answered the survey. Due to the low response rate from the mayors, the final analysis is based solely on the feedback from CAOs and those responsible for strategic communication. We tested statistically (gamma and chi square tests) whether significant differences in the answers of the two types of actors were evident. As this was the case for only one single question (with the gamma test), we merged the two questionnaires according to the following principle: If there was a CAO, we included their answers; if not, we included the answer from the person responsible for communication. Priority was given to the CAOs due to the fact that, formally, they stand "at the interface of the political and administrative spheres" (Mouritzen and Svara 2002, 9) of the local governments and hence can be expected to give more valid answers to questions involving the politicians' behavior. Overall, we reached an 82 percent response rate, although for most of the questions it falls to around 50–60 percent.

As reflected in Table 11.1, reputation management seems highly relevant to investigate in the Danish local government. Eighty-three percent of the local governments state that they either have some kind of official reputation strategy or are working strategically with their reputation in a less formal manner.

Table 11.1 Reputation strategies in Danish local governments

The local government has a specific reputation strategy	22%* (18)**
The local government has a reputation strategy as part of a general communication strategy	24.4% (20)
The local government has no reputation strategy, but we work strategically with our reputation anyway	36.6% (30)
The local government has no reputation strategy	14.6% (12)
Others	2.4% (2)

n = 82

* Valid percent

** Number of respondents

212 *Heidi Salomonsen and Jeppe Nielsen*

Table 11.2 The year local governments began working strategically with their reputations

Year	1990 or before	1995	1998	2000	2004	2005	2006	2007	2008	2009	2010	2011
Valid percent (numbers in brackets)	5.2 (3)	1.7 (1)	1.7 (1)	3.5 (2)	3.5 (2)	1.7 (1)	10.5 (6)	22.8 (13)	14.0 (8)	7.0 (4)	8.7 (5)	19.3 (11)

$n = 57$

Further reputation management seems to have become subjected to strategic considerations since around 2006–2007 (Table 11.2), where most local governments were in the process of being merged due to a radical reform that came into force in 2007 and that significantly reduced the number of bodies of local government . During and after this reform, strategic communication in general became an institutional element in the local governments. During the reform, communication was seen as the answer to the challenges involved in merging two or more local governments; after the reform, however, it became seen as a more generic answer to a number of the challenges facing local government, including reputation management (Nielsen and Salomonsen 2012, 58–60).

EMPIRICAL FINDINGS

Each of the four outlined expectations is assessed in this section. The first expectation relates to the extent to which politicians are involved in reputation management. Our data suggest that reputation management has reached the political agenda of the local governments. Seventy-five percent (35) of the local governments state that reputation has been a specific subject for discussion in the city council within the last two years (2011–2012). And 80 percent (41) state that the reputation of the local government has been the subject of discussion in relation to other political issues in the city council within the last two years (2011–2012). In the local governments with an official reputation strategy, almost all of the cases have been politically decided by either the mayor or the city council (see Table 11.3).

But the political level is not only discussing and formally deciding the reputation of the local government and strategies for its improvement. As reflected in Tables 11.4 and 11.5, reputation management is anything but a depoliticized activity, neither when it comes to the development of strategies targeting the reputation of the local government nor when it comes to

Table 11.3 Actors who have formally decided the reputation strategy

The mayor	77.5%* (31)**
The city council	17.5% (7)
The CAO	0% (0)
Others	5.0% (2)

n = 40

* Valid percent

** Number of respondents

Table 11.4 Stakeholders' involvement in the development of reputation strategies

	To a very high degree	To a high degree	To some degree	To a low degree	Not at all	Total
Mayor	41.0* (25)**	29.5 (18)	24.6 (15)	3.3 (2)	1.6 (1)	100 (61)
City council members	4.8 (3)	32.3 (20)	41.9 (26)	17.7 (11)	3.2 (2)	100 (62)
Local government CAO	45.2 (28)	43.5 (27)	8.1 (5)	3.2 (2)	0.0 (0)	100 (62)
Other members of the executive board of the local government	21.0 (13)	53.2 (33)	19.4 (12)	4.8 (3)	1.6 (1)	100 (62)
The manager and/ or person responsible for the strategic communication of the local government	61.3 (38)	30.6 (19)	6.5 (4)	1.6 (1)	0.0 (0)	100 (62)
Other communication professionals	27.9 (17)	32.8 (20)	29.5 (18)	9.8 (6)	0.0 (0)	100 (61)
Other employees	10.0 (6)	16.7 (10)	46.7 (28)	21.7 (13)	5.0 (3)	100 (60)
External consultants	5.0 (3)	16.7 (10)	23.3 (14)	35.0 (21)	20.0 (12)	100 (60)
Citizens or other external stakeholders	5.1 (3)	27.1 (16)	40.7 (24)	18.6 (11)	8.5 (5)	100 (59)
Others	3.3 (1)	10.0 (3)	10.0 (3)	3.3 (1)	73.3 (22)	100 (30)

n = 62–30

* Valid percent

** Number of respondents

214 Heidi Salomonsen and Jeppe Nielsen

Table 11.5 Stakeholder's involvement in reputation management practice

	To a very high degree	To a high degree	To some degree	To a low degree	Not at all	Total
Mayor	46.4* (26)**	23.2 (13)	26.8 (15)	3.6 (2)	0.0 (0)	100 (56)
City council members	7.1 (4)	23.2 (13)	39.3 (22)	26.8 (15)	3.6 (2)	100 (56)
Local government CAO	39.3 (22)	33.9 (19)	21.4 (12)	5.4 (3)	0.0 (0)	100 (56)
Other members of the executive board of the local government	23.2 (13)	46.4 (26)	21.4 (12)	8.9 (5)	0.0 (0)	100 (56)
The manager and/or person responsible for the strategic communication of the local government	48.2 (27)	42.9 (24)	7.1 (4)	1.8 (1)	0.0 (0)	100 (56)
Other communication professionals	25.9 (14)	40.7 (22)	24.1 (13)	7.4 (4)	1.9 (1)	100 (54)
Other employees	9.3 (5)	14.8 (8)	48.1 (26)	22.2 (12)	5.6 (3)	100 (54)
Others	14.3 (4)	7.1 (2)	14.3 (4)	10.7 (3)	53.6 (15)	100 (28)

n = 56–28

* Valid percent

** Number of respondents

being involved with the strategic work regarding the reputation of the local government in practice.

The mayor is more involved than the other city council members (Tables 11.4 and 11.5). Reputation-management activities are primarily performed in a triangle between the mayor, the CAO, and the person responsible for strategic communication, although the other members of the executive board of the local government are also involved. Hence, the expectation that reputation management is a depoliticized activity—where the politicians' involvement in (a) developing strategies and (b) performing reputation management in practice is low compared to the administrations' involvement—is not confirmed in Danish local government. Hence, reputation management

The Politics of Reputation Management 215

appears to be a rather centralized activity, developed and performed at the apex of the local government hierarchy.

To investigate whether differences in the interests and worldviews of politicians and administrators may result in different approaches to reputation management, we expected the politicians and administrators to disagree on the (a) identities of the local governments upon which they base their reputation strategy, (b) strategies for performing reputation management *per se,* and (c) purposes for performing reputation management. As seen in Table 11.6, this expectation is not confirmed. Most respondents state that they find that the politicians and administration agree upon the identity to a very high or high degree (74.4 percent [38]), as well as the purpose of reputation management (70.5 percent [36]). However, 54.2 percent (26) of the respondents state that they agree to some degree or to a low degree with the statement that the two types of actors agree upon the strategy for performing reputation management. Whether this reflects responsiveness from the administration towards political goals regarding the reputation work and the identity upon which this is based, or maybe responsiveness from the politicians toward reputation advice from the administration, is not possible to identify on the basis of these data. But it does reflect a relationship marked by "overlapping" or "complementary"—not conflicting—interests and worldviews when it comes to reputation management. As seen in Table 11.7, we

Table 11.6 Agreement/disagreement between the politicians and administration in reputation management

	To a very high degree	To a high degree	To some degree	To a low degree	To a very low degree	Total
To what extent do the politicians and administration agree on the *identity*, which is the basis of the reputation management?	21.6* (11)**	52.9 (27)	23.5 (12)	2.0 (1)	0.0 (0)	100 (51)
To what extent do the politicians and administration agree on the *purpose* of reputation management?	17.6 (9)	52.9 (27)	25.5 (13)	3.9 (2)	0.0 (0)	100 (51)
To what extent do the politicians and administration agree on the *strategy* of reputation management?	6.3 (3)	39.6 (19)	50.0 (24)	4.2 (2)	0.0 (0)	100 (48)

n = 51–48

* Valid percent

** Number of respondents

216 Heidi Salomonsen and Jeppe Nielsen

Table 11.7 Agreement/disagreement between the politicians on reputation management

	To a very high degree	To a high degree	To some degree	To a low degree	To a very low degree	Total
To what extent do the politicians agree on the *identity*, which is the basis of reputation management?	20.4* (10)**	49.0 (24)	26.5 (13)	2.0 (1)	2.0 (1)	100 (49)
To what extent do the politicians agree on the *purpose* of reputation management?	14.0 (7)	44.0 (22)	38.0 (19)	2.0 (1)	2.0 (1)	100 (50)
To what extent do the politicians agree on the *strategy* of reputation management?	8.7 (4)	19.6 (9)	58.7 (27)	10.9 (5)	2.2 (1)	100 (46)

n = 50–46

* Valid percent

** Number of respondents

find an almost identical picture for a supplementary analysis of reputation management among the politicians, although there tends to be slightly more disagreement. Most respondents state that they find to a very high or a high degree that the politicians agree upon the identity (69.4 percent [34]) and purpose of reputation management (58 percent [29]). Seventy-one percent (33) of the respondents state that they support to some degree or to a low or very low degree the statement that the politicians agree on the reputation-management strategy.

The next expectations are based on the concept of bureaucratic politics (Peters 2001), the idea being that the administration prefers to minimize the involvement of the politicians in the reputation-management process, partly to avoid potential politicization in the form of political disagreements regarding—and disloyalty to—the local government's reputation and its management. Hence, we expected that the administration would try to 'keep politics out' of the reputation management; not necessarily to safeguard and preserve their self-interest but to safeguard the continuity in reputational work.

As reflected in Table 11.8, this expectation is not confirmed. Of the respondents, 92 percent (46) find it important for politicians to be involved in the local government work with its reputation, whereas 80 percent (40) find that working with the reputation of the local government should be performed in close collaboration between the politicians, public managers, and communication professionals. However, many of the respondents agree to a very high, high, or some degree with statements saying that the development of strategies (84 percent [42]) and the practice of working strategically

Table 11.8 Should politicians be involved in reputation management?

	To a very high degree	To a high degree	To some degree	To a low degree	To a very low degree	Total
It's important that politicians are involved in the local government's work with its reputation	42.0* (21)**	50.0 (25)	8.0 (4)	0.0 (0)	0.0 (0)	100 (50)
The development of strategies targeting the reputation of the local government should primarily be performed by public managers and communication professionals	8.0 (4)	20.0 (10)	56.0 (28)	6.0 (3)	10.0 (5)	100 (50)
The practice of working strategically with the reputation of the local government should primarily be performed by public managers and communication professionals	6.0 (3)	34.0 (17)	44.0 (22)	6.0 (3)	10.0 (5)	100 (50)
It's important that the work with the reputation of the local government is performed in close collaboration between the politicians, public managers, and communication professionals	38.0 (19)	42.0 (21)	18.0 (9)	0.0 (0)	2.0 (1)	100 (50)

n = 50

* Valid percent

** Number of respondents

with the reputation of the local government (84 percent [42]) are primarily to be performed by public managers and communication professionals. This may indicate that some political involvement is important but that the strategic aspects of developing and performing reputation management should be left to the administration. This reflects elements of the autonomous administrative role, but not in the sense of public managers working separately, 'beyond control,' and without political guidance and collaboration, as 98 percent (49) find it to a very high, high, or some degree that this should be performed in close collaboration with the different parties, reflecting the complementary relationship.

As reflected in Table 11.9, however, does the analysis support the dimension that expects the administration to prefer political loyalty to the

218 *Heidi Salomonsen and Jeppe Nielsen*

Table 11.9 Should reputation management be subject to (party) politics?

	To a very high degree	To a high degree	To some degree	To a low degree	To a very low degree	Total
The local government's work with its reputation should not be a subject for politics	14.9* (7)**	38.3 (18)	25.5 (12)	14.9 (7)	6.4 (3)	100 (47)
It's important that the politicians remain loyal to the local government's work with its reputation, no matter what	29.2 (14)	35.4 (17)	29.2 (14)	4.2 (2)	2.1 (1)	100 (48)
It's okay that the politicians sometimes disagree on the local government's strategic work with its reputation	8.0 (4)	34.0 (17)	40.0 (20)	12.0 (6)	6.0 (3)	100 (50)
It's okay that the politicians sometimes criticize the local government in public, even though it damages its reputation	6.0 (3)	12.0 (6)	38.0 (19)	14.0 (7)	30.0 (15)	100 (50)
There's a formal agreement prescribing that the politicians should remain loyal to the local government's work with its reputation despite partisan disagreements	7.3 (3)	14.6 (6)	31.7 (13)	29.3 (12)	17.1 (7)	100 (41)
There's an informal agreement prescribing that the politicians should remain loyal to the local government's work with its reputation despite partisan disagreements	9.8 (4)	22.0 (9)	46.3 (19)	14.6 (6)	7.3 (3)	100 (41)

n = 50–41

* Valid percent

** Number of respondents

reputation platform, even in times where partisan differences and disagreement could be involved and salient?

Moreover, Table 11.9 shows that most of the respondents prefer that the local government's work with its reputation does not become a subject for politics—'politicized'—and it is vital for the politicians to remain loyal to the reputation and not criticize the local government in public if doing so involves a risk of damaging the reputation of the local government.

The Politics of Reputation Management 219

However, some political disagreement and discussion is accepted. Further, many of the local governments have an informal agreement prescribing that the politicians should remain loyal to the local government's work with its reputation regardless of partisan disagreements.

To further investigate the potential differences between the politicians *per se,* we expected that politicians are loyal to the reputation and strategy only as long as it is not against their legitimate partisan interests. We investigate this expectation as questions of both the degree to which the politicians remain loyal to the local government's reputation as well as whether disagreement in relation to reputation management reflects partisan interests. As reflected in Table 11.10, more than half of the respondents find to a very high or high degree that the politicians are loyal to the work with the reputation when discussing the reputation of the local government in public (54.9 percent [28]). Conversely, around half of the respondents support to a high or some degree the statement that the politicians are loyal to the work with the reputation only as long as it supports their partisan interests (54 percent [27]). Further, more than half of the respondents agree to a very high, high, or some degree that political disagreements when working with reputation reflect partisan differences (63.8 percent [30]). However, this should be read against the fact that there is, in general, a prevailing agreement between the politicians on this subject matter (cf. Table 11.7 above). Hence, the expectation that reputation management may be subject to party politicization is only partly confirmed.

Table 11.10 Political loyalty in reputation management

	To a very high degree	To a high degree	To some degree	To a low degree	To a very low degree	Total
The politicians are loyal to the work with reputation when discussing the reputation of the local government in public	15.7* (8)**	39.2 (20)	37.3 (19)	5.9 (3)	2.0 (1)	100 (51)
The politicians are loyal to the work with reputation only as long as it supports their partisan interests	0.0 (0)	18.0 (9)	36.0 (18)	22.0 (11)	24.0 (12)	100 (50)
Political disagreements when working with reputation reflect partisan differences	2.1 (1)	21.3 (10)	40.4 (19)	23.4 (11)	12.8 (6)	100 (47)

n = 51–47

* Valid percent

** Number of respondents

220 *Heidi Salomonsen and Jeppe Nielsen*

DISCUSSION AND CONCLUSION

This chapter has investigated the politics of reputation management in the context of Danish local government by asking: What are the interests, roles of, and relationships between the politicians and administration in the development of reputation strategies and performing reputation management in practice? This section reviews the empirical results and discusses how this study contributes to the literature on reputation management in the public sector.

Overall, whereas we expected reputation management in local governments to be loaded with potential conflicting interests, our empirical data does not support such a scenario. Instead, politicians and administrators seem to share the same interests or worldviews on reputation issues, for which reason the general conclusion from the survey is that reputation management is performed in practice as a 'complementary' relationship (Svara 2006a) and in an alliance across partisan differences and between politicians and the administration rather than in a process of vested conflicting interest and politics of individualistic maneuvering. Top politicians are engaged in (and seem to agree on) reputation-management practices, and they work in close collaboration with the CAO and those responsible for strategic communication. Accordingly, reputation management does not appear as a depoliticized activity in which the administration tries to 'keep politics out'; instead, administrators emphasize the usefulness of having politicians engaged in the local government work with its reputation, although they prefer (at least to some degree) keeping party politics out and politicians remaining loyal to the reputation work in the local government. Further, although politicians often formally decide on strategies, the strategizing and practical performance of reputation management should, according to the CAOs, be performed by the administration.

However, whether this conclusion is valid for all public organizations is questionable. Essentially being politically decided, the formal organization of public organizations at least ideally reflects politicians' structural choices (Moe 1990). These choices sometimes include various forms of "agency strategies" (Hood 2011) and "agencification reforms" (Verhoest et al. 2012) whereby politicians create more or less autonomous agencies insulated from political authority to secure policy continuation despite shifts in governments (Moe 1990, 124) and to delegate blame downward in the ministerial hierarchy (Hood 2011, chapter 4; see also Hood 2002). Seen from the perspective of the politicians in central government, a certain degree of distance to and a 'separated,' or distinct, relationship with the public agencies are preferable in times of policy failure and other types of public and media crises and storms, where 'scapegoats' are needed (Hood 2011, 18). Further, as noted by Maor (this volume, 25):

> [T]he protection of an agency reputation may be an interest shared by both agency and elected officials in normal practice. When the latter are

The Politics of Reputation Management 221

faced with the successful building of an agency reputation among pivot groups, and recognize the derived electoral benefits for themselves, they may do their utmost to maintain the agency's good reputation.

Interference in reputational work and strategies on the agency level would therefore be not only irrelevant but also irrational as long as the agency performs according to political preferences and the agency strategy is effective in terms of shielding the politicians in the blame games performed in such times. Although 'agencies' represents a very diverse group of public organizations, both in terms of functions, formal and de facto autonomy, and so forth (Pollitt et al. 2001), we may expect that agency heads, like their colleagues in local government, prefer to avoid public criticism and blame from their political principals in central government. Further, some of the agency heads who strategically cultivate their reputation to multiple actors in their environment (Carpenter and Krause 2012; Gilad, Maor, and Ben-Nun Bloom 2013; Maor and Sulitzeanu-Kenan 2013; Maor, Gilad, and Ben-Nun Bloom 2013) would often prefer not having politicians interfering in their reputation-related efforts, as such interference may pose a threat to their reputation as being formally autonomous and in a 'separated' relationship from their political principal. Hence, a too close and 'overlapping' relationship could pose a threat to both their 'performative' and 'moral' reputations (Carpenter and Krause 2012, 27) in relation to stakeholders other than their political principals. The most rational choice for agency heads in many cases would therefore be to not only 'keep politics out' but also 'keep politicians out' of their reputational work.

The analysis contributes to a political science perspective on reputational efforts, as it first expands the empirical domain and investigates not agencies but local governments and then indicates that the rational choice of relationship between the political authority and the public administration may differ depending on contextual factors, such as the level of government as well as the formal and actual functioning of the politico-administrative relationship of, in this case, local governments. Further, the analysis contributes to the organizational perspective's discussion of the distinctiveness of the reputation-related work carried out by public sector organizations. Here, our analysis generally does not lend support to the expectation that the politics problem proposed by an organizational perspective may pose a serious challenge to the basic premise of reputation management, the premise of performing a consistent self-presentation, and behave loyally in accordance to the same corporate identity. More generally, we may conclude that—seen from the perspective of the administration—there are no distinct challenges for the performance of reputation management related to the politics aspects of the public sector reputation management investigated here in the local government context. This is not to say that reputation management is not subject to politicization in the sense of politicians—and especially the mayor—being involved in the processes and that there are not some political

222 *Heidi Salomonsen and Jeppe Nielsen*

interests, discussions, and disagreements (also of a party political nature) involved. It is just not conceived as a major challenge by the CAOs.

So how can we understand this 'missing' politics problem in the context of Danish local government? There are at least four possible explanations.

First, related to the polity of the local governments, we expected the politics problems to be salient in local governments, but there might be some counterarguments to this statement. Local government in Denmark is generally characterized by a relatively high degree of consensus decision making among the different political parties (Berg and Kjær 2007, 14). This may help explain why our data did not demonstrate disagreement between politicians *per se* in reputation practices. It is also worth mentioning that there is a pragmatic relationship between politicians and the administrative realm in Danish local government (Mouritzen and Svara 2002, chapter 9), which among other things implies that the 'complementary' model largely based on the 'overlapping roles,' although prevailing in many local governments across Western democracies (Mouritzen and Svara 2002; Svara 2006b), is especially evident in the Danish context (Svara 2006a, 969). This is among others reflected in the fact that Danish CAOs are "the least anxious" to be in "the political room" and provide political sparring regarding policy (Mouritzen and Svara 2002, 168). This may help explain why reputation management is largely without political and administrative struggles. This has implications in terms of generalizability, as not all local governments may be characterized as consensual (regarding the relationships among the politicians) and pragmatic and overlapping (regarding the relationships between the politicians and the administration). Further, this relatively prominent role of the mayor corresponds with existing studies of the political leadership of the Danish mayors (Berg and Kjær 2007), but whether this is also the case for other types of local governments with less prominent political leadership and different politico-administrative relations is a subject on which only future comparative research can shed light.

Second, related to the governance structure of local governments vis-à-vis the central government, we have witnessed an increase in the central steering and subsequently a reduction in the autonomy of local government in terms of making political priorities in the Danish context (Christensen 2013, 161). This means that the 'policy domain' for partisan interests to be articulated is narrowed, which may add to the consensual nature of the local governments. It may also add to the common interest of politicians both across partisan differences and across politics and administration to preserve or strive for a good reputation in order to secure the autonomy remaining for the local governments.

Third, related to the policy area, both politicians and local government administrators may have obvious interests in ensuring a good reputation, albeit for somewhat different reasons. For politicians, a good reputation may help recruit more citizens (which means more revenue through taxes) and eventually lead to re-election. For CAOs, a good reputation may attract better employees and serve as a general integrating and positive identification mechanism among the public officials in the administrative part of the organization. Further, representing a novel and potentially innovative idea, reputation management may not only be attractive to the local government CAOs, as they have a "vested interest in continuity," but also give "greater emphasis to policy innovation" (Svara 2006a, 963) than as recognized in the traditional theoretical ideas of administrative behavior and preferences. Hence, a good reputation may serve a number of the interests forwarded in the theoretical section across the political and administrative realms of local government organizations.

Fourth, related to the research design, other data sources could have proven useful in identifying possible politics problems. We have relied solely on survey data from an administrative perspective, but data from politicians could lead to alternative conclusions in keeping with Allison's idea of "where you stand depends on where you sit" (1971, 176). Generally speaking, however, the same patterns identified in this analysis are revealed in the answers we received from the one-fifth of the mayors, although there were minor differences. For instance, they tend to agree more with the statement that it is all right that politicians sometimes criticize the local government in public, even though doing so damages its reputation. Reputation management may be more subject to politics if the politicians are asked. However, the general patterns are the same. Although standing on each side of the politico-administrative divide, the CAOs and mayors seem to share many interests and views on reputational issues regarding local government. This may be due to the fact that they share a position at the apex of the local government organization, for which reason investigations further down the hierarchy may reveal that reputation strategies, identity, and reputational platforms may be not only translated (Wæraas and Sataøen 2014) but also subject to bureaucratic politics by public officials placed further away from city hall.

In sum, the main findings in this chapter can be summarized as follows: (1) Whereas recent research suggests that politics problems may pose a serious challenge to the promise of public sector reputation management, our study does not support such a view; and (2) the analysis of Danish local government demonstrates that reputation management is by no means a depoliticized activity that is decoupled from the political authority.

REFERENCES

Aberbach, Joel D., Robert D. Putnam, and Bert A. Rockman. 1981. *Bureaucrats and Politicians in Western Democracies.* Cambridge: Harvard University Press.

Aberbach, Joel D., and Bert A. Rockman. 1994. "Civil Servants and Policy Makers: Neutral or Responsive Competence?" *Governance* 7:461–9.

Allison, Graham T. 1971. *Essence of Decision: Explaining the Cuban Missile Crisis.* Boston: Harper Collins Publishers.

224 Heidi Salomonsen and Jeppe Nielsen

Berg, Rikke, and Ulrik Kjær. 2007. *Lokalt politisk lederskab.* Odense: Syddansk Universitetsforlag.

Bryman, Alan. 2004. *Social Research Methods,* 2nd ed. Oxford: Oxford University Press.

Byrkjeflot, Haldor, Heidi Houlberg Salomonsen, and Arild Wæraas. 2013. "Offentlig omdømmeledelse." In *Offentlig ledelse og strategisk kommunikation,* edited by Heidi Houlberg Salomonsen, 149–168. Copenhagen: DJØF Publishing.

Carpenter, Daniel P. 2010. "Institutional Strangulation: Bureaucratic Politics and Financial Reform in the Obama Administration." *Perspectives on Politics* 8:825–846.

Carpenter, Daniel P. 2012. *Reputation and Power.* Princeton/Oxford: Princeton University Press.

Carpenter, Daniel P., and George A. Krause. 2012. "Reputation and Public Administration." *Public Administration Review* 72:26–33.

Christensen, Jørgen G. 2013. "Det administrative system." In *Det demokratiske system,* edited by Jørgen Grønnegård Christensen and Jørgen Elklit, 130–170. Copenhagen: Hans Reitzels Forlag.

Deephouse, David L., and Suzanne M. Carter. 2005. "An Examination of Differences between Organizational Legitimacy and Organizational Reputation." *Journal of Management Studies* 42:329–60.

de Vaus, David. 2002. *Surveys in Social Research,* 5th ed. London: Routledge.

Fombrun, Charles J. 2012. "The Building Blocks of Corporate Reputation: Definitions, Antecedents, Consequences." In *The Oxford Handbook of Corporate Reputation,* edited by Michael L. Barnett and Timothy G. Pollock, 94–113. Oxford: Oxford University Press.

Fombrun, Charles J., and Cees B.M. van Riel. 2004. *Fame and Fortune: How Successful Companies Build Winning Reputations.* Upper Saddle River, NJ: Prentice Hall.

Frandsen, Finn, and Winni Johansen. 2009. "Institutionalizing Crisis Communication in the Public Sector: An Explorative Study in Danish Municipalities." *International Journal of Strategic Communication* 3:102–115.

Gilad, Sharon, Moshe Maor, and Pazit Ben-Nun Bloom. 2013. "Organizational Reputation, the Content of Public Allegations, and Regulatory Communication." *Journal of Public Administration Research.* doi: 10.1093/jopart/mut041.

Hatch, Mary J., and Majken Schultz. 2000. "Scaling the Tower of Babel: Relational Differences between Identity, Image, and Culture in Organizations." In *The Expressive Organization,* edited by Majken Schultz, Mary Jo Hatch, and Mogens H. Larsen, 11–35. Oxford: Oxford University Press.

Heclo, Hugh. 1975. "OMB and the Presidency: The Problem of 'Neutral Competence.'" *The Public Interest* 38:80–98.

Hood, Christopher. 2002. "The Risk Game and the Blame Game." *Government and Opposition* 37:15–37.

Hood, Christopher. 2011. *The Blame Game: Spin, Bureaucracy and Self-Preservation in Government.* Princeton/Oxford: Princeton University Press.

Hood, Christopher, and Martin Lodge. 2006. *The Politics of Public Service Bargains: Reward, Competency, Loyalty—and Blame.* Oxford: Oxford University Press.

Luoma-aho, Vilma. 2007. "Neutral Reputation and Public Sector Organizations." *Corporate Reputation Review* 10:124–43.

Maor, Moshe, and Raanan Sulitzeanu-Kenan. 2013. "The Effect of Salient Reputational Threats on the Pace of FDA Enforcement." *Governance* 26:31–61.

Maor, Moshe, Sharon Gilad, and Pazit Ben-Nun Bloom. 2013. "Organizational Reputation, Regulatory Talk, and Strategic Silence." *Journal of Public Administration Research and Theory* 23:581–608.

The Politics of Reputation Management 225

Moe, Terry M. 1990. "The Politics of Structural Choice: Toward a Theory of Public Bureaucracy." In *From Chester Barnard to the Present and Beyond,* edited by Oliver E. Williamson, 116–153. New York/Oxford: Oxford University Press.

Mouritzen, Poul E., and James H. Svara. 2002. *Leadership at the Apex: Politicians and Administrators in Western Local Governments.* Pittsburgh: University of Pittsburgh Press.

Mulgan, Richard. 2008. "How Much Responsiveness Is Too Much or Too Little?" *The Australian Journal of Public Administration* 67:345–56.

Nielsen, Jeppe A., and Heidi H. Salomonsen. 2012. "Why All This Communication? Explaining Strategic Communication in Danish Local Governments from an Institutional Perspective." *Scandinavian Journal of Public Administration* 16:69–89.

Parry, Ken W. 1999. "Enhancing Adaptability: Leadership Strategies to Accommodate Change in Local Government Settings." *Journal of Organizational Change Management* 12:134–57.

Peters, Guy B. 2001. *The Politics of Bureaucracy: An Introduction to Comparative Public Administration,* 5th ed. London/New York: Routledge.

Pollitt, Christopher, Karen Bathgate, Janice Caufield, Amanda Smullen, and Colin Talbot. 2001. "Agency Fever? Analysis of an International Policy Fashion." *Journal of Comparative Policy Analysis: Research and Practice* 3:271–90.

Porter, Michael E. 1996. "What Is Strategy?" *Harvard Business Review* 74:61–78.

Rainey, Hal G. 2009. *Understanding and Managing Public Organizations,* 4th ed. San Francisco: Jossey-Bass.

Røvik, Kjell A. 2007. *Trender og translasjoner. Ideer som former det 21. århundrets organisasjon.* Oslo: Universitetsforlaget.

Salomonsen, Heidi H. 2008. "Kommunernes kommunikation i et politisk og administrativt perspektiv." In *De nye kommuner i støbeskeen,* edited by Karin Hansen, Bente Bjørnholt, Peter Kragh Jespersen, Jeppe Agger Nielsen, and Heidi H. Salomonsen, 147–190. Copenhagen: DJØF Publishing.

Salomonsen, Heidi H. 2011. "Strategisk kommunikasjon og organisasjonsidentiteter i kommunene." In *Substans og fremtreden. Omdømmehåndtering i offentlig sector,* edited by Arild Wæraas, Haldor Byrkjeflot, and Svein Ivar Angell, 202–219. Oslo: Universitetsforlaget.

Svara, James H. 2001. "The Myth of the Dichotomy: Complementarity of Politics and Administration in the Past and Future of Public Administration." *Public Administration Review* 61:176–83.

Svara, James H. 2006a. "Introduction: Politicians and Administrators in the Political Process—A Review of Themes and Issues in the Literature." *International Journal of Public Administration* 29:953–76.

Svara, James H. 2006b. "The Search for Meaning in Political-Administrative Relations in Local Government." *International Journal of Public Administration* 29:1065–90.

Tewdwr-Jones Mark, Janice Morphet, and Philip Allmendinger. 2006. "The Contested Strategies of Local Governance: Community Strategies, Development Plans, and Local Government Modernization." *Environment and Planning A* 38:533–551.

van Riel, Cees B.M., and Charles J. Fombrun. 2007. *Essentials of Corporate Communication: Implementing Practices for Effective Reputation Management.* Oxon/New York: Routledge.

Verhoest, Koen, Sandra Van Thiel, Geert Bouckaert, and Per Lægreid, eds. 2012. *Government Agencies: Practices and Lessons from 30 Countries.* Basingstoke: Palgrave and Macmillan.

Wæraas, Arild, and Haldor Byrkjeflot. 2012. "Public Sector Organizations and Reputation Management." *International Public Management Journal* 15:186–206.

Wæraas, Arild, and Hogne L. Sataøen. 2014. "Trapped in Conformity? Translating Reputation Management into Practice." *Scandinavian Journal of Management* 30:242–253.

Walker, Kent. 2010. "A Systematic Review of the Corporate Reputation Literature: Definition, Measurement, and Theory." *Corporate Reputation Review* 12:357–87.

Watson, Tom. 2007. "Reputation and Ethical Behaviour in a Crisis: Predicting Survival." *Journal of Communication Management* 11:317–84.

Weber, Max. 1971. *Makt og byråkrati.* Oslo: Gyldendal.

Worrall, Les, Chris Collinge, and Tony Bill. 1998. "Managing Strategy in Local Government." *International Journal of Public Sector Management* 11:472–93.

12 Municipal Reputation Building in Norway

A Reputation Commons Tragedy?

Arild Wæraas

INTRODUCTION

It is generally acknowledged that a strong reputation has beneficial implications for public sector organizations. However, for many public organizations, a pressing challenge is a huge discrepancy between aspirations and realities. Whereas they would benefit from a strong and favorable reputation, they suffer varyingly from being members of a category that is associated with negative characteristics and stereotypes. Public sector organizations are often depicted as slow, wasteful, too big, rigid, not sufficiently transparent, and inefficient. Bureaucracy bashing, declined levels of trust in government, and a negative media image are evidence of a problematic reputation that is common to all public sector organizations simply because they are 'public.' This is not to say that some public organizations cannot enjoy strong reputations. In general, though, the negative shared reputation represents a challenge for public organizations that seek to improve their reputations for two reasons: First, when organizations are tarred with the same brush, negative spillover effects reduce the possibility of building unique and strong reputations. As long as an organization is defined and understood as part of the public sector, it inherits the negative image associated with this category. Second, improving the shared reputation is beneficial for those that share it, but few incentives exist to do so. Because everyone benefits from an improved shared reputation without participating, while outcomes are highly uncertain, free-riding issues may block initiatives.

When a reputation is shared and affects all category members in general, it serves as a common resource, here referred to as a reputation commons (Barnett 2007, 2006; King, Lenox, and Barnett 2002). Such commons can exist at various levels of the public sector. In this chapter, the focus is on the local level of government. More specifically, I explore the significance of the regional reputation commons for Norwegian municipalities as they seek to improve their own reputation vis-à-vis the other municipalities of the region to which they belong. Rising stakeholder expectations combined with intense negative media scrutiny (local newspapers in Norway are widely read

228 *Arild Wæraas*

and tend to be critical); problems of funding services; competition for new residents, tourists, and business; and stereotypes of the municipal worker as lazy, procrastinating, and anything but service-minded stimulate Norwegian municipalities to try to stand out and be perceived as different from their peers (Wæraas 2014). Regions, however, tend to have stronger reputations than the municipal sector in the sense that they are associated with more specific and positive characteristics and experiences. Spanning across county borders, regional reputations are not tied to a specific level of government, but more to the unique history, traditions, and local attractions of the area. As a result, municipalities within a region may benefit from collaborative work to build a strong and unique reputation for the region in the hopes of achieving a positive spillover effect. Their mutual involvement in doing so is referred to as a *communal* strategy in this chapter, as opposed to a strategy of differentiation (King, Lenox, and Barnett 2002; Barnett 2006).

Taking an organizational perspective as its point of departure (see Wæraas and Maor in this volume), this research rests on the assumption that reputations are socially constructed at different levels, yet affect each other in significant ways. I first seek to determine to what extent Norwegian municipalities experience a reputation commons at the regional level. Using the results from a survey of 171 municipal chief administrative officers, I examine the perceived interdependencies between municipalities and regions concerning their reputations. Are the reputations of Norwegian municipalities believed to be contingent on the region's reputation? Second, I analyze how the municipalities respond to the problem of shared reputations. If there is a reputation commons at the regional level, how do municipalities deal with it? Do they seek to differentiate? Or, do they engage in communal strategies?

The results from this study contribute to our understanding of reputation in the public sector by providing evidence of how one entity's reputation may depend on the reputation of others. Obviously, this is likely to be the case in the private sector as well (King, Lenox, and Barnett 2002; Barnett 2006). Every firm is a member of an industry and may have to balance its own reputation-building efforts against the needs of the entire industry. However there is an important difference between the public and the private sector context in this respect: Public organizations have traditionally been intertwined at various levels such that it is difficult to see where one begins and the other ends (Christensen et al. 2007). This reinforces the ties between the entities and increases the probability and impact of a reputation commons. Furthermore, whereas private firms are expected to stand out from each other and provide unique services in order to be attractive in a market, public organizations within a sector or category are generally expected to provide similar services. If they differentiate too much from what is acceptable, their legitimacy may be at stake (c.f. Deephouse 1999). Consequently, a shared reputation may exert stronger constraints and pressures on public sector organizations than on private firms.

THE REPUTATION COMMONS

The concept of *commons* is derived from studies of exhaustible and scarce resources such as pasture lands, water, fish, and nonrenewable energy sources such as coal and oil. A commons exists if the resource is shared and all actors are equally affected by its exploitation. An individual member benefits from depleting the resource, but the costs of doing so are shared by all members. As a result, the resource is subject to "the tragedy of the commons" (Hardin 1968, 1243).

A shared reputation serves as a common resource in the sense that it affects all sector members. When stakeholders cannot distinguish between the character, actions, or relative performance of each member, all of them are judged equally by stakeholders and are equally vulnerable to criticism and sanctions. Errors committed by one member are likely to hurt everyone's reputation. As observed by Fombrun and Rindova (2000, 85), "a crisis for one is a loss for all; your reputation is partly your company's, partly your industry's." Although each member can take action to improve its reputation, the benefits of doing so are only marginal if stakeholders cannot distinguish effectively between category members. As a result, each member will profit from either seeking to stand out, or from engaging in a communal strategy aimed at improving category reputation (Barnett 2006). If the communal strategy is the preferred one, benefits are non-excludable in the sense that all members of the category will benefit from the improved reputation regardless of their participation. This opens up the possibility of free-riding.

Just like firms within an industry often find that their reputation is tied to other firms (King, Lenox, and Barnett 2002; Barnett 2006; Barnett and Hoffmann 2008; Fombrun and Rindova 2000), Norwegian municipalities must concern themselves with the fate they share with each other concerning their reputation. It is possible to distinguish between two levels at which the municipal reputation commons makes itself known—the municipal sector as a whole, and the clusters of municipalities that form regions.

The municipal sector in Norway serves as a reputation commons for all its 428 municipalities in the sense that they all share the same reputation as members of the Norwegian municipal sector. Any municipality that seeks to improve its own reputation does so as a member of the sector and is constrained or enabled by the sector's reputation, depending on its strength. Perceived similarity enhances the impact of the reputation commons. Although there is great variation between municipalities in terms of size, geographic location, industry density, and demographics, it is difficult for them to stand out with a different identity. Most municipalities are small, rarely in the national news, and rather unknown, and therefore easy to label and define by virtue of simply 'being' a municipality. The more similar they are, the more likely they are to be tarred by the same brush.

The significance of the reputation commons is further enhanced by the impact of errors committed by one member. If a municipality acts

230   *Arild Wæraas*

unethically, fails to adhere to laws and regulations, or engages in flawed financial ventures, the entire sector's reputation could be at stake. This possibility is captured by the Ministry of Municipal and Regional Development in a report to the Norwegian Storting (national parliament):

> Recently, the media has begun to focus on multiple undesired incidents in some municipalities. . . . In some cases, questions of inappropriate mix-up of functions, 'camaraderie,' 'bribery,' and possible corruption of a punitive character. . . . Even if these incidents may turn out not to be many, such cases may generate serious damages to the reputation of the entire municipal sector.
>
> (St. prp. nr 61 2005–2006, 45, author's translation)

Municipalities also face a reputation commons at the regional level, which is the object of attention for this study. Neighboring municipalities, regardless of their county affiliation, share the same reputation by virtue of their geographic location. Spillover effects from region to municipality can be assumed to be just as strong as those from the entire municipal sector, if not stronger, because each municipality is more strongly connected to its region than to the municipal sector. The effect can be either positive or negative depending on the region's reputation and the strength of the association between the municipality and the region. This means that municipalities inevitably 'inherit' some of the reputation that is associated with the region. This can, but does not have to, be problematic: Because regions tend to have stronger reputations and are often more well known than the municipalities themselves, municipalities within a region may use the affiliation with that region as a way of building their own reputations and attracting visitors, residents, and businesses. For example, on its web page, the Norwegian municipality of Sør-Aurdal describes itself as "a vigorous municipality in Valdres." Valdres is the region in which Sør-Aurdal is located. Whereas Valdres is a well-known tourism, hiking, skiing, and fishing destination, Sør-Aurdal is unknown to most people in Norway. As a result, it could accrue reputational benefits by becoming associated with Valdres. However, Sør-Aurdal shares the affiliation with Valdres with the other five municipalities in the region (Etnedal, Nord-Aurdal, Vang, Vestre Slidre, and Øystre Slidre), making the regional reputation a common resource for all of them.

Although there can be positive spillover effects from region to municipalities, there may also be negative spillover effects from one municipality to others if this municipality's reputation is weakened. Each municipality, therefore, must consider how closely it wants to build its reputation with its region, how much it wants to invest in a positive reputation for the region—taking into account the possibility that others may not contribute—or whether it should seek an independent reputation by differentiating from the others.

Municipal Reputation Building in Norway 231

In this chapter the focus is on the significance of the reputation commons at the regional level, and on how the municipalities handle the challenge of managing their own reputations while at the same time sharing a reputation with others. As noted previously, there are two strategies for coping with the reputation commons problem that potentially may be followed. The first is the *differentiation* strategy, whereby a municipality seeks to stand out. If this strategy is successful, one municipality's mistake will not spill over to its peers. As noted by King et al., organizations can 'privatize' the reputation commons by "building 'mental fences' in the minds of stakeholders to distinguish the reputation of individual or groups of firms" (King, Lenox, and Barnett 2002, 399). They may, for example, reveal individual performance, team with credible stakeholders, make credible investments, adopt standardized reporting, or form an elite club.

The other strategy is to engage in communal strategies. A communal strategy is undertaken to enhance the reputation of the entire region. Barnett (2006; Barnett and King 2008) notes that the more similar organizations within a group are to each other, the more resources they will tend to allocate to communal strategy. This could be the case with Norwegian municipalities, and perhaps especially within a region. Municipalities that belong to the same region may find that their reputation is tied much more strongly to each other than to the municipal sector as a whole. However, in these cases, free-riding issues may be significant. A municipality that does not participate in the communal strategy of improving regional reputation will still benefit from other actors' efforts because of potentially positive spillover effects. If a communal strategy cannot be agreed upon, the result may be a reputation commons tragedy in the sense that everyone is interested in reaping the benefits of a strong reputation, but no one does anything to cultivate it.

METHODOLOGY

Empirical Context

Municipalities are not just geographical places but also agents of the national government in carrying out public policies. The responsibilities of Norwegian municipalities are given and regulated by the Norwegian Municipal Act (1993), whose purpose is to secure a "rational and efficient use of municipal and county interests within the framework of the national community" (§1). However, Norwegian municipalities are free to undertake any activity that is not mentioned in the Norwegian Municipal Act and develop strategies to meet goals independently of it.

The municipal organization is typically characterized by an administrative hierarchy where the chief administrative officer sits at the top and commands a diversified municipal organization that serves to implement

232   Arild Wæraas

policies enacted by the municipal council. About 40 percent of the Norwegian municipalities have introduced a two-level administrative structure based on extensive horizontal specialization in performance units that have both budget and human resources responsibilities (Hovik and Stigen 2008). The performance units report directly to the chief administrative officer (hence the two-level structure). Examples of performance units include day care centers, primary and secondary schools, and nursing homes. The larger the municipality in terms of population, the more complex the municipal administration concerning the number of performance units. Municipalities that have not implemented a two-level administrative structure usually have a sectorial structure based on major purpose, such as education, roads, water, and sewage, parks and recreation, and so on (Gulick 1937), or a combination of performance and sector units.

The municipal sector is an important part of Norway's public sector. About a quarter of the workforce is employed in the municipal sector, and municipal service production amounts to about 15 percent of the total Norwegian economy (Hanssen, Klausen, and Vabo 2006). For Norwegian citizens it is virtually impossible not to be a user of municipal services in one way or another. The legitimacy of the entire municipal sector is thus affected by the sum of reputations of the municipalities.

During the last 10 to 15 years, Norwegian municipalities have become increasingly interested in the benefits of a strong reputation (Wæraas 2014; Wæraas, Bjørnå, and Moldenæs 2014). There are several reasons for this interest. First, competitive pressures have become more pronounced. Even though they are not competing in a defined market characterized by supply and demand, structural arrangements and transparency regimes established by the Norwegian central government offer incentives for Norwegian municipalities to outperform each other. The most important measure is KOSTRA ("Municipality-State-reporting"), a national statistics database to which all municipalities are required to reveal how they perform on multiple indicators. For example, municipalities must report the share of children having day care center access, per capita expenditures on primary schooling, share of medical doctors per capita, and so on. The database not only serves as a benchmarking system in the sense that Norwegian municipalities can see how they compare to their peers, but also provides information for the general public, businesses, and the media that can be used for purposes of reputation rankings and decision making.

Second, municipalities suffer from a reputation paradox in the sense that most users of municipal services are generally satisfied, yet do not attribute the municipality as a whole with a positive reputation (Hind et al. 2001; Nesheim 2006; Wæraas and Bjørnå 2011). This paradox is characteristic of not only the municipal sector but also the public sector as a whole (Katz et al. 1977; Goodsell 2004). As a result, any municipality has much to gain from improving its reputation. Norwegian municipalities currently participate in educational programs to learn how to build an attractive municipality

Municipal Reputation Building in Norway 233

reputation, define their distinct reputation platforms, organize reputation seminars and slogan contests, have their reputation measured and defined on various reputation rankings, and seek help from external communication consultancies to define municipal identity and desired reputation—in competition with their peers (Wæraas 2014; Wæraas, Bjørnå, and Moldenæs 2014).

For Norwegian municipalities, reputation management revolves around two important aspects. On the one hand, it is about developing a strong track record with the local population. Having a strong reputation for providing good services means developing an internal focus on how to improve services and connect with the residents and their needs. On the other hand, municipal reputation management is also about influencing the social construction of reputation through initiatives that shape overall perceptions of the municipality as a coherent unit. These initiatives, which imply an external focus and are undertaken in competition with other municipalities, revolve more around the strategic communication and presentation of unique value propositions. A municipality may, for example, promote itself through identity or brand descriptions that emphasize beautiful surroundings, recreational opportunities, industries and business, or good services. There are, probably, noticeable differences between large and small municipalities in this respect. Because large municipalities are likely to be well known, they may not need to stand out. As a result, they can direct their energy and resources to the internal aspects of reputation management instead.

Data Collection and Variables

This study is primarily exploratory, aimed at revealing the significance and prevalence of the reputation commons in the Norwegian municipal sector and mapping the strategies used by municipalities for handling this commons. I draw on two data sources. The first is a questionnaire distributed in May 2012 to 428 Norwegian municipalities (one municipality is not included because it refused to disclose the email of its chief administrative officer) and administered online through QuestBack. The survey was presented as a research project on municipal branding and reputation management. The target respondent was the chief administrative officer, which means that the responses, opinions, and more or less subjective viewpoints of this person serve as the only source of information concerning the municipality's reputational strategies. This is an important limitation of this study that should be taken into account when assessing the empirical findings. However, it was possible for the chief administrative officer to forward the questionnaire to a staff member. A total of 171 respondents completed the survey, of which 81.8 percent were chief administrative officers. The rest were communication or information directors, project managers, senior analysts, policy directors, and so on. The total response rate was 40 percent.

234   *Arild Wæraas*

In order to assess the significance and impact of the reputation commons, I relied on four sets of questions. All of them were formulated as statements for which the respondent was asked to indicate his or her level of agreement on a scale of 1 to 5. The first set of statements measured the relationship between the respondent's municipality and the municipal sector as a whole concerning reputation interdependency. The second set measured the relationship between the respondent's municipality and the region. The third set concerned the strategies used by the municipalities regarding the possibility of differentiating from their peers. The fourth set dealt with free-riding issues and the municipalities' willingness to build a regional reputation. The statements are presented in Table 12.1.

The survey served as an important gateway into the municipalities' strategic thinking. However, in order to increase the trustworthiness of the study and obtain a more complete picture of reputation-building efforts in Norwegian municipalities, I supplemented the survey with qualitative interviews with 11 selected interviewees from nine municipalities. Five of them had participated, or were participating, at the Reputation School ("Omdømmeskolen") initiated by the Norwegian Ministry of Municipal and Regional Development (for more on the Reputation School, see Bjørnå in this volume). Two of them had completed the reputation survey sent out in May 2012.

The interviews were conducted in 2012. Four of the interviewees were chief administrative officers, one was a deputy administrative officer, three were communication or information directors, two were project managers, and one was a mayor. Three interviewees represented large municipalities, i.e., with more than 20,000 residents. I asked them questions about how they related to their neighboring municipalities in their reputation-management work, potential forms of collaboration, the significance of the regional reputation, and free-riding issues. The interviews followed a semi-structured form, and I varied the questions according to whether the interviewee was from a large or small municipality. For large municipalities I focused more on their willingness to moderate their reputation-building efforts to accommodate neighboring municipalities' need for a favorable reputation. When talking to smaller municipalities, I inquired more about the possibilities and their ambitions concerning the prospect of building a reputation independently of the region.

FINDINGS

The Municipal Reputation Commons

Table 12.1 presents the results from the survey. It gives an overview of the share of respondents that checked the two highest values on the self-placement scales. Looking first at the relationship between each municipality

Municipal Reputation Building in Norway 235

Table 12.1 Percentages of respondents who agree with the statements. N = 171

Statement	Percentage	Mean score
Relationship with municipal sector as a whole		
We are in many ways similar to the other municipalities in Norway	37.4	3.15
The weak reputation of the municipal sector negatively affects the reputation of our municipality	15.5	3.11
The reputation of our municipality could have been better if the reputations of the other municipalities were better	26.3	2.88
When we succeed in building the reputation of our municipality, the reputation of the entire municipal sector is positively affected	50.3	3.45
Relationship with region		
The reputation of our municipality is tightly connected to the reputation of our region	65.5	3.71
The reputation of our municipality is affected by the reputation of our neighboring municipalities	31.5	2.98
We have strong ties to the other municipalities in our region	71.3	3.92
When we succeed in building the reputation of our municipality, the reputation of our region is positively affected	83.1	4.05
Strategies		
We seek to differentiate from the other municipalities in Norway	54.4	3.52
We seek to differentiate from our neighboring municipalities	45.6	3.26
We prioritize the reputation of our municipality over the region's reputation	42.7	3.11
Free-riding		
We want our region to have a strong reputation	91.8	4.47
As long as our neighboring municipalities make an effort to build the region's reputation, we do not have to contribute	7.0	2.11
We contribute actively to the region's reputation	82.5	4.14

and the municipal sector as a whole, a somewhat surprising tendency can be observed. A general finding is that Norwegian municipalities—according to the respondents—neither perceive themselves to be very similar to the other municipalities nor feel that their reputation is much affected by the negative reputation of the municipal sector as a whole. Only 37.4 percent

236   *Arild Wæraas*

of the respondents acknowledge being similar to the other municipalities in Norway, and less than 16 percent feel that their reputation is negatively affected by the municipal sector's reputation. Not more than 26.4 percent agree that their reputation could have been better if the other municipalities' reputations were better. These findings suggest that the municipalities downplay the significance of the sector's reputation for their own reputation-management work.

However, these findings do not necessarily imply that there is no reputation commons at all. If external observers tar municipalities with the same brush, it matters less what the municipalities think of their own relative standing. Also, although the data cannot confirm it, the respondents' inclination to think of reputation in strategic terms may lead them to overestimate the impact of their own municipality's reputation on the reputation of the entire sector, while at the same time underestimating the impact of the sector's reputation on their reputation. About half the respondents agree that their successful reputation-management work has had a positive impact on the reputation of the entire municipal sector. Thus, they claim to influence others, but, paradoxically, also claim to not be influenced by others.

Furthermore, the respondents tend to acknowledge having closer ties to their neighboring municipalities at the regional level than to the municipal sector as a whole. Whereas 31.5 percent recognize being affected by the reputation of their neighboring municipalities, 65.5 percent of them agree that their reputation is tightly connected to the regional reputation, and 71.3 percent acknowledge having strong ties to the others. There is also a large majority (83.1 percent) that emphasize the positive effects of their own reputation-building efforts on the regional reputation. Thus, there is slight ambivalence in the respondents' answers, but much less so compared to the ones pertaining to the national level.

STRATEGIC DIFFERENTIATION VERSUS COMMUNAL STRATEGY

The results presented in Table 12.1 show that 54.4 percent of the municipalities seek to differentiate from other municipalities in Norway. This represents the majority, but it is by no means an overwhelming majority. Given the proliferation of reputation management in Norwegian municipalities, and the weak reputation of the municipal sector in general, it is a bit surprising that the share is not larger. It seems that Norwegian municipalities seek a strong reputation but are, nevertheless, somewhat reluctant to 'dare' to differentiate from their peers. At the regional level, the share is even lower. Not more than 45.6 percent of them seek to stand out as different from their peers, and perhaps even more surprisingly, only 42.7 percent agree that they prioritize the reputation of their municipality over the region's reputation. There is no significant correlation between perception of similarity and the desire to stand out from other municipalities

Municipal Reputation Building in Norway 237

($r = -.10$, $p = -.18$) or from neighboring municipalities ($r = -.06$, $p = .42$), which means that the feeling of being similar to others is not likely to be a reason for engaging in a differentiation strategy. These findings stand in contrast to the curriculum taught at the Ministry of Municipal and Regional Development's Reputation School, where competitive advantage and differentiation are important keywords.

Standing out can be conceived of as an act of disloyalty to others within a group where expectations of similarity are strong (Sataøen and Wæraas 2011). This reluctance toward differentiation seems understandable when considering the municipalities' emphasis on building the regional reputation. Almost all of the respondents (91.8 percent) want a strong regional reputation, and 82.5 percent claim to contribute actively to building the region's reputation.

A large number of quotes from the qualitative interviews support and shed light on these findings. Multiple interviewees highlight the need to work together to maintain a positive regional reputation:

> I think it's much more fun being a strong municipality in an area of the country that is able to make the wheels turn around, rather than trying to make it in an area that stands still. I think that [we] benefit from being part of a strong region. Surely you would feel good if you are able to achieve something that your neighbors are unable to achieve . . . but if your neighboring areas prosper, there is mutual reinforcement.
>
> (Chief administrative officer, small municipality)

> We do focus on attracting new residents to [us]. But we also see very clearly that when things are going well for *Mountaintown*, things are good for us.
>
> (Chief administrative officer, small municipality)

> I think that we must promote the strengths of the region, its qualities, and then we must consider our own specific qualities. I think that if you look totally isolated at your own municipality, your own qualities. . . . Well I am more interested in looking at the entire region and its qualities.
>
> (Chief administrative officer, small municipality)

When asked directly about the relative importance of building the reputation of his own municipality versus the regional reputation, one mayor from a small municipality answered the following:

> It's [our region], our common reputation that is the most important. And that's what we are trying to build through the creation of the common culture and natural park, it is to brand the region of *Northvalley*.
>
> (Mayor, small municipality)

238 *Arild Wæraas*

The above quotes are from interviewees representing small municipalities. It is quite understandable that they are interested in a strong regional reputation, because for most of them, their region is likely to be more well known than they are and thus may enable them to acquire a positive spillover effect from their membership in the region. The following quote from the municipality of *Snowtown* catches the point:

> Nobody has heard about *Snowtown*. That's what we are struggling with. . . . The point isn't necessarily to sell *Snowtown* in our reputation management work. I don't think that that is the most essential. The most important thing is that visitors use our brand *Resortpeak* for whatever it's worth, and *Northvalley* as a region.
>
> (Mayor, small municipality)

On the other hand, when the region is unknown as well, seeing where to start can be difficult. One interviewee pointed to the challenges of putting his municipality on the map because his region, *Inner Valley Region,* could easily be confused with a neighboring region, the *Valley Region*. Whereas the name of the other region is very well known and associated with specific characteristics and experiences, the identity of *Inner Valley Region* is not clear. As explained by the interviewee, a deputy chief administrative officer, "*Inner Valley Region* is not associated with anything. It is an undercommunicated region." The reputation-building efforts of his municipality suffered accordingly.

For large municipalities, there are certainly cases where they carry out their strategies without much concern for their surrounding neighbors. This is illustrated by one of the interviewees who describes their relationship with the larger neighbor as rather competitive:

> *Largetown* sometimes offers our employees better deals than we can afford. They give them an offer right before our salary negotiations. It has happened that highly educated staff come to us, work for two years, build up their practical expertise, and are recruited thereafter to *Largetown. . . . Largetown* has not been a big brother to us.
>
> (Deputy chief administrative officer, small municipality)

However, the general impression from the data is that large municipalities also see the value of a strong regional reputation for their own reputation. There is no difference between small and large municipalities concerning their willingness to prioritize the region's reputation over their own reputation. The relationship between municipal size and willingness to prioritize the region's reputation is statistically insignificant ($r = -.02$, $p = .81$). In most cases, large municipalities clearly signal a willingness to work together with their neighbors to secure a favorable regional reputation. This is noted by the following interviewees:

Municipal Reputation Building in Norway   239

So, within the municipal sector, we must raise it, that is, the prestige of working for the municipality, and promote the value that public or municipal work has. And the next thing, then, is place branding. But we must see this in a regional perspective. *Fjordtown* and us, we must work together.

(Communication director, large municipality)

It is good for us when *Smallfjord* and *Tinyfjord* are doing well. It is bad for us when things are bad in *Tinyfjord*.

(Chief administrative officer, large municipality)

In some cases, large municipalities impose restrictions on themselves so as to not deprive their smaller neighbors of resources that are needed for reputation building. This is despite the fact that from a purely competitive viewpoint they could have deprived their neighbors of vital resources had they wanted to do so. The following interviewees illustrate the general argument:

As a regional center, we must be much more careful compared to what our neighboring municipalities can allow themselves to do. If we do selfish things, we will be perceived negatively by the neighboring municipalities that surround us. We must be more generous than the neighboring municipalities.

(Communication director, large municipality)

We depend on all our neighboring municipalities, just like they depend on us. But we must lay lower.

(Chief administrative officer, large municipality)

The above quotes from large municipalities suggest that large municipalities assume responsibility for the region's reputation and their smaller neighbors' chances of building up their own reputations. This is somewhat of a paradox, because spillover effects from a region to a large municipality are likely to be rather limited, if not nonexistent. Many large municipalities, such as Oslo, Bergen, and Kristiansand, are more well known than their regions. It is possible for such municipalities to completely disregard and out-compete the other municipalities in the region, building up their own reputations independently of their neighboring peers and the region's reputation. From this viewpoint, differentiation strategies should be more prevalent in large than small municipalities. The quotes suggest that this is not the case. They are also supported by the fact that there is no statistically significant relationship between municipal size and the desire to stand out from other municipalities in general ($r = .04$, $p = .64$) or from neighboring municipalities ($r = -.01$, $p = .85$).

240 *Arild Wæraas*

Finally, it is interesting to note the survey respondents' answers to the questions concerning free-riding issues. Very few of them admit to deferring regional reputation building to their peers whereas they themselves do little or nothing. Overall, 91.8 percent want a strong regional reputation, and 82.5 percent claim to be actively involved in building a region's reputation. Only 7 percent prefer to leave regional reputation building to others. These findings are consistent with statements made by the interviewees. During the interviews, no one complained about a lack of contribution from others. As noted already, the interviewees preferred to emphasize the strong bonds between themselves and the other municipalities of their region.

DISCUSSION AND CONCLUSION

This chapter has focused on the relationship between Norwegian municipalities and their regions as it pertains to the reputation work of the municipalities. We have seen that the municipalities downplay the significance of the municipal sector's reputation as a whole, but greatly emphasize their bonds with their region and the importance of its reputation. Whereas they highlight their own abilities to build their reputation independently of the municipal sector as a whole, they acknowledge sharing a regional reputation on which they are dependent. The dependence is particularly pronounced for small municipalities. However, large municipalities also point to the significance of the regional reputation and in some cases even modify their behavior so as to avoid preventing their smaller neighbors from managing their reputations effectively. The findings suggest that Norwegian municipalities favor communal strategies over strategies of differentiation as a general rule, although they are interested in building up their own reputations as well. Expectations of similarity and compliance within the region are strong, but also expectations of collaboration, which have long and strong traditions in the Norwegian municipal sector where over 100 municipalities have less than 5,000 inhabitants. Without collaboration, some municipal services required by law are simply not possible to provide. With collaboration, services such as schooling, renovation, water supply, and electricity can be provided across municipal borders. The municipalities are also able to achieve things that go beyond the requirements of the law. This was noted by, for example, the interviewee who highlighted the role of the cultural and national park as a way of promoting the region. As a result, it is not surprising that the municipalities reported that they contribute to the region's reputation, and that almost all of them denied being a free-rider. Without collaboration, the result would be a tragedy of the reputation commons, in which case they all would suffer.

The findings contribute to research on reputation and reputation management in the public sector in several ways. First, by pointing to the existence of a reputation commons, the findings add important insights into our understanding of the constraints under which public organizations operate in order to achieve their goals. Whereas previous studies have focused on structural and political constraints (e.g., Wilson 1989), this chapter identifies the reputation commons as an additional constraining factor. Even if almost half of the respondents in this study acknowledge seeking to differentiate from their neighboring municipalities, they also clearly highlight the strong ties they have with the region. This emphasis is particularly evident in the qualitative interviews, where the informants point to the benefits of being associated with the region and the importance of the region having a strong reputation. Thus, inferring from the findings, public sector organizations are not free to build their reputation in any way they see fit. The reputation commons prevents them from focusing exclusively on themselves in their reputation-management work, suggesting that differentiation strategies are moderated and toned down. They must take into account the reputation of their peers and that of the category of which they are members.

Second, although there is a burgeoning body of research on public sector reputation, most of it has ignored reputation interdependency and the possibility of reputation management occurring simultaneously at different levels. The data presented here suggests that public organizations must manage their own reputation, but they also have a responsibility for the reputation of the group or category to which they belong. The general implications of the findings are that the reputation of a public organization and its efforts to manage it should be seen in connection with a superordinate structure or category of which the organization is member. Public organizations within a category are likely to share a reputation and end up in a situation characterized by reputation interdependency. As a result, they build up, maintain, and protect their reputations within a structural context through their membership in the larger category, whose reputation must also be protected. The extent of their involvement at the category level is affected by the strength of that category's reputation. If it is weak, they may prefer to distance themselves from it, or they may engage in communal strategies in order to improve it. If it is strong, it may represent an opportunity.

Despite constraints and interdependencies, managing reputation at two levels does have its benefits. In the case of Norwegian municipalities, no differentiation philosophy can change the fact that membership in the regional category is an asset for some of them. Indeed, the reputation commons may have positive spillover effects in cases where the region is associated with a positive reputation and the municipality is not, or is not well known. Municipalities with a weak or unknown status may seek to be associated with the region's reputation in an effort to acquire a positive spillover effect. Such a strategy may not be viable only for municipalities but also for other public sector organizations that are members of clearly defined categories, such as public hospitals, regulatory agencies, public schools, colleges, and police units.

242   *Arild Wæraas*

As public sector organizations continue to develop their reputation-management strategies, their membership in superordinate categories are likely to increase in importance. In a time that has been characterized by structural devolution and decentralization of authority, splitting up of large public organizations into single-purpose organizations, and growing reliance on performance management, one might expect that every public organization has become more focused on itself, its own results, and its own reputation. The data presented here add important nuances to this view by highlighting the prevalence of collaborative strategies. A public sector organization that ignores completely its category peers runs the risk of becoming unpopular and jeopardizing the collaboration that it already has with them. As a result, interdependencies are likely to continue to be a reality in the public sector context and shape future reputation-management initiatives.

REFERENCES

Barnett, Michael L. 2006. "Finding a Working Balance between Competitive and Communal Strategies." *Journal of Management Studies* 43:1753–1773.
Barnett, Michael L. 2007. "Tarred and Untarred by the Same Brush: Exploring Interdependence in the Volatility of Stock Returns." *Corporate Reputation Review* 10:3–21.
Barnett, Michael L., and Andrew J. Hoffmann. 2008. "Beyond Corporate Reputation: Managing Reputational Interdependence." *Corporate Reputation Review* 11:1–9.
Barnett, Michael L., and Andrew A. King. 2008. "Good Fences Make Good Neighbors: A Longitudinal Analysis of an Industry Self-Regulatory Institution." *Academy of Management Journal* 51:1150–1170.
Christensen, Tom, Per Lægreid, Paul G. Roness, and Kjell A. Røvik, eds. 2007. *Organization Theory and the Public Sector. Instrument, Culture and Myth.* Oxford: Routledge.
Deephouse, David L. 1999. "To Be Different, or To Be the Same? It's a Question (and Theory) of Strategic Balance." *Strategic Management Journal* 20:147–166.
Fombrun, Charles J., and Violina Rindova. 2000. "The Road to Transparency: Reputation Management at Royal Dutch/Shell." In *The Expressive Organization. Linking Identity, Reputation, and the Corporate Brand,* edited by Majken Schultz, Mary Jo Hatch, and Mogens Holten Larsen, 77–96. Oxford: Oxford University Press.
Goodsell, Charles T. 2004. *The Case for Bureaucracy. A Public Administration Polemic.* Washington, DC: CQ Press.
Gulick, Luther. 1937. "Notes on the Theory of Organization." In *Papers on the Science of Administration,* edited by Luther Gulick and Lyndall Urwick, 3–35. New York: Columbia University.
Hanssen, Gro, Jan E. Klausen, and Signy I. Vabo. 2006. "Traces of Governance: Policy Networking in Norwegian Local Government." In *Legitimacy and Urban Governance: A Cross National Comparative Study,* edited by D. Heinelt and P Getimis, 90–101. London: Routledge.
Hardin, Garrett. 1968. "The Tragedy of the Commons." *Science* 162:1243–1248.
Hind, Roar, Reidar Jenssen, Per J. Tehel, and Ole Fr. Ugland. 2001. *Befolkningens vurdering av bostedskommunen og de offentlige tjenester.* Norsk Gallup Insti-

Municipal Reputation Building in Norway 243

tutts nasjonale befolknings- og brukerundersøkelse 2000. Oslo: Norsk Gallup og Arbeids- og Administrasjonsdepartementet.

Hovik, Sissel, and Inger Marie Stigen. 2008. *Kommunal organisering 2008. Redegjørelse for kommunal og regionaldepartementets organisasjonsdatabase.* Oslo: NIBR.

Katz, Daniel, Barbara A. Gutek, Robert L. Kahn, and Eugenia Barton. 1977. *Bureaucratic Encounters: A Pilot Study in the Evaluation of Government Services.* Ann Arbor, MI: Institute for Social Research.

King, Andrew A., Michael Lenox, and Michael L. Barnett. 2002. "Strategic Responses to the Reputation Commons Problem." In *Organizations, Policy, and the Natural Environment: Institutional and Strategic Perspectives,* edited by Andrew Hoggmann and Marc Ventresca, 393–404. Stanford: Stanford University Press.

Nesheim, Torstein. 2006. *Framtidens ledelse i kommunene.* SNF report 26/06. Bergen: Samfunns- og næringslivsforskning AS.

Norwegian Municipal Act. 1993. *Lov om kommuner og fylkeskommuner.* Oslo: Norwegian Ministry of Municipal and Regional Development.

Sataøen, Hogne Lerøy, and Arild Wæraas. 2011. "Part of the Big Family? The Ambiguity of Brand Leadership in the Public Sector." In *Public Leadership,* edited by Justin Ramirez, 39–54. New York: Nova Publishers.

St. prp. nr 61. 2005–2006. *Om lokaldemokrati, velferd og økonomi i kommunesekoren 2007.* Oslo: Ministry of Local Government and Regional Development.

Wæraas, Arild. 2014. "Making a Difference: Strategic Positioning in Municipal Reputation-Building." *Local Government Studies.* doi: 10.1080/03003930.2014. 930025.

Wæraas, Arild, and Hilde Bjørnå. 2011. "Kommunegrå eller unik? Omdømmebygging i kommunesektoren." In *Substans og framtreden. Omdømmehåndering i offentlig sektor,* edited by Arild Wæraas, Haldor Byrkjeflot, and Svein Ivar Angell, 230–245. Oslo: Universitetsforlaget.

Wæraas, Arild, Hilde Bjørnå, and Turid Moldenæs. 2014. "Place, Organization, Democracy: Three Strategies for Municipal Branding." *Public Management Review.* doi: 10.1080/14719037.2014.906965.

Wilson, James Q. 1989. *Bureaucracy: What Government Agencies Do and Why They Do It.* New York: Basic Books.

Contributors

Hilde Bjørnå is Professor of Political Science at the University of Tromsø—The Arctic University of Norway. Her main research interests are local government, reputation management, NPM, democratic theory, and local leadership.

Maria Blomgren is an Associate Professor of Business Studies at Uppsala University, Sweden. Her research is mainly focused on new control systems in public sector reforms.

Jan Boon is a PhD researcher in the Research Group on Public Administration and Management at the University of Antwerp. His research focuses on the implementation of shared services in the public sector and their effect on the relationships among and between (reputation-conscious) bureaucratic and political actors.

Haldor Byrkjeflot (haldor.byrkjeflot@sosgeo.uio.no) is Professor of Sociology at the Department of Sociology and Human Geography at the University of Oslo. He has directed research programs on comparative management and public sector reforms, publishing on topics related to comparative employment systems, comparative management, health care reform, and the globalization of the MBA.

Tom Christensen is a Professor in the Department of Political Science, University of Oslo. He has published extensively on public sector reform and institutional change from a comparative perspective.

Tina Hedmo is an Assistant Professor at the Department of Business at Uppsala University, Sweden. Her research focuses on the organizing and management of public sector reforms.

Per Lægreid is Professor in the Department of Administration and Organization Theory, University of Bergen. He has published extensively on public sector reform and institutional change from a comparative perspective.

246   *Contributors*

Moshe Maor is Professor of Political Science at the Hebrew University of Jerusalem and holder of the Wolfson Family Chair of Public Administration. His areas of expertise are bureaucratic politics, public sector reforms, public policy dynamics, and comparative politics.

Jeppe Agger Nielsen is currently an Assistant Professor at the Department of Political Science, Center for Organization, Management & Administration, at Aalborg University, Denmark. His research focuses on public management reform and innovation, including e-government, performance management, and strategic communication.

Ciara O'Dwyer, PhD, is a Post-Doctoral Research Fellow at the Collegio Carlo Alberto in Turin. She specializes in research on ageing and social policy and on the use of regulation to improve quality standards in care services.

Lucio Picci is Professor of Economics, University of Bologna, and holds a PhD from the University of California at San Diego. His latest book is *Reputation-Based Governance* (Stanford University Press, 2011).

Jan Rommel is at the Public Governance Department of the Flemish Government and received a PhD at the Public Governance Institute at the KU Leuven, Belgium.

Heidi Houlberg Salomonsen is Associate Professor at the Department of Political Science, Center for Organization, Management & Administration, at Aalborg University, Denmark. Her research focuses on relations between top civil servants, ministers, and political advisers in a comparative perspective, political communication, and strategic communication in the public sector, including reputation management.

Yael Schanin is a graduate of the Honors Graduate Program in Public Policy in Federmann School of Public Policy and Government at the Hebrew University of Jerusalem. Her thesis focused on reputation strategies of bureaucratic organizations.

Koen Verhoest is Research Professor in the Research Group on Public Administration and Management at the University of Antwerp, Belgium.

Arild Wæraas is Professor of Organization Studies and Leadership in the School of Economics and Business at the Norwegian University of Life Sciences, and Adjunct Researcher at the University of Tromsø—The Arctic University of Norway.

Caroline Waks is an Associate Professor of Business Studies at Uppsala University, Sweden. Her research interest focuses primarily on the role of professionals in public sector reforms.

Index

accountability 80, 91, 101, 110, 112, 201
advertising 49
Agency for the Cooperation of Energy Regulators (ACER) 128
authenticity (authentic) 187–8, 192–4, 196, 198, 200
autonomy 77–81, 90–1; bureaucratic 118; de facto 118–20, 125, 134, 221

banking 139–56
Banking Supervisor Department of the Bank of Israel (BSD) 139–56
Bayes' theorem 41
Belgium 118–38
Bergen 239
blame avoidance 32, 111, 139, 141
branding 54, 58, 163, 169–70, 174, 176; municipal 233; place 55, 239; products 56
bureaucracy 17, 21, 32, 60, 63, 169, 207; bashing 227; professional 181
bureaucratic politics 26, 207, 209, 216, 223

Care and Welfare Regulations of Ireland 83
chief administrative officer (CAO) 192, 196, 210–11, 220, 231–33, 237–39
chief executive officer (CEO) 128
China 44
city hall 195, 237
clientelist administrative system 81
committee: executive 210; standing 210
Committee on Socioeconomic Reform, Israel 144

communication: integrated 66, 69; strategic 167–78, 170, 176–9, 206, 211, 214, 220, 233
communication strategy 25, 29, 37, 48–9, 78, 90, 96
communicators 169–73
competency 78
competition 68, 73, 76, 157–8, 160
competitive game 185, 187, 201
Congress (U.S.) 22, 25, 43
consistency 40, 68, 78, 96, 167–8, 198
content analysis 83, 97, 139
control 18, 22, 64, 78–92, 100–1, 108, 110, 119, 125, 165–6, 181, 207; variables 149
cooperation 112, 127; regional 193
corporate reputation *see* reputation
corporate social responsibility (CSR) 60, 188
corruption 46, 63, 230
criminal record 61
culture: administrative 30; blame 18; informal 130; of health care 175; macho 100; national 65; organizational 56, 98; police 101, 110, 112
customers 40, 63, 143, 146, 152, 155

democracy 58, 61–3, 69, 201, 207
Denmark 203–23
differentiation 10, 56, 187–8, 198, 207, 228, 231, 236–7, 239–41
disloyalty 237

economic theory 38
economics 2, 6, 166; perspective 3–4, 38, 56, 198
education 68, 188, 205, 232
effectiveness 19, 24, 25, 48, 62, 85, 103

248 Index

efficiency 19, 78, 97, 99, 179, 211
European Commission 127, 129–30
European networks 123
European Regulators Group for
    Electricity and GAS (ERGEG)
    127
European regulatory networks 129
evaluation 19, 28, 99, 103, 105, 126;
    self- 102, 106–8, 111
externalities 43, 58

Federal Emergency Management
    Agency (U.S., FEMA) 31
Federal Reserve (U.S.) 59
financialization 58
Flanders 119
Flemish Regulator for Electricity and
    Gas (VREG) 119, 120, 125–33
Food and Drug Administration (U.S.,
    FDA) 23–8, 31
for-profit 86, 185–6, 198, 200–1

game theory 37
Gjørv commission 106–9
globalization 24
Globes 145–6
Greenspan, A. 59–60

Halvorsen, K. 60
Health Act of 2007 83, 87–8
health care 78, 81–2, 91, 164, 166–81
hierarchy 42, 58, 62, 142, 215, 220,
    223, 231
HIQA 81–91
hospitals 163–6, 168–81
hybridity: organizations 165; norms,
    98, roles 207

identity 56, 58, 69, 98, 124, 187,
    205, 215–16, 223, 229, 233,
    238; base 208; bureaucratic
    180; corporate 205, 208, 221;
    local democratic 208; desired
    173; expression 167; municipal
    233; organizational 141, 166,
    173, 180; of public officials 40;
    shared 124, 167–8
impression management 96, 99, 195
inconsistencies 164, 168, 178
institutional persistence 17, 23
institutional perspectives 3–4, 12, 98
institutional theory 166
investment 25, 58, 79, 119, 122, 231

Ireland 27, 78–89
Israel 27, 139–56
Israeli Minister of Finance 144

jurisdictions 48, 82

knowledge 81, 164, 175, 177, 181,
    203; collective 3–4; society 18,
    technology 171
Kristiansand 239

labor 185; force 188; minister of 60;
    Party 102
legibility 47–8, 50
legitimacy 19, 63, 96–7, 108, 112–13,
    118, 164, 167, 179, 228, 232
local government 185, 190, 203–23
logic of appropriateness 61
Lom Municipality 63
loyalty 64; political 209, 217; to
    reputation platform 209

marketing 2, 64, 166, 175, 194
Marketing Practices Act 174
mayor 192–6, 210–12, 214, 222–3, 234
media: coverage 26–8, 31–2, 61, 125,
    146, 149–51, 154; salience 28,
    139, 146, 149, 154–5
medical profession: 171, 176, 178, 180
migration 191; in- 189
misconduct 101, 209
mistrust 55, 64, 67, 69, 80, 82, 90
monopoly 99, 114; natural 61

National Aeronautics and Space
    Administration (U.S., NASA)
    31, 46
National Security Agency (U.S., NSA)
    43
neoinstitutionalists 57–8
neoinstitutional perspective 98
neoliberalism 58
New Public Management 57, 62, 67,
    166; post- 67–8; reforms 166
New York Times 44
niche 200, 202
Nike 186
norms 98; cultural 97, 99, 110,
    120, 123; institutional 177;
    international 60; of local
    democracy 63; professional 164,
    178, 180; of reciprocity 32; of
    social responsibility 189

Index 249

Norway 95–114, 185–201, 227–42
Norwegian Ministry of Justice and Police 101
Norwegian Ministry of Municipal and Regional Development 190, 230, 234
Norwegian Municipal Act of 1993 231
Norwegian Municipal Reputation School 62, 190, 192, 234, 237

OECD 77, 80
Oslo 102, 106, 239

Pew Research 44
pluralism 167
political principal 8, 38, 46–7, 118–23, 127–34, 207
political science 6, 17–18, 54, 203; approach 78, 122, 141, 167, 185, 198; institutional 18, 30; perspectives 203, 221; research tradition 4; theory 97
police 95–114, 241; Oslo 110
policing 61
pooling equilibrium 41
president 22
presidential decision 17, 23
psychiatric patient 61; ward 61
public administration 38, 43, 63, 68, 95, 108, 118, 166, 203, 221
public interest 79, 81, 85, 90, 105, 175
public protest 139–56
public relations (PR) 29, 60, 106, 180, 194

quantitative analysis 139, 148

re-election 209, 222
regulation 23, 47, 60–1, 82–6, 88–9; drug approval 27; EU 119; lack of 59; over- 31, self- 59–61, super-national 60
regulatory: communication 139–56; policy 119, 127–8, 139–56
Reich, R. 60
relational strategies 120–34
reputation: bureaucratic 17–32, 125; capital 98; commons 227–42; crisis 66; economic view of 187; game 37–51; moral 123, 127, 129, 134; neutral 51, 91,

performative 122; procedural 78, 123; rankings 25, 57, 232–3; risk 142; satisficing 46, strong 19, 29, 77–81, 87, 91, 114, 227; technical 96, 123, 127, 134
reputation management recipe 54; diffusion of 6

separating equilibrium 41
signaling 41, 49, 129, 132, 139–40, 155–6, 198
social constructivism 3, 18
Socialist Left Party 60
spillover effects 227–8, 230, 239, 241
stakeholders 163, 166, 173; external 95, 164, 186, 189, 196, 204; internal 186, 193, 196, 201, 204
strategic communication 167–70; 176–9, 206, 211, 214, 220, 233
Statistics Norway 191
status 23, 62, 79, 81, 83, 87, 155, 165, 241
Sweden 168–9, 171
symbols 97–9, 113

tariffs 119
tax: agency 62; collection 61; payers 189, 192
taxes 119, 189, 205, 222
tent city 144
terrorism, counter- 109
tourism 189, 202, 230
transparency 48, 61, 65, 70, 175, 187–9, 193–4, 198–201, 232
trust: active 124; competence-based 124, 127–8, 132; identity-based 121, 124, 129, 132
trustworthiness 118, 120–4, 127, 132, 134, 200, 234
TV2 114

uncertainty 19, 22, 24–5, 37, 91, 123, 167–8, 181
United States 23, 27, 45
Utøya 102, 104–7

values: bureaucratic 63; Christian 174; core 168–71, 173–4, 177, 179, 187, 198; inconsistent 163, 165, 167, 180; institutional 178; intangible 58–9; internal 167,

250 Index

181; multiple 168; professional
165, 179–80; public 69
VG 109
visibility 46, 154
vision 56, 67, 193–6; authentic 196;
common long-term 128; idealized
168; joint 168; shared 82, 208;
reputational 192; statement 169
Volvo 186

Washington Post 43
web 176; managers 169; pages 191,
230; sites 177
Weber, M. 63, 205
welfare state 61, 177
wicked issues 61
World Economic Forum 59

zero-sum game 62

An environmentally friendly book printed and bound in England by www.printondemand-worldwide.com

This book is made of chain-of-custody materials; FSC materials for the cover and PEFC materials for the text pages.

#0015 - 031215 - C0 - 229/152/14 [16] - CB - 9780415729772